Graphical Models for Machine Learning and
Digital Communication

Adaptive Computation and Machine Learning

Thomas G. Dietterich, Editor

Christopher M. Bishop, David Heckerman, Michael I. Jordan, and Michael J. Kearns, Associate Editors

Bioinfomatics: The Machine Learning Approach, Pierre Baldi and Søren Brunak

Reinforcement Learning: An Introduction, Richard S. Sutton and Andrew G. Barto

Graphical Models for Machine Learning and Digital Communication, Brendan J. Frey

Graphical Models for Machine Learning and Digital Communication

Brendan J. Frey

A Bradford Book
The MIT Press
Cambridge, Massachusetts
London, England

Second printing, 1999

© 1998 Massachusetts Institute of Technology

This book was set in Times Roman by the author using TEX and was printed and bound
in the United States of America.

Library of Congress Cataloging-in-Publication Data

Frey, Brendan J.
  Graphical models for machine learning and digital communication / Brendan J. Frey.
    p. cm.—(Adaptive computation and machine learning)
  Includes bibliographical references and index.
  ISBN 0-262-06202-X (alk. paper)
  1. Machine learning. 2. Digital communications. 3. Graph theory. I. Title.
II. Series.
Q325.5.F74   1998
006.3′1—dc21   98-13414
                                                                CIP

In memory of Granny Frey

Contents

Series Foreword

The goal of building systems that can adapt to their environments and learn from their experience has attracted researchers from many fields, including computer science, engineering, mathematics, physics, neuroscience, and cognitive science. Out of this research has come a wide variety of learning techniques that have the potential to transform many industrial and scientific fields. Recently, several research communities have begun to converge on a common set of issues surrounding supervised, unsupervised, and reinforcement learning problems. The MIT Press Series on Adaptive Computation and Machine Learning seeks to unify the many diverse strands of machine learning research and to foster high quality research and innovative applications.

This book by Brendan Frey is a perfect illustration of the convergence of these fields around a common set of mathematical and computational tools. Frey studies hierarchical probabilistic models, algorithms for learning and reasoning with them, and applications of these models to problems in supervised learning, unsupervised learning, data compression, and perhaps most surprisingly, error-control coding. The recent discovery that certain algorithms for decoding error-correcting codes are performing belief propagation over Bayesian belief networks is thrilling. Not only does it provide yet another connection between information theory and machine learning, but it also suggests new approaches to the design of improved error-correcting codes and to the design and analysis of learning algorithms. Frey provides the reader with a beautifully written introduction to graphical models and their associated algorithms. Then he takes us on a tour of the research frontier and of his recent work, which has advanced this frontier significantly. The book concludes with a thought-provoking assessment of future directions in this exciting research area.

Thomas G. Dietterich

Preface

What is this book about?

A variety of problems in machine learning and digital communication deal with complex but structured natural or artificial systems. Natural patterns that we wish to automatically classify are a consequence of a hierarchical causal physical process. Learning about the world in which we live requires that we extract useful sensory features and abstract concepts and then form a model for how these interact. Universal data compression involves estimating the probability distribution of a data source, which is often produced by some natural hierarchical process. Error-correcting codes used in telephone modems and deep-space communication consist of electrical signals that are linked together in a complex fashion determined by the designed code and the physical nature of the communication channel. Not only are these tasks characterized by complex structure, but they also contain random elements. Graphical models such as Bayesian belief networks and Markov random fields provide a way to describe the relationships between random variables in a complex stochastic system.

In this book, I use graphical models as an overarching framework to describe and solve problems in the areas of pattern classification, unsupervised learning, data compression, and channel coding. This book covers research I did while in my doctoral program at the University of Toronto. Rather than being a textbook, this book is a treatise that covers several leading-edge areas of research in machine learning and digital communication.

The book begins with a review of graphical models and algorithms for inferring probabilities in these models, including the probability propagation algorithm, Markov chain Monte Carlo (Gibbs sampling), variational inference, and Helmholtz machines. I then turn to the practical problem of learning models for pattern classification. Results on the classification of handwritten digits show that Bayesian network pattern classifiers outperform other standard methods, such as the k-nearest neighbor method.

In the area of unsupervised learning, I show that with just a simple local delta-rule learning algorithm (the "wake-sleep" algorithm) Bayesian network – neural network hybrids can learn hierarchical structure from images.

When Bayesian networks with hidden variables are used as source models for data compression, an exponentially large number of codewords are associated with each input pattern. However, it turns out that the code can still be used efficiently, if a new technique called "bits-back coding" is used.

The current *best* error-correcting decoding algorithms (*e.g.*, turbodecoding) are instances of "probability propagation" in various graphical models. These new schemes are rapidly closing the gap between the performances of practical channel coding systems and Shannon's fifty-year-old channel coding limit. The graphical model framework exposes the similarities between these codes and leads the way to a new class of "trellis-constrained codes" which also operate close to Shannon's limit.

The book concludes with suggestions by myself and other experts for future directions of research in graphical models for machine learning and digital communication.

Nomenclature

Vectors, matrices, high-dimensional matrices and sets of variables are written in boldface type. (Vectors are usually written in lower-case type.) Sets are quite different from vectors, but this abuse of notation permits set operations (*e.g.*, "$\subseteq$", "$\backslash$") while at the same time permitting cardinal access to the set members (*e.g.*, weighted sum of the elements via indexing). I use curly braces $\{\dots\}$ to write the elements in a set or vector of variables. $\{z_k\}$ is the set containing a singleton variable z_k, whereas $\{z_k\}_{k=1}^K = \{z_1, \dots, z_K\}$. Extra labels on variables usually appear as upper-case type in superscripts (*e.g.*, θ^V), whereas vector, matrix, and high-dimensional matrix indices usually appear as subscripts (*e.g.*, θ_{ik}^V). For example, we can write the following with respect to the set of parameters $\boldsymbol{\theta}$: $\{\theta_{ik}^V\}_{k=1}^K = \boldsymbol{\theta}_i^V \subseteq \boldsymbol{\theta}^V \subseteq \boldsymbol{\theta}$, and $\sum_j \theta_{ij}^V h_j$. Some types of index (notably training case indices) appear as superscripts in parentheses (*e.g.*, $\mathbf{v}^{(t)}$).

Probability mass functions are usually written in upper-case italics (*e.g.* $P(\cdot)$, $Q(\cdot)$) whereas probability density functions are usually written in lower-case italics (*e.g.* $p(\cdot)$, $q(\cdot)$). The distribution is identified by the random variable, so the distribution $P(\mathbf{v})$ is different from $P(\mathbf{x})$. Also, to keep the formulas short, the symbols for a random variable and its value are usually the same. So, $P(u_k|\mathbf{y})$ sometimes refers to the probability that the random variable U_k takes on the value u_k, and at other times refers to the set of probabilities corresponding to the values that U_k can take on. In cases where a random variable and its value must be distinguishable, I write an assignment. So, $P(u_k = u_k'|\mathbf{y})$ means $P_{U_k|\mathbf{Y}}(u_k'|\mathbf{y})$. A distribution subscripted with "r" refers to the correct, or "real" distribution. For example, if $P(\mathbf{v})$ is a model distribution, we hope that $P(\mathbf{v}) \approx P_r(\mathbf{v})$. $\mathrm{E}[\cdot]$ is an expectation with respect to the stated distribution.

I use $\log(\cdot)$ for the natural logarithm and $\log_x(\cdot)$ for the logarithm to the base x.

Acknowledgments

The material in this book is a consequence of the interactions I have had with several excellent researchers. I thank my doctoral advisor Geoffrey Hinton for his guidance; I greatly value his open-mindedness, his inspirational discussions, and his honest criticisms. I also thank Radford Neal, whose creativity and persistent pursuit of precision has certainly enhanced my research and this book. I am very grateful to Frank Kschischang for valuable discussions on error-correcting coding and for introducing me to the information theory community. Glenn Gulak was very helpful in suggesting that there might be similarities between my research on machine learning and the turbodecoding algorithm for error-correcting codes. I also greatly appreciate recent energetic collaborations with David MacKay, who I find is lots of fun to work with.

Thanks also go to the following people for valuable conversations: Peter Dayan, Zoubin Ghahramani, Tommi Jaakkola, Michael Jordan, Carl Rasmussen, Virginia de Sa, Brian Sallans, Lawrence Saul, and Chris Williams.

My love goes to my wife Utpala for being supportive of my interest in research and to my children Shardul and Sarth for motivating me to get some work done. Last, but not least, I also thank my parents John and Cecelia for providing me with an environment conducive to curiosity and exploration, while I was growing up.

I was financially supported by a Natural Sciences and Engineering Research Council 1967 Science and Engineering Scholarship, a Walter C. Sumner Memorial Fellowship, and a University of Toronto Open Fellowship. My work was financially supported by grants from the Natural Sciences and Engineering Research Council, the Institute for Robotics and Intelligent Systems, and the Arnold and Mabel Beckman Foundation.

Graphical Models for Machine Learning and Digital Communication

1 Introduction

In this book, I explore algorithms for pattern classification, unsupervised learning, data compression, and channel coding. At first, it may be hard to imagine how these different research areas can be brought into focus under a single theme that is both novel and of practical value. My hope is to convince the reader that these problems can be attacked in an interesting and fruitful manner using a recently developed class of algorithms that make use of *probabilistic structure*. These algorithms take advantage of a graphical description of the dependencies between random variables in order to compute, or estimate, probabilities derived from a joint distribution. As simple and well-known examples, the forward-backward algorithm [Baum and Petrie 1966] and the Viterbi algorithm [Forney 1973] make use of a chain-like Markovian relationship between random variables.

The roots of probabilistic structure reach far back to the beginning of the 20th century. In 1921, Sewall Wright [1921] developed "path analysis" as a means to study statistical relationships in biological data. Few new developments were made until the 1960's when statisticians began using graphs to describe restrictions in statistical models called "log-linear models" [Vorobev 1962; Goodman 1970]. In 1963, the idea of hierarchical probabilistic structure briefly reared its head in the engineering research community when Gallager [1963] invented an error-correcting decoding algorithm based on a graphical description of the probabilistic relationships between variables involved in channel coding. Most likely because of the primitive computers available at the time, his algorithm was quickly overlooked by his peers, only to be rediscovered nearly 35 years later independently by at least three research groups, and to be shown to yield unprecedented performance in error-correcting coding applications [Berrou, Glavieux and Thitimajshima 1993; Wiberg, Loeliger and Kötter 1995; MacKay and Neal 1995]. A simpler chain-type Markovian graphical structure later became popular and very useful in the engineering community, largely due to a good tutorial paper by Forney [1973], in which the notion of a "trellis" was introduced. Probabilistic structure has been extensively developed in the artificial intelligence literature, with applications ranging from taxonomic hierarchies [Woods 1975; Schubert 1976] to medical diagnosis [Spiegelhalter 1990]. In the late 1980's, Pearl [1986] and Lauritzen and Spiegelhalter [1988] independently published a general algorithm for computing probabilities based on a graphical representation of probabilistic structure. This algorithm is practical and exact for only a special type of probabilistic structure that is characterized by a relatively small "state space". Over the last decade, there has also been a tremendous increase in interest in estimating the parameters of models with fixed graphical structure. In the mid 1980's, Hinton and Sejnowski [1986] introduced a maximum likelihood algorithm for learning the parameters of a graph-based log-linear model called a "Markov random field". More recently, approximate algorithms for general models based on directed graphical models called "Bayesian networks" have been introduced. These include Markov chain Monte Carlo methods [Pearl 1987; Neal 1992], "Helmholtz machines" [Hinton *et al.* 1995; Dayan *et al.* 1995], and variational techniques [Ghahramani and Jordan 1998; Saul, Jaakkola and Jordan 1996; Jaakkola, Saul and Jordan 1996].

1.1 A probabilistic perspective

Offhand, it is not obvious that sophisticated probability models are needed to solve problems in machine learning and digital communication. Given a segment of speech, a classifier outputs a decision, say, as to whether or not the speaker has security clearance. It appears there are no random variables in this model. The classifier may also output a measure of reliability regarding the decision it makes. In this case, it appears there is just one binary random variable that captures the variability in the decision. The mean of this Bernoulli random variable must somehow be related to the input, and this task can be viewed as some sort of function approximation. Similarly, in response to a series of sensory inputs, an animal makes a single motor action. Given a highly redundant image, a data compression algorithm usually produces a unique sequence of codeword symbols. Given the output of a noisy telephone line, a channel decoder (telephone modem) makes a deterministic decision about the contents of the transmitted data file.

The above modelling approaches either require only very low-dimensional probability models or do not use random variables at all, and so they are clearly not representing the true underlying structure in each problem. For example, in reality each speaker has a unique glottis that interacts in a random way with a unique shape of vocal tract and a unique random style of articulation to produce a speech segment. It seems that a fruitful approach to speaker identification would involve representing these random variables and the probabilistic relationships between them. In the following four sections, I give some general ideas about what is missing in the above approaches to pattern classification, unsupervised learning, data compression, and channel coding.

1.1.1 Pattern classification

A soft-decision *classifier* estimates the probability that a given pattern $\mathbf{v}$ belongs to each class $j \in \{0, \dots, J-1\}$. That is, the classifier estimates

$$P_r(j|\mathbf{v}), \tag{1.1}$$

where the subscript "r" in P_r indicates a true (real) probability (as opposed to one produced by a model). If these probabilities can be accurately estimated, Bayes' decision theory tells that a minimum error rate is achieved by choosing the class j that maximizes $P_r(j|\mathbf{v})$ [Chow 1957; Duda and Hart 1973].

We could use a logistic regression model to estimate $P_r(j|\mathbf{v})$. For example, regression with a flexible neural network has been successfully used to classify individual digits extracted from handwritten United States ZIP codes [Le Cun *et al.* 1989]. Alternatively, support vector techniques can be used to obtain conditional probability estimates [Vapnik 1998]. However, these approaches ignore the *causal structure* in the physical production of the input patterns.

In order to faithfully capture the actual physical process that produces each digit, we first ought to specify an *a priori* distribution $P(j)$ over the digit classes $j \in \{0, \dots, 9\}$ — maybe some digits are more common than others. Next, for a given class of digit j, we expect there to be a distribution $P(\mathbf{h}|j)$ over a set of digit attributes $\mathbf{h}$. These attributes are called "hidden variables", because they are not part of the classifier inputs or outputs. Each element of $\mathbf{h}$ might specify the presence or absence of a particular line segment or flourish. Given a set of features $\mathbf{h}$, we expect there to be a distribution $P(\mathbf{v}|\mathbf{h})$ over possible images — this distribution models the way in which features combine to make an image, as well as noise such as ink spots. The joint distribution given by this model of the real world can be written

$$P(j, \mathbf{h}, \mathbf{v}) = P(j)P(\mathbf{h}|j)P(\mathbf{v}|\mathbf{h}), \tag{1.2}$$

and the distribution over classes given a pattern can be obtained using Bayes' rule with $\mathbf{h}$ marginalized out:

$$P(j|\mathbf{v}) = \frac{P(j, \mathbf{v})}{\sum_{j'} P(j', \mathbf{v})} = \frac{\sum_{\mathbf{h}} P(j, \mathbf{h}, \mathbf{v})}{\sum_{j'} \sum_{\mathbf{h}} P(j', \mathbf{h}, \mathbf{v})}. \tag{1.3}$$

So, it appears that to properly model the structure of the problem, we need a more sophisticated probabilistic description than (1.1). In general, a *correct* model of this sort, where $P(j|\mathbf{v}) \approx P_r(j|\mathbf{v})$, will perform optimally in terms of classification error.

1.1.2   Unsupervised learning

The goal of unsupervised learning is for a machine to process a set of training data and then extract structure which cognitive scientists believe to be relevant to perception and conception. For example, given a training set containing examples of handwritten digits, we would like our machine to learn to represent digit class without being told what the digit classes are. When the machine is given a new test image of, say, a 3, we hope that somewhere within the machine there will be a flashing light saying "I think this is a 3!"

One powerful approach to developing unsupervised learning algorithms is to suppose that in addition to the input sensory variables $\mathbf{v}$ there are hidden "concept" variables $\mathbf{h}$, and that all the variables are linked together by a *parameterized* probability model $P(\mathbf{v}, \mathbf{h}|\boldsymbol{\theta})$, with parameters $\boldsymbol{\theta}$. This probability model has a form that we believe to be appropriate for the task of cognition. For example, we may believe that given the hidden variables, the sensory inputs are independent:

$$P(\mathbf{v}, \mathbf{h}, \boldsymbol{\theta}) = P(\mathbf{h}|\boldsymbol{\theta}) \prod_{i=1}^{N} P(v_i|\mathbf{h}, \boldsymbol{\theta}). \tag{1.4}$$

The model is fit to a set of training examples $\mathbf{v}^{(1)}, \dots, \mathbf{v}^{(T)}$ using maximum-likelihood parameter estimation:

$$\boldsymbol{\theta}^{\mathrm{ML}} = \operatorname*{argmax}_{\boldsymbol{\theta}} \prod_{t=1}^{T} P(\mathbf{v}^{(t)}|\boldsymbol{\theta}), \tag{1.5}$$

where the marginal probability of the sensory inputs is computed from

$$P(\mathbf{v}^{(t)}|\boldsymbol{\theta}) = \sum_{\mathbf{h}} P(\mathbf{v}^{(t)}, \mathbf{h}|\boldsymbol{\theta}). \tag{1.6}$$

We hope that the maximum likelihood model will represent the true physical process that produced the patterns; *i.e.*, that the hidden variables will come to represent meaningful concepts.

For example, in the case of unsupervised learning of digits, when a new pattern $\mathbf{v}$ is presented to the trained machine, we hope that in the posterior distribution over the hidden variables,

$$P(\mathbf{h}|\mathbf{v}, \boldsymbol{\theta}) = \frac{P(\mathbf{v}, \mathbf{h}|\boldsymbol{\theta})}{\sum_{\mathbf{h}} P(\mathbf{v}, \mathbf{h}|\boldsymbol{\theta})}, \tag{1.7}$$

high probability will be given to a representation that correctly identifies the digit.

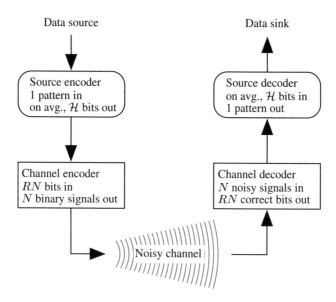

Figure 1.1
An ideal distortion-free digital communication system.

1.1.3 Data compression

Figure 1.1 shows an ideal distortion-free digital communication system. We assume the data source produces patterns that are independent and identically drawn (i.i.d.) with true information content (entropy) $\mathcal{H}$ bits per pattern. Each source pattern $\mathbf{v}$ is fed into an ideal *source encoder*, which on average produces a block of $\mathcal{H}$ information bits that look perfectly random. An ideal *channel encoder* takes in a block of these random-looking information bits (with a length that is usually different from $\mathcal{H}$) and produces a longer block of binary signals. The redundant signals in the longer block identify relationships between the information bits, so that an information bit that is received in error can be corrected using the "redundant" signals. To produce a block of N binary signals, the channel encoder takes in a block of RN bits, where R is called the "rate".

An ideal *channel decoder* takes in a block of N noise-corrupted signals, which are in general now real-valued instead of binary (*e.g.*, if the channel noise is Gaussian). The decoder produces RN information bits that are *error-free*. An ideal *source decoder* on average takes in $\mathcal{H}$ error-free information bits and produces a distortion-free source pattern. Notice that memory may be needed at each stage in this block diagram since, *e.g.*, several source patterns may be needed to obtain enough information bits for the channel encoder to produce a block of signals.

It is important to recognize that digital communication can be broken down into two stages [Cover and Thomas 1991]: compressing data to obtain random-looking information bits and then communicating this compressed data in an error-free fashion.

A *source code* maps each input pattern $\mathbf{v}$ to a source codeword $\mathbf{u}$, such that for each valid $\mathbf{u}$ there is a unique pattern. I will consider sources where i.i.d. patterns are generated from $P_r(\mathbf{v})$. The purpose of noiseless source coding, or lossless data compression, is to losslessly represent the source patterns by codewords, so that the expected codeword length is as small as possible. Shannon's noiseless source coding theorem [Shannon 1948] states that the average codeword length per source pattern cannot be less than the source entropy:

$$E[\ell(\mathbf{v})] \geq \mathcal{H}, \tag{1.8}$$

where $\ell(\mathbf{v})$ is the length of the codeword for $\mathbf{v}$ in bits, and $\mathcal{H}$ is the entropy of the source in bits:

$$\mathcal{H} = -\sum_{\mathbf{v}} P_r(\mathbf{v}) \log_2 P_r(\mathbf{v}). \tag{1.9}$$

Shannon's theorem also states that if the input patterns are processed in blocks, there exists a source code with an average codeword length per input pattern that is arbitrarily close to $\mathcal{H}$.

Arithmetic coding [Rissanen and Langdon 1976; Witten, Neal and Cleary 1987] is a practical algorithm for producing near-optimal codewords when the source distribution $P_r(\mathbf{v})$ is known. Sometimes, *e.g.*, if $\mathbf{v}$ is binary-valued, these probabilities can be easily estimated from the source. Often, however, the distribution is too complex, and so a more sophisticated parametric model or flexible model must be used to estimate the probabilities. For example, consider a high-dimensional binary image $\mathbf{v}$ that is produced by the physical process described in Section 1.1.1, so that

$$P(j, \mathbf{h}, \mathbf{v}) = P(j)P(\mathbf{h}|j)P(\mathbf{v}|\mathbf{h}). \tag{1.10}$$

The probabilities used by the arithmetic encoder are obtained by marginalizing out j and $\mathbf{h}$:

$$P(\mathbf{v}) = \sum_{j}\sum_{\mathbf{h}} P(j, \mathbf{h}, \mathbf{v}). \tag{1.11}$$

Thus, probabilistic descriptions can also be very useful for source coding.

1.1.4 Channel coding

A *channel code* maps a vector of information bits **u** to a vector of codeword signals **x**. This mapping adds redundancy to **u** in order to protect the block against channel noise. (As a simple example, the codeword might consist of three repetitions of the information vector.) After **x** is transmitted across the channel, the decoder receives a noise-corrupted version **y** and produces an estimate of the information block **û**. We say that a *block error* or a *word error* has occurred if **û** $\neq$ **u**. In its simplest form, Shannon's channel coding theorem [Shannon 1948] states that for any given channel, there *exists*[1] a channel code that can achieve an arbitrarily low probability of block error when the signal-to-noise ratio is greater than a channel-dependent threshold called the Shannon limit. Roughly speaking, the codewords are kept far apart in codeword symbol space, so that when a moderately noise-corrupted codeword is received, it is still possible to determine with high probability which codeword was transmitted.

From a probabilistic perspective, the decoder can minimize the word error rate by choosing an estimate **û** that maximizes $P_\mathrm{r}(\hat{\mathbf{u}}|\mathbf{y})$, or minimize the symbol error rate by choosing an estimate **û** that maximizes $\prod_k P_\mathrm{r}(\hat{u}_k|\mathbf{y})$. A probabilistic model can be constructed by examining the encoding process and the channel. We first specify a (usually uniform) distribution for the information blocks, $P(\mathbf{u})$. Often, the encoder uses a set of *state* variables, **s**, in order to produce the codeword. These variables are determined from the information block using a distribution $P(\mathbf{s}|\mathbf{u})$ — although this relationship is usually deterministic, this probabilistic description will come in handy later on when we study probabilistic decoding. The transmitted codeword is determined from the information block and state variables by $P(\mathbf{x}|\mathbf{u},\mathbf{s})$. Finally, the real-valued channel outputs are related to the transmitted codeword by a probability density function $p(\mathbf{y}|\mathbf{x})$ that models the channel. The joint distribution given by the model is

$$P(\mathbf{u},\mathbf{s},\mathbf{x},\mathbf{y}) = P(\mathbf{u})P(\mathbf{s}|\mathbf{u})P(\mathbf{x}|\mathbf{u},\mathbf{s})p(\mathbf{y}|\mathbf{x}), \qquad (1.12)$$

and the distribution over information symbol u_k given the channel output can be obtained by marginalizing out **s**, **x** and u_j, for all $j \neq k$, and using Bayes' rule:

---

[1]Shannon was quite the tease. He proved the code exists, but did not show us a practical way to encode or decode it.

$$P(u_k|\mathbf{y}) = \frac{\sum_{u_j \forall j \neq k} \sum_{\mathbf{s}} \sum_{\mathbf{x}} P(\mathbf{u}, \mathbf{s}, \mathbf{x}, \mathbf{y})}{\sum_{\mathbf{u}'} \sum_{\mathbf{s}} \sum_{\mathbf{x}} P(\mathbf{u}', \mathbf{s}, \mathbf{x}, \mathbf{y})}. \tag{1.13}$$

Although this probabilistic formulation may seem strange compared to many of the strongly algebraic traditional approaches, it is this formulation that I view as the foundation of the recently proposed high-performance *turbocodes* [Berrou and Glavieux 1996].

1.1.5 Probabilistic inference

As presented above, pattern classification, unsupervised learning, data compression, and channel coding are all similar in that some type of marginal (and possibly conditioned) distribution is sought for a given joint distribution. Consider a set of random variables $\mathbf{z} = (z_1, z_2, \ldots, z_N)$ that covary according to a joint distribution $P(z_1, z_2, \ldots, z_N)$. For any two subsets of variables $\mathbf{z}^1 \subseteq \mathbf{z}$ and $\mathbf{z}^2 \subseteq \mathbf{z}$, I will refer to the computation or estimation of $P(\mathbf{z}^1|\mathbf{z}^2)$, or a decision based on $P(\mathbf{z}^1|\mathbf{z}^2)$, as *probabilistic inference*.

Examples of probabilistic inference include the computation of the class probabilities for pattern classification (1.3), the computation of the distribution over concepts in unsupervised learning (1.7), the computation of the input probability for data compression (1.11), and the information symbol decisions based on the information symbol probabilities for channel coding (1.13). Notice that in these different cases of probabilistic inference, the joint distributions can be decomposed in different ways. In fact, if we decompose the joint distributions at the level of individual variables instead of vector variables, we can envision a wide variety of rich structures. In the next section, I describe graphical models, which can be used to describe this structure.

1.2 Graphical models: Factor graphs, Markov random fields and Bayesian belief networks

Often, the joint distribution associated with a probabilistic inference problem can be decomposed into locally interacting factors. For example, the joint distributions involved in the applications of Bayes' rule in (1.3), (1.7), (1.11), and (1.13) can be expressed in the forms given in (1.2), (1.4), (1.10), and (1.12). By taking advantage of such *probabilistic structure*, we can design inference algorithms that are more efficient than the blind application of Bayes' rule.

Probabilistic structure can be characterized by a set of *conditional independence* relationships. (This structural description does not fix the values of the probabilities.) For example, in the case of channel coding, we can use the chain rule of probability to write out the joint distribution:

$$P(\mathbf{u}, \mathbf{s}, \mathbf{x}, \mathbf{y}) = P(\mathbf{u})P(\mathbf{s}|\mathbf{u})P(\mathbf{x}|\mathbf{u}, \mathbf{s})p(\mathbf{y}|\mathbf{u}, \mathbf{s}, \mathbf{x}). \qquad (1.14)$$

The probability density function (the last factor) can be simplified, since the received vector $\mathbf{y}$ is conditionally independent of the information vector $\mathbf{u}$ and the state vector $\mathbf{s}$, given the transmitted codeword $\mathbf{x}$:

$$p(\mathbf{y}|\mathbf{u}, \mathbf{s}, \mathbf{x}) = p(\mathbf{y}|\mathbf{x}). \qquad (1.15)$$

By substituting this conditional independency relationship into (1.14), we obtain the more structured form of the joint distribution given in (1.12).

The general idea is to express the joint distribution as a product of factors, where each factor depends on a subset of the random variables. In the simplest case, each factor depends on a single random variable, making marginalization easy. Most distributions that describe practical problems cannot be broken up in this way, and the subsets overlap. Within this richer set of models, some structures lead to highly efficient exact algorithms (*e.g.*, the forward-backward algorithm for a chain-type structure). Other structures are not tractable and lead to approximate algorithms.

It turns out that graph theory provides a succinct way to represent probabilistic structure. A graphical representation for probabilistic structure, along with functions that can be used to derive the joint distribution, is called a *graphical model*. Examples of graphical models include *Markov random fields*, *Bayesian networks* (a.k.a., belief networks, causal networks, or influence diagrams), *chain graphs* [Lauritzen and Wermuth 1989], and *factor graphs*. Not only does the graphical representation concisely capture probabilistic structure, but it forms a framework for computing useful probabilities.

1.2.1   Factor graphs

A factor graph [Frey *et al.* 1998] explicitly indicates how a joint function of many variables factors into a product of functions of smaller sets of variables. Here, we will consider global functions that are probability distributions, although in general factor graphs can be used to describe the decomposition of any function that evaluates to a semi-ring [Wiberg, Loeliger and Kötter 1995; Aji and McEliece 1997; Frey *et al.* 1998]. Consider a distribution over a set of variables $\mathbf{z}$ that can be written as follows:

$$P(\mathbf{z}) = \alpha \prod_{j=1}^{J} f_j(\mathbf{z}_j), \qquad (1.16)$$

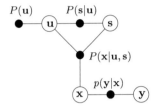

Figure 1.2
The factor graph for the global probability distribution, $P(\mathbf{u}, \mathbf{s}, \mathbf{x}, \mathbf{y})$ = $P(\mathbf{u})P(\mathbf{s}|\mathbf{u})P(\mathbf{x}|\mathbf{u}, \mathbf{s})p(\mathbf{y}|\mathbf{x})$.

where $\mathbf{z}_j \subseteq \mathbf{z}$ is the subset of variables that the jth *local function* $f_j(\cdot)$ depends on and α is a normalization constant. The local functions may be marginal distributions or conditional distributions (as in (1.12)), or they may be "potentials" like the ones used for Markov random fields (see Section 1.2.2). A *factor graph* is a bipartite graph (meaning there are two types of vertex and edges may only connect vertices of differing type), with one set of vertices corresponding to the variables in $\mathbf{z}$ and another set of vertices corresponding to the local functions, $f_1(\cdot), \ldots, f_J(\cdot)$. Each local function is connected to the variables on which it depends. For example, Figure 1.2 shows the factor graph for the channel coding model given by (1.12). Notice that the function $P(\mathbf{u})$ can be included with $P(\mathbf{s}|\mathbf{u})$ or $P(\mathbf{x}|\mathbf{u}, \mathbf{s})$ if we wish.

A factor graph may have directed edges in order to indicate conditional dependence as is done in Bayesian networks (see Section 1.2.3). It turns out that in terms of expressing factorization of the global distribution, factor graphs are more general than Markov random fields and Bayesian networks.

1.2.2 Markov random fields

A *Markov random field* (MRF) (see Kinderman and Snell [1980] for a tutorial) is an undirected graph with vertices corresponding to variables (there aren't any local function vertices as there are in factor graphs). Let $\mathbf{n}_i$ be the neighbors of variable z_i in the MRF. Then, the MRF defines a local Markov property with respect to the global distribution:

$$P(z_i|\mathbf{z} \setminus \{z_i\}) = P(z_i|\mathbf{n}_i), \qquad (1.17)$$

where $\mathbf{z} \setminus \{z_i\}$ are all the variables in $\mathbf{z}$, except z_i. That is, given its neighbors, each variable is independent of all other variables. The global distribution for an MRF can be written in terms of a product of *clique potentials*, as long as the distribution is positive. A *clique* is a fully-connected subgraph that cannot

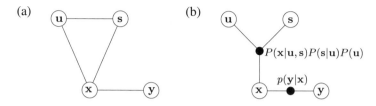

Figure 1.3
(a) The Markov random field (MRF) for the global probability distribution, $P(\mathbf{u}, \mathbf{s}, \mathbf{x}, \mathbf{y}) = P(\mathbf{u})P(\mathbf{s}|\mathbf{u})P(\mathbf{x}|\mathbf{u}, \mathbf{s})p(\mathbf{y}|\mathbf{x})$. (b) The MRF drawn as a factor graph.

remain fully connected if more variables are included. For example, in the MRF shown in Figure 1.3a, there are two cliques: $\mathbf{z}_1 = (\mathbf{u}, \mathbf{s}, \mathbf{x})$ and $\mathbf{z}_2 = (\mathbf{x}, \mathbf{y})$. If there are C cliques and $\mathbf{z}_j$ are the variables in clique j, then the distribution can be written

$$P(\mathbf{z}) = \alpha \prod_{j=1}^{C} \psi_j(\mathbf{z}_j), \tag{1.18}$$

where $\psi_j(\cdot)$ is the potential for clique j and α is a normalization constant.

Notice that the factorization of $P(\cdot)$ implied by *any* MRF can also be represented by a factor graph (compare (1.16) and (1.18)). We simply create one local function vertex for each clique and connect it to the clique variables. For example, Figure 1.3b shows the factor graph for the MRF shown in Figure 1.3a.

In contrast, *not* all factorizations that can be represented by factor graphs can be represented by MRFs. Factor graphs are more explicit about factorization than are MRFs. For example, both the factor graph shown in Figure 1.2 and the factor graph shown in Figure 1.3b correspond to the MRF shown in Figure 1.3a. In fact, it is not possible to construct an MRF that explicitly gives the factorization $P(\mathbf{u}, \mathbf{s}, \mathbf{x}, \mathbf{y}) = P(\mathbf{u})P(\mathbf{s}|\mathbf{u})P(\mathbf{x}|\mathbf{u}, \mathbf{s})p(\mathbf{y}|\mathbf{x})$.

1.2.3 Bayesian networks

Unlike MRFs, Bayesian networks [Pearl 1988] are specified in terms of *directed acyclic graphs*, in which all edges are directed and in which there are no closed paths when edge directions are followed. A *Bayesian network* for a set of random variables $\mathbf{z} = (z_1, z_2, \ldots, z_N)$ consists of a directed acyclic graph with one vertex for each variable, and a set of probability functions $P(z_k|\mathbf{a}_k)$, $k = 1, \ldots, N$, where the *parents* $\mathbf{a}_k$ of z_k are the variables that have directed edges connecting *to* z_k. If z_k has no parents, then $\mathbf{a}_k = \varnothing$. For now, we can think of each function $P(z_k|\mathbf{a}_k)$ as an exhaustive list of probabilities corre-

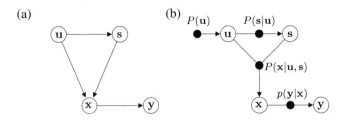

Figure 1.4
(a) The Bayesian network for the global probability distribution, $P(\mathbf{u}, \mathbf{s}, \mathbf{x}, \mathbf{y}) = P(\mathbf{u})P(\mathbf{s}|\mathbf{u})P(\mathbf{x}|\mathbf{u}, \mathbf{s})p(\mathbf{y}|\mathbf{x})$. (b) The Bayesian network drawn as a factor graph.

sponding to the possible configurations of z_k and $\mathbf{a}_k$. The global probability distribution is written

$$P(\mathbf{z}) = \prod_{k=1}^{N} P(z_k|\mathbf{a}_k). \tag{1.19}$$

For example, Figure 1.4a shows the Bayesian network for the coding model discussed above.

A Bayesian network can be drawn as a factor graph by introducing one function vertex for each conditional probability function (effectively producing a *moral* graph [Lauritzen and Spiegelhalter 1988]). The edges of the factor graph may be directed to indicate that the local functions are conditional probabilities, as shown in Figure 1.4b.

As with MRFs, we can actually define a Bayesian network in terms of its independence properties and then derive (1.19). Several definitions will be useful for making this connection. The *children* $\mathbf{c}_k$ of z_k are the variables that have directed edges connecting *from* z_k. The *descendents* $\mathbf{d}_k$ of z_k are its children, its children's children, *etc.* The *nondescendents* $\mathbf{n}_k$ of z_k are the variables in $\{z_1, z_2, \ldots, z_{k-1}, z_{k+1}, \ldots, z_N\}$ that are not in $\mathbf{d}_k$, *i.e.*, $\mathbf{n}_k = \mathbf{z} \setminus (\mathbf{d}_k \cup \{z_k\})$. Note that $\mathbf{n}_k \neq \mathbf{z} \setminus \mathbf{d}_k$, since z_k is *not* included in the nondescendents. From these definitions, it follows that $\mathbf{a}_k \subseteq \mathbf{n}_k$. Figure 1.5 shows an example of a Bayesian network, along with the parents, children, descendents and nondescendents of variable z_5.

The defining conditional independence property of a Bayesian network is that given the parents of any variable z_k, the distribution over z_k will not change if any combination of the nondescendents of z_k are also given:

$$P(z_k|\mathbf{a}_k, \mathbf{w}) = P(z_k|\mathbf{a}_k), \quad \forall \, \mathbf{w} \subseteq \mathbf{n}_k. \tag{1.20}$$

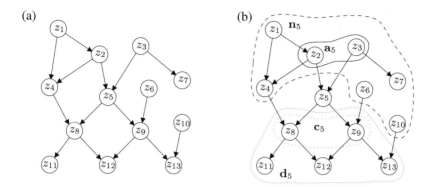

Figure 1.5
(a) An example of a Bayesian network. (b) The parents $\mathbf{a}_5$ of z_5 are shown by a solid loop; the children $\mathbf{c}_5$ are shown by a sparse dotted loop; the descendents $\mathbf{d}_5$ are shown by a dense dotted loop; the nondescendents $\mathbf{n}_5$ are shown by a dashed loop.

In other words, z_k is conditionally independent of any combination of its non-descendents, given its parents. To take the family hierarchy (not necessarily a tree) analogy further, given the genetic code of Susan's parents, determining the genes of her siblings, her grandparents, her grandparents' children, her children's other parents or any combination of the above does not influence our prediction of Susan's genetic make-up. This is not true for descendents. For example, determining the genes of Susan's grandchildren *does* influence our prediction of her genetic make-up, even though determining the genes of those parents of Susan's grandchildren who are not Susan's children *does not* (notice that the latter are nondescendents).[2]

The expression for the global distribution (1.19) is derived from (1.20) in the following way. Since a Bayesian network contains no directed cycles, it is always possible to choose an *ancestral ordering* $z_{\pi(1)}, z_{\pi(2)}, \ldots, z_{\pi(N)}$, where $\pi(\cdot)$ is a permutation map, so that the descendents of each variable come later in the ordering: $\mathbf{d}_{\pi(k)} \subseteq \{z_{\pi(k+1)}, \ldots, z_{\pi(N)}\}$. For example, the variables in the network shown in Figure 1.5 were assigned so that $z_1, z_2, \ldots, z_{13}$ is an ancestral ordering. Using the general chain rule of probability applied to the ancestral ordering, we have

---

[2]Interestingly, if we have previously determined the genes of Susan's grandchildren, then determining the genes of those parents of Susan's grandchildren who are not Susan's children *does* influence our prediction of Susan's genetic make-up. See Section 1.2.5 for more details.

Figure 1.6
An example of a chain-type Bayesian network, or a *Markov chain*.

$$P(\mathbf{z}) = \prod_{k=1}^{N} P\big(z_{\pi(k)}\big|z_{\pi(1)}, \cdots, z_{\pi(k-1)}\big). \tag{1.21}$$

From the definition of the ancestral ordering, it follows that the set of variables that precede $z_{\pi(k)}$ is a subset of its nondescendents and that the parents of $z_{\pi(k)}$ are a subset of the variables that precede $z_{\pi(k)}$:

$$\mathbf{a}_{\pi(k)} \subseteq \{z_{\pi(1)}, \cdots, z_{\pi(k-1)}\} \subseteq \mathbf{n}_{\pi(k)}. \tag{1.22}$$

For this reason, $\{z_{\pi(1)}, \cdots, z_{\pi(k-1)}\} = \mathbf{a}_{\pi(k)} \cup (\{z_{\pi(1)}, \cdots, z_{\pi(k-1)}\} \backslash \mathbf{a}_{\pi(k)})$, and taking $\mathbf{w} = \{z_{\pi(1)}, \cdots, z_{\pi(k-1)}\} \backslash \mathbf{a}_{\pi(k)}$ in (1.20), we have

$$\begin{aligned}
P\big(z_{\pi(k)}\big|z_{\pi(1)}, \cdots, z_{\pi(k-1)}\big) &= P\big(z_{\pi(k)}\big|\mathbf{a}_{\pi(k)}, \{z_{\pi(1)}, \cdots, z_{\pi(k-1)}\} \backslash \mathbf{a}_{\pi(k)}\big) \\
&= P\big(z_{\pi(k)}\big|\mathbf{a}_{\pi(k)}\big). \tag{1.23}
\end{aligned}$$

Inserting this result into (1.21), we obtain the form given in (1.19).

If the probability functions for a Bayesian network are not specified, the network is meant to represent *all* distributions that can be written in the form given in (1.19). For the network with ancestral ordering $z_1, z_2, \ldots, z_{13}$ shown in Figure 1.5, (1.19) gives a joint distribution

$$\begin{aligned}
P(\mathbf{z}) = &P(z_1)P(z_2|z_1)P(z_3)P(z_4|z_1, z_2)P(z_5|z_2, z_3)P(z_6)P(z_7|z_3) \\
&\cdot P(z_8|z_4, z_5)P(z_9|z_5, z_6)P(z_{10})P(z_{11}|z_8)P(z_{12}|z_8, z_9)P(z_{13}|z_9, z_{10}). \tag{1.24}
\end{aligned}$$

This product could have been written in any order, but using an ancestral ordering helps clarify the dependencies. In this equation, each variable z_k is conditioned on variables whose distributions appear to the *left* of the distribution for z_k. Note that a Bayesian network may have more than one ancestral ordering. In this case, $z_{10}, z_6, z_3, z_7, z_1, z_2, z_4, z_5, z_8, z_{11}, z_9, z_{13}, z_{12}$ is also an ancestral ordering. An interesting special case of a Bayesian network is the chain-type network shown in Figure 1.6, also known as a first-order *Markov chain.* Applying (1.19) to this network, we obtain

$$P(\mathbf{z}) = P(z_1)P(z_2|z_1)P(z_3|z_2)P(z_4|z_3)P(z_5|z_4). \qquad (1.25)$$

This type of structure is frequently used to model time series data, where it is often assumed that the next state of a physical system depends only on the previous state. Comparing this network to the more complex networks that appear later in this book, the Bayesian network can be thought of as a generalization of the Markov chain.

1.2.4 Ancestral simulation in Bayesian networks

It is often practically very difficult to simulate vectors $\mathbf{z}$ that are distributed according to $P(\mathbf{z})$. For example, in a Markov random field it can take a very long time for a stochastic simulation to reach equilibrium. However, if the joint distribution can be described by a Bayesian network, and if a value for each z_k can be drawn from its conditional probability $P(z_k|\mathbf{a}_k)$ in a practical manner, then the ancestral ordering can be used to draw an entire vector. Starting with $k = 1$, we draw $z_{\pi(1)}$ from $P(z_{\pi(1)})$. We continue to draw $z_{\pi(k)}$ from $P(z_{\pi(k)}|\mathbf{a}_{\pi(k)})$ for $k = 2, \ldots, N$ until an entire vector $\mathbf{z}$ has been drawn. In this way, the probabilistic structure implied by the graph allows us to decompose the simulation problem into local pieces.

1.2.5 Dependency separation in Bayesian networks

In Section 1.2.3, we saw that a Bayesian network implies that variable z_k is conditionally independent of any subset of its nondescendents, given its parents. This is expressed mathematically by (1.20). A convenient way to describe this scenario is to say that "z_k is dependency-separated from any combination of its nondescendents by its parents".

Consider the uncountable set of distributions $\mathcal{P}$ that can be described by a given Bayesian network. In general, I will say that $\mathbf{z}^A$ is dependency-separated from $\mathbf{z}^B$ by $\mathbf{z}^S$ ("S" for separation), if and only if

$$P(\mathbf{z}^A|\mathbf{z}^S, \mathbf{z}^B) = P(\mathbf{z}^A|\mathbf{z}^S), \quad i.e. \quad P(\mathbf{z}^A, \mathbf{z}^B|\mathbf{z}^S) = P(\mathbf{z}^A|\mathbf{z}^S)P(\mathbf{z}^B|\mathbf{z}^S),$$

$$(1.26)$$

for all $P \in \mathcal{P}$. (See Pearl [1988] for an extensive discussion of dependency-separation.) Notice that dependency-separation is symmetric with respect to $\mathbf{z}^A$ and $\mathbf{z}^B$. The type of dependency-separation that can we used to define a Bayesian network in Section 1.2.3 is special, in that $\mathbf{z}^S$ was the set of parents of the single variable $\mathbf{z}^A$, and $\mathbf{z}^B$ was a subset of the nondescendents of $\mathbf{z}^A$.

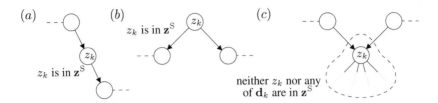

Figure 1.7
The three ways in which a path may be blocked. If all paths from all variables in $\mathbf{z}^A$ to all variables in $\mathbf{z}^B$ are blocked, then $\mathbf{z}^A$ and $\mathbf{z}^B$ are dependency-separated by $\mathbf{z}^S$.

It is possible to ascertain dependency separation in the general case simply by inspecting the Bayesian network. If $\mathbf{z}^A$, $\mathbf{z}^B$, and $\mathbf{z}^S$ are three disjoint subsets of $\mathbf{z}$, then $\mathbf{z}^S$ dependency-separates $\mathbf{z}^A$ from $\mathbf{z}^B$ if, in every path connecting any variable in $\mathbf{z}^A$ to any variable in $\mathbf{z}^B$, there is at least one variable z_k that satisfies one or more of the following three conditions:

1. z_k acts as both a parent and a child in the path and $z_k \in \mathbf{z}^S$ (Figure 1.7a), or

2. z_k acts as the parent of two variables in the path and $z_k \in \mathbf{z}^S$ (Figure 1.7b), or

3. z_k acts as the child of two variables in the path and neither z_k nor any of its descendents are in $\mathbf{z}^S$ (Figure 1.7c).

(Note that the identification of a path does not depend on edge directions.) A path for which one of these conditions is met is said to be *blocked*. In order to ascertain dependency-separation, we need to consider only paths that do not intersect themselves, since those conditions that hold for any given path will also hold for the path when extra variables that form a loop are considered.

For example, in Figure 1.5a we have the following dependency separation relationships. z_6 is dependency-separated from z_{10} (by nothing), since the sole path z_6, z_9, z_{13}, z_{10} is blocked by z_{13} in condition 3. What if z_9 is observed? Then, z_6 is still dependency-separated from z_{10}, by condition 1 applied to the sole path z_6, z_9, z_{13}, z_{10}. In contrast, if only z_{13} is observed, then z_6 is *not* dependency-separated from z_{10}, since there exists a path z_6, z_9, z_{13}, z_{10} for which none of the three conditions can be met. This means that once z_{13} is observed, z_6 and z_{10} *may* become dependent. Note that there *may* exist a distribution in $\mathcal{P}$ where z_6 and z_{10} are *independent* given z_{13}, but there exists at least one distribution in $\mathcal{P}$ where z_6 and z_{10} are dependent given z_{13}.

Here are some more complicated examples. z_2 is dependency-separated from z_9 by z_5, since path z_2, z_5, z_9 is blocked by z_5 in condition 1, paths

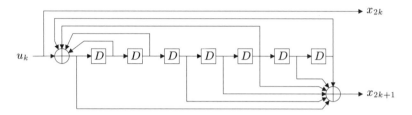

Figure 1.8
The LFSR for a systematic recursive convolutional code that has a minimum distance of 10.

$z_2, z_4, z_8, z_{12}, z_9$ and $z_2, z_1, z_4, z_8, z_{12}, z_9$ are blocked by z_{12} in condition 3, paths z_2, z_4, z_8, z_5, z_9 and $z_2, z_1, z_4, z_8, z_5, z_9$ are blocked by z_5 in condition 2 *and* by z_8 in condition 3, path $z_2, z_5, z_8, z_{12}, z_9$ is blocked by z_5 in condition 1 *and* by z_{12} in condition 3. z_2 is dependency-separated from $\{z_3, z_7\}$ (by nothing), since the paths z_2, z_5, z_3 and z_2, z_5, z_3, z_7 are blocked by z_5 in condition 3. This means that in the absence of observations z_2 and $\{z_3, z_7\}$ are independent. z_2 is not dependency-separated from $\{z_3, z_7\}$ by z_{12}, since there exists a path z_2, z_5, z_3 for which none of the conditions can be met. Condition 3 applied to z_5 fails, because z_{12} is a descendent of z_5. This means that once z_{12} is observed, z_2 and $\{z_3, z_7\}$ may *become* dependent.

1.2.6 Example 1: Recursive convolutional codes and turbocodes

Recall from Section 1.1.4 that the purpose of channel coding is to communicate over a noisy channel in an error-free (or nearly error-free) fashion. To do this, we encode a given binary information vector **u** as a longer codeword vector **x**, which contains extra bits whose purpose is to "protect" the information from the channel noise. (An example is a repetition code, where each information bit is simply transmitted several times.) The codeword is converted to a physical form (*e.g.*, radio waves) and then sent over a channel. A vector of noisy signals **y** is received at the output of the channel. Given **y**, the decoder must make a guess **û** at what the original **u** was.

One very popular class of channel codes (you probably have one of these in your telephone modem) can be described using Bayesian networks. The encoder for a *recursive convolutional code* is simply a linear feedback shift register (LFSR) that takes in information bits and generates codeword bits. See Lin and Costello [1983] for an extensive treatment of convolutional codes. Figure 1.8 shows the LFSR for the convolutional code that is described below. Each box represents a 1-bit memory element and D indicates a delay buffer.

The discs represent addition modulo 2 (XOR). For this particular convolutional code, every second output is actually just a copy of the input bit. This type of code is called *systematic*. Notice that for each input bit, two output bits are produced, so this is a rate 1/2 code. If there are K information bits, then there will be $N = 2K$ codeword bits. The device shown in Figure 1.8 is called a *linear* feedback shift register because the output sequence generated by the sum of two input sequences is equal to the sum of the two output sequences that are generated by the individual input sequences (where summation is modulo 2). The details of how to choose the feedback delay taps and the output taps in order to produce a good code can be found in Lin and Costello [1983; 1996]. However, the operation of an encoder of this type is quite simple. The LFSR is initialized so that all memory elements contain 0's. Then, the information bits u_k are fed into the LFSR, producing codeword bits x_k. Signals that represent the codeword bits are then transmitted over the channel. For example, on a twisted pair of wires, we might apply $+1$ volts if $x_k = 1$ and -1 volts if $x_k = 0$.

Figure 1.9a shows the Bayesian network for a recursive systematic convolutional code. Normally, the number of information bits K is much larger than 6 (typical numbers range from 100 to 100,000 bits). s_k is the state of the LFSR at time k, extended to include the input bit (this makes the network simpler). To fully specify the Bayesian network, we must also provide the conditional distributions. Assuming the information bits are uniformly distributed,

$$P(u_k) = 0.5, \quad \text{for } u_k \in \{0, 1\}. \tag{1.27}$$

Let $S(s_{k-1}, u_k)$ be a function (determined from the LFSR) that maps the previous state and current input to the next state, and let $g(s_k)$ be a function that maps the state to the nonsystematic output bit. Then, the deterministic conditional distributions for the states and state outputs are

$$P(s_0|u_0) = \delta(s_0, S(0, u_0))$$

$$P(s_k|u_k, s_{k-1}) = \delta(s_k, S(s_{k-1}, u_k))$$

$$P(x_{2k}|u_k) = \delta(x_{2k}, u_k)$$

$$P(x_{2k+1}|s_k) = \delta(x_{2k+1}, g(s_k)), \tag{1.28}$$

where $\delta(a, b) = 1$ if $a = b$ and 0 otherwise. Assuming that the channel simply adds independent Gaussian noise with variance σ^2 to the $+1/-1$ signals described above, the conditional distributions for the received channel output signals are

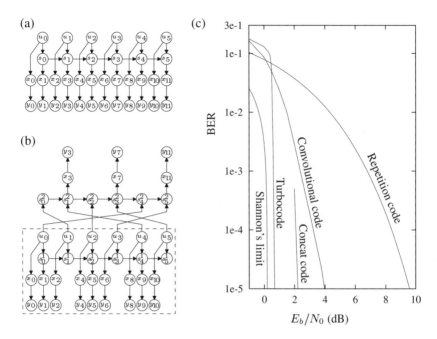

Figure 1.9
(a) The Bayesian network for a recursive systematic convolutional code. (b) The Bayesian network for an example of the recently proposed turbocode. (c) The bit error rate (BER) performance for instances of these two codes.

$$p(y_k|x_k) = \begin{cases} \frac{1}{\sqrt{2\pi\sigma^2}}e^{-(y_k-1.0)^2/2\sigma^2} & \text{if } x_k = 1 \\ \frac{1}{\sqrt{2\pi\sigma^2}}e^{-(y_k+1.0)^2/2\sigma^2} & \text{if } x_k = 0. \end{cases} \quad (1.29)$$

Given an information vector **u**, encoding and channel transmission can be simulated by one sweep of ancestral simulation. For example, we first directly copy u_0 into x_0, which is then used to draw a noisy channel output value y_0. Then, we use u_0 to determine s_0, which is then used to determine x_1, which is then used to draw a noisy channel output value y_1. Then, we directly copy u_1 into x_2 and so on until the entire channel output vector **y** has been obtained.

The decoder sees only the vector **y**, and ideally would infer the most likely value of each information bit, *i.e.*, determine for each k the u_k that maximizes $P(u_k|\mathbf{y})$. In general such a probabilistic inference is very difficult, but if we take advantage of the graphical structure of the code it turns out it can be done quite easily. In fact, it is possible to compute $P(u_k|\mathbf{y})$ $k = 0, \ldots, K-1$ *exactly* using the forward-backward (a.k.a. BCJR) algorithm [Baum and Petrie 1966; Bahl *et al.* 1974], which is just a special case of the general *probability propagation* algorithm discussed in Section 2.1. Once the block is decoded, we can compare the decoded information bit values with the true ones to determine the number of bit errors made for the block transmission. If we simulate the transmission of many blocks, we can obtain an estimate of the bit error rate (BER).

This procedure was carried out for the convolutional code shown in Figure 1.8. This recursive systematic convolutional code was designed to maximize the smallest Hamming distance between all pairs of codewords [Viterbi and Omura 1979; Lin and Costello 1983] ($d_{\min} = 10$). The information vector length was $K = 5000$ (giving a codeword length of $N = 10000$), and 5000 vectors (25×10^6 information bits in all) were transmitted for a fixed noise variance. It is common practice to give BER results as a function of the noise level measured by a signal-to-noise ratio E_b/N_0 in decibels. For any system with $N = 2K$ and transmission power (variance) of unity, E_b/N_0 is related to σ^2 by $E_b/N_0 = -10 \log_{10} \sigma^2$. Figure 1.9c shows the BER as a function of E_b/N_0 for this recursive systematic convolutional code.[3] Notice that as E_b/N_0 increases (σ^2 decreases), the BER drops.

In the same figure, I also give the BER curve for a simple repetition code, where each information bit is transmitted twice, maintaining $N = 2K$. If the information bit is 0, a pair of -1's are sent; if the information bit is 1, a pair of +1's are sent. Each pair of received noisy signals is then averaged before a threshold of 0.0 is applied to detect the information bit. The curve on the far left shows Shannon's limit; for a given E_b/N_0, it is impossible to communicate with a BER below this curve using binary signalling. (See Sections. 6.1.6 and 6.1.7 for a derivation of this curve.) So, systems of practical interest give performance points that lie between the Shannon limit curve and the curve for the repetition code. Performance points to the left of the Shannon limit are impossible, and performance points to the right of the curve for the repetition code are not of practical interest.

Recently, a code and decoding algorithm were discovered that give unprecedented BER performance. It turns out that the *turbodecoding* algorithm for these *turbocodes* [Berrou and Glavieux 1996] is just the probability propagation algorithm discussed in Section 2.1 applied to a code network like the one shown in Figure 1.9b [Frey and Kschischang 1997; Kschischang and Frey 1998; McEliece, MacKay and Cheng 1998]. This Bayesian network contains two recursive convolutional code networks that are connected to the infor-

---

[3]Trellis termination [Lin and Costello 1983] was used to improve the performance of the code.

mation bits in different ways. The information bits feed directly into one of the chains (s^1), but feed into the second chain (s^2) in a *permuted order* as shown. In order to produce the same number of codeword bits per codeword as would be produced by the recursive systematic convolutional encoder described above, every second output of each LFSR is alternately not transmitted (a procedure called *puncturing*).

Figure 1.9c shows the BER performance for a turbocode system with $K = 65,536$ and $N = 131,072$. 530 vectors ($\sim 35 \times 10^6$ information bits) were transmitted to determine the BER for each noise level. Each of the two LFSRs had 4 bits of memory and used identical feedback and output delay taps. All four delayed bits were fed back to the input of the LFSR. Only the bit entering the first delay element and the most-delayed bit were fed forward to the output. (This block length and these constituent LFSRs were proposed by Berrou, Glavieux and Thitimajshima [1993]). The decoding complexity per information bit for the turbocode was roughly twice that for the convolutional code described above. The information bit permuter was chosen at random. The turbocode system clearly outperforms the computationally comparable single convolutional code system. At a BER of 10^{-5}, the turbocode system is tolerant to 3.3 dB more noise than the single convolutional code system, and is only 0.5 dB from the Shannon limit. Also shown on this graph is the performance of a concatenated Reed-Solomon convolutional code described in Lin and Costello [1983], which had been considered to be the best practical code until the proposal of turbocodes. The turbocode system is tolerant to 1.5 dB more noise than the concatenated system.

In Chapter 6, I explore some of the exciting new applications of Bayesian networks to channel coding problems, with a focus on using the probability propagation algorithm discussed in Section 2.1 for inference.

1.2.7 Parameterized Bayesian networks

It is sometimes convenient to represent the conditional distributions $P(z_k|\mathbf{a}_k)$ in parametric form. That is, the distribution over z_k given its parents $\mathbf{a}_k$ is specified not by an exhaustive list of probability masses, but by a function of z_k, $\mathbf{a}_k$, and a set of parameters $\boldsymbol{\theta}_k$. (The subscript k indicates that $\boldsymbol{\theta}_k$ is a set of parameters associated with z_k.) In this case, we write the conditional distribution as $P(z_k|\mathbf{a}_k, \boldsymbol{\theta}_k)$. The total set of parameters is $\boldsymbol{\theta} = \{\boldsymbol{\theta}_1, \dots, \boldsymbol{\theta}_N\}$, and the parameterized joint distribution is expressed as $P(\mathbf{z}|\boldsymbol{\theta})$. Such a parametric form can be useful in applications such as density estimation, pattern classification, and data compression, where the distribution $P(\mathbf{z}|\boldsymbol{\theta})$ is to be estimated from a data set. In this case, the parametric form can act as a regularizer. Since the number of possible configurations of each z_k and $\mathbf{a}_k$ is usually quite large, we would need an extremely large data set to estimate all probabilities

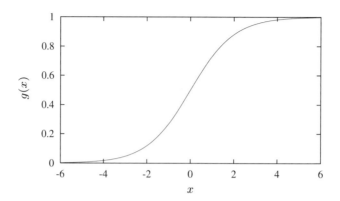

Figure 1.10
The logistic function $g(x) = 1/(1 + \exp[-x])$.

accurately. Using the parametric form, however, we need only estimate each parameter. As described in Section 2.3, a parametric form is also useful when formulating variational inference algorithms.

A common parametric Bayesian network is the sigmoidal Bayesian network [Neal 1992; Jordan 1995; Saul, Jaakkola and Jordan 1996], whose random variables are all binary. The conditional probability function $P(z_k|\mathbf{a}_k, \boldsymbol{\theta}_k)$ can be viewed as a regression model that is meant to predict z_k from a set of attributes $\mathbf{a}_k$. A standard statistical method for predicting a binary-valued variable is *logistic regression* [McCullagh and Nelder 1983], in which the conditional probability for z_k given $\mathbf{a}_k$ is

$$P(z_k|\mathbf{a}_k, \boldsymbol{\theta}_k) = \begin{cases} 1/(1 + \exp[-\theta_{k0} - \sum_{\forall j: z_j \in \mathbf{a}_k} \theta_{kj} z_j]) & \text{if } z_k = 1, \\ 1 - 1/(1 + \exp[-\theta_{k0} - \sum_{\forall j: z_j \in \mathbf{a}_k} \theta_{kj} z_j]) & \text{if } z_k = 0, \end{cases} \tag{1.30}$$

where the parameter θ_{k0} represents a constant *bias* in the exponent. The logistic function $g(x) = 1/(1 + \exp[-x])$ is used to restrict the probability to lie between 0 and 1. (This function is shown in Figure 1.10.) In terms of log-odds,

$$\log \frac{P(z_k = 1|\mathbf{a}_k, \boldsymbol{\theta}_k)}{P(z_k = 0|\mathbf{a}_k, \boldsymbol{\theta}_k)} = \theta_{k0} + \sum_{\forall j: z_j \in \mathbf{a}_k} \theta_{kj} z_j, \tag{1.31}$$

which shows how each parent $z_j \in \mathbf{a}_k$ independently increases or decreases the log-odds for z_k, depending on the sign of θ_{kj}.

Sometimes, for the sake of notational simplicity, I will assume that the set of parents for each variable z_k is specified by some parameter constraints. Assume without loss of generality that for a given network, the random variables $\mathbf{z}$ have an ancestral ordering $z_1, z_2, \ldots, z_N$. I take $P(z_k|\mathbf{a}_k, \boldsymbol{\theta}_k) = P(z_k|\{z_j\}_{j=1}^{k-1}, \boldsymbol{\theta}_k)$, where in the second expression the parameters are constrained so that the function does not depend on nonparents. Also, in order to succinctly account for the bias, I will usually assume that there is a dummy variable z_0 that is set to $z_0 = 1$. (Thus the notation θ_{k0} for the bias in the summations above.) Using these notational simplifications and using $g(\cdot)$ for the logistic function, the sigmoidal model described above can be written

$$P(z_k|\{z_j\}_{j=1}^{k-1}, \boldsymbol{\theta}_k) = z_k g(\textstyle\sum_{j=0}^{k-1}\theta_{kj}z_j) + (1 - z_k)(1 - g(\textstyle\sum_{j=0}^{k-1}\theta_{kj}z_j)),$$

(1.32)

where θ_{kj} is set to 0 for each nonparent z_j.

1.2.8 Example 2: The bars problem

Bayesian networks provide a useful framework for specifying *generative models*. A generative model can be used to generate data vectors that exhibit interesting structure. The generative models discussed in this book can also be used for pattern classification and data compression, in the fashion described in Sections. 1.1.1 and 1.1.3. If the Bayesian network is parameterized, we can estimate the parameters of the network from a training set by making the generative distribution "close" (say, in the Kullback-Leibler pseudo-distance) to the training set distribution. We hope that in this fashion, we can extract the "true" underlying generative process, or at least one that is equally efficient at describing the data.

For example, the 4×4 binary images shown in Figure 1.11a were generated by first selecting an orientation (horizontal or vertical) with equal probability, and then randomly instantiating each of the four possible bars with that orientation with probability 0.5. (The all-on images were removed from the training set, since the orientation of the bars in an all-on image is ambiguous.) Using the Helmholtz machine and the wake-sleep algorithm (described in Sections. 2.4 and 3.4.4), I fit the parameterized network shown in Figure 1.11b to a large training set of 2×10^6 images produced in this way. The network has three layers of binary variables: 1 in the top layer, 8 in the middle layer, and 16 in the visible layer (the image). The variables in adjacent layers are fully-connected, and the conditional distributions are modelled using logistic regression, as described in the previous section. After parameter estimation

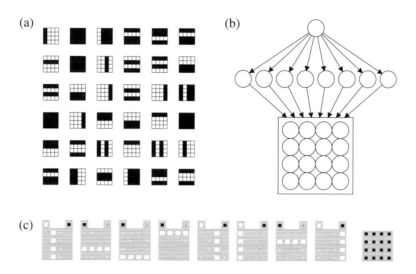

Figure 1.11
(a) Examples of training images typical of the "bars problem". (b) The graph for a parameterized Bayesian network that was estimated from a large training set using the wake-sleep algorithm. Edges that terminate on the box are connected to all vertices within the box. (c) The parameters of the Bayesian network clearly show that the network has learned the notion of horizontal and vertical bars (see the main text for a more complete description).

(see Hinton, *et al.* [1995] for details), ancestral simulation of the network produces output images that are indistinguishable from the training images.

After learning, the bias for the top-layer variable is nearly zero, so that under the joint distribution it has the value 1 as often as it has the value 0. The values of the other parameters are depicted in Figure 1.11c. The eight large blocks on the left show the parameters associated with the connections that feed into and out of the middle-layer variables. The bias for a variable is shown by the small black or white square on the top right of the block for each middle-layer variable. Positive parameters are white, negative parameters are black, and the area of the square is proportional to the magnitude of the parameter. (The largest parameter shown in the figure is 14.1.) The parameter associated with the connection from the top-layer variable to a middle-layer variable is shown by the small square on the top left of the block for each middle-layer variable. Finally, the parameters associated with the connections from a middle-layer variable to the visible variables are shown by the 4×4 grid of squares in the block for each middle-layer variable. The biases for the 16 visible variables are shown by the 4×4 grid of squares on the far right of Figure 1.11c.

It is clear from these parameter values that each middle-layer variable represents the presence (value of 1) or absence (value of 0) of a particular horizontal or vertical bar. If the top-layer variable is 1, the probability that a horizontal bar is present is nearly 0, since the biases for these variables are nearly 0 and the parameters that connect these variables to the top-layer variable are large and negative. On the other hand, if the top-layer variable is 0, the probability that a horizontal bar is present is 0.5. In this way, the network captures the true generative model that produced the training data.

In Chapters 3 and 5, I show how Monte Carlo inference, variational inference, and Helmholtz machines can be used to fit Bayesian networks to training data for the purposes of pattern classification, unsupervised learning, and data compression.

1.3   Organization of this book

In the remainder of this book, I use graphical models (mostly Bayesian networks) as a platform to develop algorithms for pattern classification, unsupervised learning, data compression, and channel coding. The last of these problems is quite different from the former ones, since we will usually *design* an error-correcting code using a graphical model and then use probabilistic inference to perform decoding. On the other hand, for pattern classification, unsupervised learning, and data compression, we will usually *estimate* a parameterized Bayesian network from some training data and then use probabilistic inference to classify a new pattern, perform perceptual inference, or produce a source codeword for a new pattern.

In Chapter 2, I discuss different ways to perform probabilistic inference, including probability propagation, Markov chain Monte Carlo, variational optimization, and the Helmholtz machine.

Several types of Bayesian networks that are suitable for pattern classification are presented in Chapter 3. I show how Markov chain Monte Carlo, variational optimization, and the Helmholtz machine wake-sleep algorithm can be used for probabilistic inference and parameter estimation in these networks. Based on a digit classification problem, I compare the performances of these systems with several standard algorithms, including the k-nearest neighbor method and classification and regression trees (CART).

Learning to extract structure from data *without* using a supervised signal such as class identity is another interesting parameter estimation problem. In Chapter 4, I examine unsupervised learning in Bayesian networks that have binary-valued and real-valued variables. It turns out that simple algorithms in neural-network type Bayesian networks can be used to learn hierarchical structure from data, such as noisy images of horizontal and vertical bars.

In Chapter 5, I consider the problem of how to efficiently compress data using Bayesian networks with hidden variables. When there are hidden variables, a Bayesian network may assign many source codewords of similar length to a particular input pattern. I present the "bits-back" coding algorithm that can be used to efficiently communicate patterns, despite this redundancy in the source code.

In Chapter 6, I present several recently invented error-correcting codes in terms of Bayesian networks and show that their corresponding iterative decoding algorithms can be derived as special cases of probability propagation. In particular, the recently proposed turbodecoding algorithm, which brought researchers a leap closer to (and almost up against) the Shannon limit, is an instance of probability propagation. Motivated by these results and the breadth in perspective offered by graphical models, I present a new class of "trellis-constrained codes", which when iteratively decoded are competitive with turbocodes. I also present two approaches for speeding up a popular class of computationally burdensome iterative decoding algorithms.

Finally, in Chapter 7, I discuss some directions which look promising for further research on graphical models in machine learning and digital communication.

2 Probabilistic Inference in Graphical Models

In this chapter, I discuss methods for probabilistic inference that make use of the graphical model description of the joint distribution. Many readers may be aware of how probabilistic inference in a Markov chain is simplified by a chain-type graphical structure that leads to the forward-backward algorithm [Baum and Petrie 1966]. A generalized form of this simplification holds for those graphical models that have only a single path (when edge directions are ignored) between any two vertices. In Section 2.1, I review an algorithm for "probability propagation", which can be used to infer the *exact* distributions over individual variables or small groups of variables in such models. It turns out that the generalized Viterbi algorithm is just probability propagation with summations replaced by minimizations ($a + b \rightarrow \min(a, b)$) and products replaced by summations ($a \cdot b \rightarrow a + b$).

For networks that have multiple paths between one or more pairs of vertices, probability propagation is not exact. Although there are procedures for attempting to convert an original network to one that is appropriate for probability propagation [Spiegelhalter 1986; Lauritzen and Spiegelhalter 1988], these procedures are not practically fruitful when the number of multiple paths is large. In these cases, approximate inference methods must be used. In Section 2.2, I discuss a Monte Carlo approach to inference, where we attempt to produce a sample from the desired distribution. Histograms based on the sample can then be used to approximate the true marginal distributions of interest. In Section 2.3, I present a variational method for approximate inference. Here, we construct a parameterized approximation to the true distribution and then attempt to optimize the parameters of this variational approximation in order to make it as close as possible to the true distribution. This technique requires that the distribution specified by the Bayesian network can be expressed in a form suitable for mathematical analysis. Finally, in Section 2.4, I present the Helmholtz machine. This method can be very efficient, and is tailored to inference in Bayesian networks whose parameters are estimated from data.

2.1 Exact inference using probability propagation (the sum-product algorithm)

In the late 1980's, Pearl [1986; 1988] and Lauritzen and Spiegelhalter [Spiegelhalter 1986; Lauritzen and Spiegelhalter 1988; Lauritzen 1996] independently

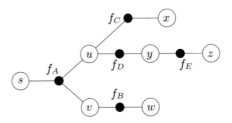

Figure 2.1
A simple factor graph that describes the factorization $P(s, u, v, w, x, y, z) = f_A(s, u, v) f_B(v, w) f_C(u, x) f_D(u, y) f_E(y, z)$.

published an exact *probability propagation* algorithm (a.k.a. the "sum-product algorithm" [Wiberg 1996; Frey *et al.* 1998]) for inferring the distributions over individual variables in singly-connected graphical models. A *singly-connected* network has only a single path (ignoring edge directions) connecting any two vertices.

It is easy to see how probability propagation works by studying a simple example. Figure 2.1 shows a singly-connected factor graph that describes the following factorization of the global distribution:

$$P(s, u, v, w, x, y, z) = f_A(s, u, v) f_B(v, w) f_C(u, x) f_D(u, y) f_E(y, z). \quad (2.1)$$

Suppose we wish to compute $P(s|z = z')$ for the observed value z' of z. First, notice that $P(s|z = z') = P(s, z = z') / \sum_s P(s, z = z')$, so that we can instead compute $P(s, z = z')$ and then normalize to get $P(s|z = z')$. If we directly compute $\sum_{u,v,w,x,y} P(s, u, v, w, x, y, z = z')$, we will have to sum over $n_u \times n_v \times n_w \times n_x \times n_y$ terms, where n_u is the number of values u can take on, and so on.

In fact, the individual summations over u, v, w, x and y distribute across the products in (2.1); *e.g.*, the summation over y can take place over just the last two factors. One distribution of sums gives

$$P(s, z = z') =$$

$$\sum_{u,v} f_A(s, u, v) \underbrace{\left\{ \underbrace{\sum_w f_B(v, w)}_{v} \right\} \left\{ \underbrace{\left[\underbrace{\sum_x f_C(u, x)}_{u} \right] \left[\underbrace{\sum_y f_D(u, y) f_E(y, z = z')}_{u} \right]}_{} \right\}}_{s}.$$

$$(2.2)$$

Each summation can be viewed as a processing stage that removes a variable and produces an output function. The underbraces indicate what the output of each summation depends on. The principle of probability propagation is to decompose the global sum into products of local sums, so that the computation is tractable. Using this procedure, the total number of additions in the example is $n_u \times n_v + n_w + n_x + n_y$. Whereas the number of additions in the brute force marginalization scales exponentially with the total number of variables, the number of additions in probability propagation scales linearly with the exponential of the number of variables in the largest local function. For example, in (2.2), the summation over u and v dominates when the number of values the variables can take on is large (say, $n_u = n_v = n_w = n_x = n_y = 100$).

There are essentially two types of computation performed in probability propagation: multiplication of local marginals; and summation over local joint distributions. Within the second set of curly braces in (2.2), the product of the terms in square braces is an example of multiplication of local marginals. The summation over the product of $f_A(s, u, v)$ and the two terms in curly braces is an example of a summation over a local joint distribution. Since these operations take place locally in the graph, we can view the edges of the graphical model as *message passing* channels for inference computations. By passing short real-valued vectors between neighboring vertices in the singly-connected graphical model, the probability propagation algorithm can perform exact probabilistic inference efficiently. One flavor of probability propagation is the *generalized forward-backward algorithm*, in which messages are passed in a highly regular way.

2.1.1   The generalized forward-backward algorithm

It is easiest to understand the operation of the generalized forward-backward algorithm in factor graphs, although the algorithm can be applied to MRFs and Bayesian networks. In fact, MRFs and Bayesian networks are special cases of factor graphs in this context. So, we will begin with a Bayesian network, convert it to a factor graph, and then see how the generalized forward-backward algorithm works.

To begin with, the singly-connected Bayesian network shown in Figure 2.2a is converted to the factor graph shown in Figure 2.2b. The marginal probabilities for the root variables are simply included in neighboring local functions. Note that the conversion from a Bayesian network to a factor graph can remove local cycles. For example, if there were an edge from z_1 to z_2 in the original Bayesian network, the singly-connected factor graph shown in Figure 2.2b is still obtained. At this point, we can ignore the edge directions, and simply interpret the parent-child conditional probabilities as local functions in the factor graph.

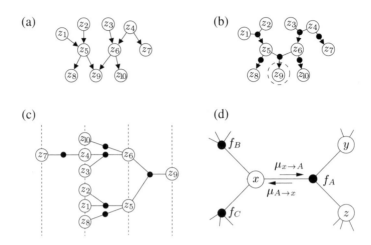

Figure 2.2
(a) shows a singly-connected Bayesian network which is easily converted to a factor
graph, as shown in (b). At this point the conditional distributions can be interpreted
simply as local functions. A tree is obtained by choosing z_9 as a root vertex as shown
in (c), where the edge directions have been left off. (d) shows a network fragment with
a variable-to-function message $\mu_{x \to A}$ and a function-to-variable message $\mu_{A \to x}$ that
are used in the generalized forward-backward algorithm.

Next, the factor graph is arranged as a horizontal tree with an arbitrarily
chosen "root" vertex on the far right. For example, if the circled vertex z_9
in Figure 2.2b is chosen as the root, we obtain the tree shown in Figure 2.2c.
(Imagine the network sits in a viscous fluid and we grasp the root vertex and
pull it down and then to the right.) Beginning at the left-most level, messages are passed level by level forward to the root, while being multiplied and
marginalized. Each vertex stores its messages for later use. Then, messages
are passed level by level backward from the root to the leaves. During these
two phases, the observed variables **v** are held constant and are not marginalized out. The total number of messages passed in this fashion is just twice
the number of edges in the graph, since each edge passes a message in both
directions. Once both passes are complete, each vertex z_i combines its stored
incoming messages to obtain $P(z_i|\mathbf{v})$.

During each of the forward and backward passes, two types of vector messages are passed: variable-to-function messages consisting of products of local
marginals; and function-to-variable messages consisting of sums of distributions over nearby variables. To make this more clear, consider the network
fragment shown in Figure 2.2d, with variables x, y and z, and local functions

$f_A(x, y, z)$, $f_B(x, \ldots)$ and $f_C(x, \ldots)$ (the other variables to which $f_B(\cdot)$ and $f_C(\cdot)$ are connected are not shown). The variable-to-function message $\mu_{x \to A}(x)$ is computed from

$$\mu_{x \to A}(x) = \mu_{B \to x}(x)\mu_{C \to x}(x), \tag{2.3}$$

unless x is observed, in which case we set

$$\mu_{x \to A}(x) = \delta(x, x'), \tag{2.4}$$

where x' is the observed value and $\delta(x, x') = 1$ if $x = x'$, $\delta(x, x') = 0$ if $x \neq x'$. The function-to-variable message $\mu_{A \to x}(x)$ is computed from

$$\mu_{A \to x}(x) = \sum_y \sum_z f_A(x, y, z)\mu_{y \to A}(y)\mu_{z \to A}(z). \tag{2.5}$$

After the generalized forward and backward phases are complete, the distribution over x conditioned on the observations $\mathbf{v}$ is computed from

$$P(x|\mathbf{v}) = \beta\mu_{A \to x}(x)\mu_{B \to x}(x)\mu_{C \to x}(x), \tag{2.6}$$

where β is computed to ensure normalization, *i.e.*, that $\sum_x P(x|\mathbf{v}) = 1$.

2.1.2 The burglar alarm problem

In order to illustrate how the generalized forward-backward algorithm works, consider a variant of the simple "burglar alarm" network described by Pearl [1988]. The network describes a shoddy burglar alarm that is sensitive not only to burglars, but also to earthquakes. (Judea Pearl lives in California.) The three binary random variables in the network are b for "burglary", e for "earthquake" and a for "alarm". A value of 0 for one of these variables indicates that the corresponding event *has not* occurred, whereas a value of 1 indicates that the corresponding event *has* occurred. Figure 2.3a shows the network, which has the following conditional probability relationships:

$$P(b{=}1) = 0.1, \qquad P(e{=}1) = 0.1,$$
$$P(a{=}1|b{=}0, e{=}0) = 0.001, \quad P(a{=}1|b{=}1, e{=}0) = 0.368,$$
$$P(a{=}1|b{=}0, e{=}1) = 0.135, \quad P(a{=}1|b{=}1, e{=}1) = 0.607. \tag{2.7}$$

Suppose that while you are away at a conference, the burglar alarm contacts you by cell phone and informs you that the alarm is ringing ($a = 1$). We would like to infer the distribution over the two causes to make a well-informed decision about whether or not you should be concerned about a bur-

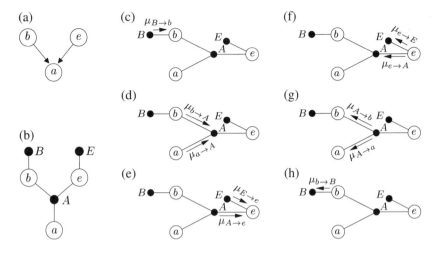

Figure 2.3
(a) The Bayesian network for the burglar alarm problem, with variables b ("burglary"), e ("earthquake") and a ("alarm"). (b) a factor graph for the network in (a). (c) - (e) and (f) - (h) show the messages passed during the generalized forward and backward passes.

glary. Since this network is quite simple, we can apply Bayes rule $P(b, e|a) = P(a|b, e)P(b)P(e)/\sum_{b', e'} P(a|b', e')P(b')P(e')$ to obtain the exact solution,

$$P(b=0, e=0|a=1) = 0.016, \quad P(b=1, e=0|a=1) = 0.635,$$
$$P(b=0, e=1|a=1) = 0.233, \quad P(b=1, e=1|a=1) = 0.116. \quad (2.8)$$

The most likely explanation for the ringing alarm is that a burglary took place. However, although an earthquake is also a likely explanation, it is relatively *unlikely* that both a burglar and an earthquake simultaneously caused the alarm.

Now, consider using the generalized forward-backward algorithm for probabilistic inference in this network. We first rewrite the Bayesian network as a factor graph, as shown in Figure 2.3b, where

$$f_B(b) = P(b), \quad f_E(e) = P(e), \quad \text{and } f_A(a, b, e) = P(a|b, e). \quad (2.9)$$

After we arbitrarily select e as the root, the generalized forward-backward algorithm sends messages in the forward direction as shown in Figures 2.3c – e, and then in the backward direction as shown in Figures 2.3f – h as follows:

(c) Since B is connected to b by one edge, the function-to-variable message $\mu_{B \to b}$ is equal to the local function $P(b)$ (see (2.5)): $\mu_{B \to b} = (0.9, 0.1)$.

(d) Since b is connected to B by one edge, $\mu_{b \to A}$ is equal to $\mu_{B \to b}$ (see (2.3)): $\mu_{b \to A} = \mu_{B \to b} = (0.9, 0.1)$. a is observed to be 1, so we set its message to $\mu_{a \to A} = (0, 1)$.

(e) This time, the function-to-variable message $\mu_{A \to e}$ will require a marginalization as indicated in (2.5):

$$\mu_{A \to e}(e) = \sum_{b,a} f_A(a, b, e)\mu_{b \to A}(b)\mu_{a \to A}(a) = \sum_b P(a = 1|b, e)\mu_{b \to A}(b)$$

$$= (.001 \cdot .9 + .368 \cdot .1, \; .135 \cdot .9 + .607 \cdot .1) = (.0377, .1822). \qquad (2.10)$$

The message $\mu_{E \to e}$ is set equal to the local function $P(e)$: $\mu_{E \to e} = (0.9, 0.1)$.

(f) The message $\mu_{e \to E}$ does not influence the distributions over e and b, so we can neglect computing it. The message $\mu_{e \to A}$ is set equal to $\mu_{E \to e}$ (see (2.5)): $\mu_{e \to A} = \mu_{E \to e} = (0.9, 0.1)$.

(g) Again, the message $\mu_{A \to a}$ is not needed, so we don't compute it. The message $\mu_{A \to b}$ requires a marginalization, as indicated in (2.5):

$$\mu_{A \to b}(b) = \sum_{e,a} f_A(a, b, e)\mu_{e \to A}(e)\mu_{a \to A}(a) = \sum_e P(a = 1|b, e)\mu_{e \to A}(e)$$

$$= (.001 \cdot .9 + .135 \cdot .1, \; .368 \cdot .9 + .607 \cdot .1) = (.0144, .3919). \qquad (2.11)$$

(h) The message $\mu_{b \to B}$ is not needed so we don't compute it.

Finally, we compute $P(b|a = 1)$ and $P(e|a = 1)$ using (2.6):

$$\big(P(b{=}0|a{=}1), P(b{=}1|a{=}1)\big) = \beta\big(\mu_{B \to b}(0)\mu_{A \to b}(0), \mu_{B \to b}(1)\mu_{A \to b}(1)\big)$$

$$= (0.249, 0.751),$$

$$\big(P(e{=}0|a{=}1), P(e{=}1|a{=}1)\big) = \beta\big(\mu_{E \to e}(0)\mu_{A \to e}(0), \mu_{E \to e}(1)\mu_{A \to e}(1)\big)$$

$$= (0.651, 0.349).$$

$$(2.12)$$

These distributions are exactly equal to the marginal posterior distributions computed from (2.8).

2.1.3   Probability propagation (the sum-product algorithm)

The highly regular way that messages are passed in the generalized forward-backward algorithm can be relaxed to obtain a more general *probability propagation* algorithm. It turns out that as long as a few simple rules are followed, messages may be passed in any order (even in parallel) to obtain conditional probabilities. These rules prescribe how the network is to be initialized for propagation, and how messages are created, propagated, absorbed and buffered. Aside from these rules, the formulas for propagating messages are identical to those in (2.3) to (2.6).

Before propagation begins, the network must be *initialized*. This procedure computes the *a priori* incoming messages for each vertex, and corresponds to a generalized forward-backward pass without any observations. After initialization, each vertex z_i has available its *a priori* probability $P(z_i)$. In some networks (such as those used for channel coding) these probabilities are uniform and so the initialization procedure can be skipped.

Messages are now *created* in response to observations. If variable y is observed to have the value y', then a message must be sent out on each of the edges connected to y, using (2.4).

Messages are *propagated* in response to other messages. If variable y receives a message on an edge, y must send out messages on all *other* edges, and similarly for the function vertices.

Messages are *absorbed* by vertices that are connected by only a single edge. This rule follows naturally from the propagation rule, since if such a vertex receives a message on its only edge, the vertex is not required to propagate it back.

It is not necessary that messages be propagated without delay. In fact, a vertex may *buffer* one or more outgoing messages and pass them at any time. (It is usually most convenient to *compute* them at a later time, too.) For example, if a vertex has just received a message and is about to receive another one, computations can often be saved by waiting for the second message before computing and sending out a set of messages.

At any time during propagation, vertex y can compute a current estimate $\hat{P}(y|\mathbf{v})$ of $P(y|\mathbf{v})$ using (2.6). If the above rules are followed and propagation continues until there are no buffered messages remaining in the network, then the estimates will equal the exact probabilities: $\hat{P}(y|\mathbf{v}) = P(y|\mathbf{v})$.

Instead of a complete initialization, it is possible to simply buffer the initial messages. Since these messages will be propagated eventually, this has the same final result as the initialization procedure described above, although the intermediate probabilities may differ.

The generalized forward-backward algorithm described in the previous section can be viewed as a special case of probability propagation. First, the network is arranged as a tree. Then, the initialization messages are buffered, as are the messages that would be created in response to any observations. (At this point, no computations have been performed.) During the forward pass, each right-going message induces a set of buffered left-going messages and a single right-going message. The latter right-going message is passed to the next level, where it too induces a set of buffered left-going messages and a single right-going message. So, once the forward pass is complete, there are no more buffered right-going messages in the network. During the backward pass, each vertex receives a left-going message from its only right-hand edge. Since an incoming message to a vertex never induces an outgoing message on the same edge, the left-going message will induce only a set of buffered left-going messages. So, there will be no buffered messages remaining in the network once the backward pass is complete. Finally, each vertex z_i can compute the exact value for $P(z_i|\mathbf{v})$.

2.1.4   Grouping and duplicating variables in Bayesian networks

Often, it is possible to convert a multiply-connected Bayesian network to a singly-connected Bayesian network, so that probability propagation can then be applied in a practical manner. To do this, we *group* variables, until there are no more multiple paths in the network. Graphically, two variables z_j and z_k are grouped by removing from the graph z_j and z_k as well as the edges to which they are connected, and then introducing a new vector variable $\{z_j, z_k\}$. The set of parents of the new vector variable is the union of the sets of parents of the two old variables. The set of parents of each child of z_j and z_k is extended to include *both* z_j and z_k. New edges are introduced to reflect these relationships. This grouping operation will produce a valid Bayesian network as long as z_k is not an indirect descendent of z_j and *vice versa*. Otherwise, a directed cycle will result from the grouping, violating the requirement that a Bayesian network have no directed cycles. Note that if z_k is a child of z_j, and at the same time *not* an indirect descendent, the grouping is still valid, since no directed cycles are produced.

It turns out that this grouping operation also preserves the representational capacity of the network. Any distribution represented by the old network can be represented by the new one. In fact, all of the conditional probabilities $P(z_k|\mathbf{a}_k)$ in the new network will be the same as in the old network, except the ones that involve either of the grouped variables. The latter conditional probabilities can quite easily be derived from the old ones.

Although grouping variables may help to produce a singly-connected network to which probability propagation can be applied, the grouping operation

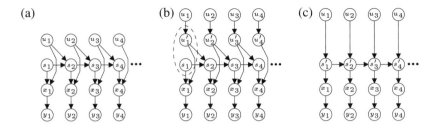

Figure 2.4
Transforming the multiply-connected Bayesian network for a recursive convolutional
code (a) into a singly-connected network (c) involves variable *duplication* (a) – (b) and
grouping (b) – (c).

also hides the structure that makes probability propagation an attractive inference method in the first place. So, it is important to produce minimal groupings
and retain as much of the structure as possible. Not surprisingly, by grouping
variables, *any* network can be made singly-connected — simply group all variables together into a single vertex. However, extreme groupings of this sort
usually eliminate too much structure. "Probability propagation" for the single
vertex is equivalent to manipulating the full joint distribution, which in most
practical cases is unwieldy.

Another useful operation is *duplicating* variables. A variable z_j can be du-
plicated by adding an extra variable z_{N+1} to the network, and creating the
following new parent-child relationships: $\mathbf{a}_{N+1} = \mathbf{a}_k^{\text{old}}$ and $\mathbf{a}_k^{\text{new}} = \{z_{N+1}\}$.
This procedure is especially useful in combination with grouping, since al-
though we may wish to group z_j and z_k in order to make the network singly-
connected, we may also wish to graphically distinguish z_j from the vector
variable $\{z_j, z_k\}$.

For example, the recursive convolutional code network shown in Figure 1.9a
can be derived from the more natural recursive convolutional code network
shown in Figure 2.4a. The latter network explicitly shows the dependence of
the encoder state variable s_k on the previous information symbol u_{k-1} and the
previous state s_{k-1}, as well as the dependence of the encoder output x_k on u_k
and s_k. This network is multiply-connected, so probability propagation cannot
be used to compute $P(u_k|\mathbf{y})$ for maximum *a posteriori* information symbol
decoding. To convert the network to a singly-connected one, we first duplicate the information symbols (so that they are graphically distinguished in the
final network) as shown in Figure 2.4b. Then, we group pairs of information
symbols and state variables as shown by the dashed loop, producing the singly-
connected network shown in Figure 2.4c. Note that by grouping variables in

this way, the number of values that each new state s'_k can take on is increased by a factor of two.

Although in many cases grouping can be used to produce a tractable network, there are cases where it is impossible to find an appropriate grouping. In fact, it turns out that inference in multiply-connected networks is a very difficult problem, in general.

2.1.5   Exact inference in multiply-connected networks is NP-hard

Probability propagation is an exact method of inference for *singly-connected* graphical models. Cooper [1990] has shown that probabilistic inference in Bayesian networks is *in general* NP-hard. The same is true for MRFs and factor graphs. Summations relevant to inference, such as the ones in (1.3), (1.7), (1.11) and (1.13), contain an exponential number of terms and it appears that in general these summations cannot be simplified. Researchers have thus focused on developing exact inference algorithms for restricted classes of graphical models (*e.g.*, probability propagation for singly-connected networks), and on developing approximate inference algorithms for networks that are intractable (assuming P $\neq$ NP). In fact, Dagum [1993] (see also Dagum and Chavez [1993]) has shown that for general Bayesian networks, approximate inference to a desired number of digits of precision is NP-hard. (*I.e.*, the time needed to obtain an approximate inference that is accurate to n digits is believed to be exponential in n.)

One obvious approach to approximate inference in a multiply-connected graphical model is to use the probability propagation algorithm while ignoring the fact that the network is multiply-connected. Each vertex propagates messages as if the network were singly-connected. In this case, the propagation procedure will never terminate, because there will be loops in which messages will endlessly circulate. Although this method has provided excellent results in the area of channel coding, it is frowned upon in other areas (such as medical diagnosis) because there is little theoretical understanding of the behavior of this iterative procedure.

Another disadvantage of the probability propagation algorithm is that it is cumbersome for inferring the *joint* distribution over several variables (*e.g.*, u_1 and u_4 in Figure 2.4c). This inference is accomplished by first computing the distribution over u_1 given the observations, using one forward-backward sweep. Then, the distribution over u_4 given the observations *and* each of the possible values for u_1 is computed using one forward-backward sweep for each possible value for u_1. (Notice that these sweeps may be partial, since they need only take into account the effects of clamping u_1 to different values.) If the variables of interest have n possible configurations, roughly n (possibly partial) forward-backward sweeps are needed. If we cannot afford the time to perform these sweeps, a faster approximate algorithm may be desirable.

In the following sections, I describe several other approaches to approximate probabilistic inference, including Monte Carlo, variational inference and Helmholtz machines. In these sections, I focus on inference in Bayesian networks.

2.2   Monte Carlo inference: Gibbs sampling and slice sampling

The Monte Carlo method [Hammersley and Handscomb 1964; Kalos and Whitlock 1986; Ripley 1987] makes use of pseudo-random numbers in order to perform computations. Monte Carlo inference uses random numbers in order to perform inference in a graphical model that describes a joint distribution $P(\mathbf{z})$. If we can somehow obtain a reasonably large sample from the distribution $P(\mathbf{h}|\mathbf{v})$ over some unobserved *hidden* variables $\mathbf{h} \subseteq \mathbf{z}$ in a graphical model, given some observed *visible* variables $\mathbf{v} \subseteq \mathbf{z}$, then relative frequencies can be used for approximate inference.

2.2.1   Inference by ancestral simulation in Bayesian networks

One brute force Monte Carlo approach is to simply simulate the network using the ancestral ordering. Then, we extract from the sample all those vectors that have the desired value for the component $\mathbf{v}$. Next, we compile a frequency histogram for the different values that $\mathbf{h}$ can take on. Although this approach is sometimes useful (notably, when using a small network to verify that a more sophisticated inference method works), in general it is not computationally efficient. The problem is that the value of $\mathbf{v}$ that we wish to condition on may occur *extremely* rarely, so that an inordinate sample size must be used in order to obtain useful results.

If we are interested in a subset $\mathbf{h}^{\mathrm{I}} \subseteq \mathbf{h}$ of the hidden variables, it so happens that in some cases ancestral simulation can be used to obtain a sample from $P(\mathbf{h}^{\mathrm{I}}|\mathbf{v})$ in an efficient manner. In general, if the parents of the visible variables are dependency-separated (see Section 1.2.5) from the hidden variables of interest by the visible variables, then ancestral simulation can be used to obtain a sample from $P(\mathbf{h}^{\mathrm{I}}|\mathbf{v})$. If the visible variables have no parents, then it follows trivially that the variables in this null set are dependency-separated from the hidden variables. Using the ancestral ordering, a value is drawn for each *hidden* variable given its parents. After one complete sweep, the value for $\mathbf{h}^{\mathrm{I}}$ will be an unbiased draw from $P(\mathbf{h}^{\mathrm{I}}|\mathbf{v})$.

Ancestral simulation can be used for inference in this case because, if the condition holds, then every path connecting each variable in $\mathbf{h}^{\mathrm{I}}$ to the parents

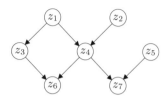

Figure 2.5
An example of a Bayesian network.

of each visible variable is blocked. This means that *disconnecting* each visible variable from its parents will not change the distribution $P(\mathbf{h}^{\mathrm{I}}|\mathbf{v})$. Since each visible variable will then have no parents, its value can be included as fixed constant in the conditional probability functions for its children. We are then left with a new Bayesian network that describes a distribution $P'(\mathbf{h})$ over the variables $\mathbf{h}$ that were not observed in the original network. Although in general $P'(\mathbf{h}) \neq P(\mathbf{h}|\mathbf{v})$, as shown above we have $P'(\mathbf{h}^{\mathrm{I}}) = P(\mathbf{h}^{\mathrm{I}}|\mathbf{v})$. So, we may simply use ancestral simulation in the new network to obtain samples from $P(\mathbf{h}^{\mathrm{I}}|\mathbf{v})$. Notice that ancestral simulation in the new network is equivalent to ancestral simulation for the unobserved variables in the original network.

For example, suppose that in the multiply-connected network with ancestral ordering $z_1, z_2, z_3, z_4, z_5, z_6, z_7$ shown in Figure 2.5, the set of visible variables is $\{z_1, z_4\}$ and we would like to infer the distribution over the subset of hidden variables $\{z_6, z_7\}$. Since $\{z_6, z_7\}$ is dependency-separated by $\{z_1, z_4\}$ from the parents $\{z_2\}$ of $\{z_1, z_4\}$, we can estimate $P(z_6, z_7|z_1, z_4)$ by ancestral simulation. We draw a value for z_2, then for z_3 given z_1, then for z_5, then for z_6 given z_3 and z_4, then for z_7 given z_4 and z_5. We can estimate $P(z_6, z_7|z_1, z_4)$ by repeating this procedure over and over while building up a histogram for $\{z_6, z_7\}$.

Notice that in the above example, it was not really necessary to draw a value for z_2, since for the ancestral simulation method to work, it was *required* that z_2 be dependency-separated from $\{z_6, z_7\}$ by $\{z_1, z_4\}$; *i.e.*, given $\{z_1, z_4\}$, z_2 does not influence $\{z_6, z_7\}$. In general, values need only be drawn for those variables in the ancestral ordering that are *not* dependency-separated from $\mathbf{h}^{\mathrm{I}}$ by $\mathbf{v}$. If we can easily identify these, we can save simulation computations.

2.2.2 Gibbs sampling

When inference by ancestral simulation is not possible, Markov chain Monte Carlo is often used (see an excellent review of these methods by Neal [1993]). Given $\mathbf{v}$, a temporal sequence $\mathbf{h}^{(1)}, \mathbf{h}^{(2)}, \ldots$ of the hidden variable values is produced by simulating a Markov chain whose stationary distribution is carefully constructed (*e.g.*, as described below) to be equal to $P(\mathbf{h}|\mathbf{v})$. By collecting these values over time, an approximate sample is obtained. Ideally, the chain is run long enough so that equilibrium is reached. In practice, the Markov chain may be terminated before equilibrium is reached, so that the simulation time can be kept within a reasonable limit. Once collected, the sample can be used to produce a frequency histogram of the variables of interest in $\mathbf{h}$.

The *Gibbs sampling* algorithm is the simplest of the Markov chain Monte Carlo methods, and has been successfully applied to Bayesian networks [Pearl 1987; Pearl 1988; Neal 1992] as well as other graphical models [Geman and Geman 1984; Hinton and Sejnowski 1986]. In this algorithm, each successive state $\mathbf{h}^{(\tau)}$ is chosen by modifying only a single variable in the previous state $\mathbf{h}^{(\tau-1)}$. The variables are usually modified in sequence. If at time τ, we have decided to modify $z_k \in \mathbf{h}$, then we draw a value $z_k^{(\tau)}$ from

$$P(z_k|\{z_j = z_j^{(\tau-1)}\}_{j=1, j \neq k}^N). \tag{2.13}$$

Usually, we cannot obtain this distribution directly, but instead must first compute the joint probability which is proportional to the conditional probability:

$$P(z_k|\{z_j = z_j^{(\tau-1)}\}_{j=1, j \neq k}^N) \propto P(z_k, \{z_j = z_j^{(\tau-1)}\}_{j=1, j \neq k}^N), \tag{2.14}$$

where the constant of proportionality does not depend on z_k. The joint probability can usually be computed easily from (1.19). If z_k is discrete, we compute the joint probability for each value that it can take on, normalize these values, and then randomly draw a value $z_k^{(\tau)}$ from this normalized distribution. When z_k is a continuous random variable, it can be quite difficult to draw a value from its distribution. Efficient sampling methods for several special types of continuous parametric distribution are given in Devroye [1986] and Ripley [1987]. In order to draw values from other types of distribution, more sophisticated techniques such as adaptive rejection sampling [Gilks and Wild 1992] must be used.

2.2.3 Gibbs sampling for the burglar alarm problem

In order to illustrate how Gibbs sampling works, I use the simple burglar alarm problem presented in Section 2.1.2, whose Bayesian network is shown in Figure 2.6a.

In order to perform Gibbs sampling, we need the probabilities for each of the hidden variables conditioned on *all* the other variables. Since these conditional probabilities are proportional to the joint probabilities, we can compute them in the following way, using $P(b=1|e=0, a=1)$ as an example:

(a)

(b)

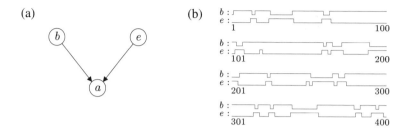

Figure 2.6
(a) The Bayesian network for the burglar alarm problem, with variables b ("burglary"), e ("earthquake") and a ("alarm"). (b) 400 steps of Gibbs sampling for the variables b and e when the alarm is observed to be ringing ($a = 1$).

$$P(b{=}1|e{=}0, a{=}1) = \frac{P(b{=}1, e{=}0, a{=}1)}{P(e{=}0, a{=}1)}$$

$$= \frac{P(b{=}1, e{=}0, a{=}1)}{P(b{=}0, e{=}0, a{=}1) + P(b{=}1, e{=}0, a{=}1)}$$

$$= \frac{0.03312}{0.00081 + 0.03312} = 0.976, \tag{2.15}$$

where $P(b, e, a) = P(a|b, e)P(b)P(e)$ is the joint distribution determined from the network specification in (2.7). Similarly,

$$P(b{=}1|e{=}1, a{=}1) = \frac{0.00607}{0.01215 + 0.00607} = 0.333,$$

$$P(e{=}1|b{=}0, a{=}1) = \frac{0.01215}{0.00081 + 0.01215} = 0.938,$$

$$P(e{=}1|b{=}1, a{=}1) = \frac{0.00607}{0.03312 + 0.00607} = 0.155. \tag{2.16}$$

Gibbs sampling proceeds by alternately visiting b and e, while sampling from $P(b|e, a{=}1)$ and $P(e|b, a{=}1)$ using the above formulas. Figure 2.6b shows the values of b and e for 400 steps of Gibbs sampling, starting from an initial configuration ($b = 0, e = 0$). (In each step, one variable is updated.) The Markov chain shows that the configurations ($b{=}0, e{=}0$) and ($b{=}1, e{=}1$) are unlikely compared to ($b{=}1, e{=}0$) and ($b{=}0, e{=}1$). The correct probabilities in (2.8) can be approximated using the relative frequencies computed from this chain:

$$\hat{P}(b=0, e=0|a=1) = 0.010,$$
$$\hat{P}(b=1, e=0|a=1) = 0.674,$$
$$\hat{P}(b=0, e=1|a=1) = 0.228$$
$$\hat{P}(b=1, e=1|a=1) = 0.088. \tag{2.17}$$

These are quite close to the correct values given in (2.8). Usually, an initial segment of the Markov chain is discarded when computing these statistics. The motivation for this procedure is that we would like to have samples that are typical of the *equilibrium* distribution, not the initial configuration.

2.2.4 Slice sampling for continuous variables

In networks with continuous variables, it is often not an easy task to sample from the conditional distribution of each hidden variable, as Gibbs sampling requires. Unlike the case for discrete variables, it is usually not possible to compute the joint distribution for every configuration of a hidden variable. There are infinitely many configurations, and it is often practically impossible to determine an effective discretization. Methods for sampling from continuous distributions include the Metropolis algorithm [Metropolis *et al.* 1953; Neal 1993] and hybrid methods that use "momentum" in order to help search the configuration space [Duane *et al.* 1987; Neal 1993]. In this section, I review a technique called *slice sampling* [Neal 1997; Frey 1997a], that can be used for drawing a value z from a univariate probability density $p(z)$ — in the context of inference, $p(z)$ is the conditional distribution $p(z_k|\{z_j = z_j^{(\tau-1)}\}_{j=1, j\neq k}^N)$. Slice sampling does not directly produce values distributed according to $p(z)$, but instead produces a Markov chain that is guaranteed to converge to $p(z)$. At each step in the sequence, the old value z^{old} is used as a guide for where to pick the new value z^{new}. When used in a system with many variables, these updates may be interleaved for greatly improved efficiency.

To perform slice sampling, all that is needed is an efficient way to evaluate a function $f(z)$ that is *proportional* to $p(z)$ — in this application, the easily computed joint probability $p(z_k, \{z_j = z_j^{(\tau-1)}\}_{j=1, j\neq k}^N)$ is appropriate. Figure 2.7a shows an example of a univariate distribution, $p(z)$. The version of slice sampling discussed here requires that all of the probability mass lies within a bounded *interval* as shown. To obtain z^{new} from z^{new}, $f(z^{\text{new}})$ is first computed and then a uniform random value is drawn from $[0, f(z^{\text{new}})]$. The distribution is then horizontally "sliced" at this value, as shown in Figure 2.7a.

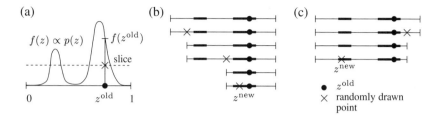

Figure 2.7
Slice sampling. After obtaining a random slice from the density (a), random values are
drawn until one is accepted. (b) and (c) show two such sequences.

Any z for which $f(z)$ is greater than this value is considered to be part of the
slice, as indicated by the bold line segments in the picture shown at the top
of Figure 2.7b. Ideally, z^{new} would now be drawn uniformly from the slice.
However, determining the line segments that comprise the slice is not easy,
for although it is easy to determine whether a particular z is in the slice, it is
much more difficult to determine the line segment boundaries, especially if the
distribution is multimodal. Instead, a uniform value is drawn from the original
interval as shown in the second picture of Figure 2.7b. If this value is in the
slice it is accepted as z^{new} (note that this decision requires an evaluation of
$f(z)$). Otherwise either the left or the right interval boundary is moved to this
new value, while keeping z^{new} in the interval. This procedure is repeated until
a value is accepted. For the sequence in Figure 2.7b, the new value is in the
same mode as the old one, whereas for the sequence in Figure 2.7c, the new
value is in the other mode. Once z^{new} is obtained, it is used as z^{new} for the
next step. As shown in Neal [1997], this procedure satisfies detailed balance
and therefore gives the desired stationary distribution $p(z)$.

2.3 Variational inference

In contrast to both the rather unprincipled approach of applying probability
propagation to multiply-connected networks, and the computationally intensive stochastic approach of Monte Carlo, variational inference is a nonstochas-
tic technique that directly addresses the quality of inference. In the Bayesian
network literature, variational inference methods [Saul, Jaakkola and Jordan
1996; Ghahramani and Jordan 1998; Jaakkola, Saul and Jordan 1996] were
introduced as an alternative variation on the central theme of Helmholtz machines [Hinton *et al.* 1995; Dayan *et al.* 1995], which are described in Sec-

tion 2.4. However, I will present variational inference first, because it is simpler to understand.

Suppose we are given a set of visible variables $\mathbf{v} \subseteq \mathbf{z}$. (This set may includes different variables on different occasions.) In order to solve the inference problem of estimating $P(\mathbf{h}|\mathbf{v})$, we introduce a parameterized variational distribution $Q(\mathbf{h}|\boldsymbol{\xi})$ that is meant to approximate $P(\mathbf{h}|\mathbf{v})$. The most appropriate form of this distribution will depend on many factors, including the network specification and the quality of inference desired. Next, the distance between $P(\mathbf{h}|\mathbf{v})$ and $Q(\mathbf{h}|\boldsymbol{\xi})$ (*e.g.*, Euclidean, relative entropy) is minimized with respect to $\boldsymbol{\xi}$, either directly or by using an optimization technique such as a Newton-like method or a conjugate gradient method [Fletcher 1987]. Once optimized, the distribution $Q(\mathbf{h}|\boldsymbol{\xi})$ is used as an approximation to $P(\mathbf{h}|\mathbf{v})$.

A main advantage of variational inference over probability propagation in multiply-connected networks is the explicit choice of a distance measure that is minimized. Although probability propagation is optimal for singly-connected networks, there is very little known theoretically about the quality of inference that results when the network is multiply-connected. On the other hand, there is no general guarantee that in multiply-connected networks, variational methods will perform better than probability propagation. An example where probability propagation in multiply-connected networks works very well for practical purposes is the celebrated turbodecoding algorithm for error-correcting coding [Berrou, Glavieux and Thitimajshima 1993; Frey and Kschischang 1997].

Compared to Monte Carlo, variational inference may provide the designer with a more structured approach to choosing a computationally tolerable approximation to $P(\mathbf{h}|\mathbf{v})$. However, variational methods do not usually provide a means to obtain exact inference. Also, variational inference can only be applied when the network is well-tailored to a sensible distance measure along with a fruitful form of variational distribution. (For example, the majority of work on variational methods for Bayesian networks to date has focused on networks that are parameterized.) In contrast, Monte Carlo methods can be applied to any Bayesian network, and can be designed so that they are guaranteed to converge to the correct solution.

2.3.1   Choosing the distance measure

Depending on the particular problem, different measures of distance may be appropriate. For example, in the case of hard-decision classification and hard-decision channel coding, a binary distance is ideal. Under this distance, the distributions are identical if they lead to the same decisions. Otherwise, the distance is incremented for each incorrect decision. In practice, this distance must be softened in order to use continuous optimization methods.

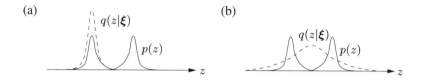

Figure 2.8
The effect of using (a) $D_{q\|p}$ versus (b) $D_{p\|q}$ when fitting a variational distribution $q(z|\boldsymbol{\xi})$ that is unimodel to a bimodal distribution $p(z)$.

As another example, we will see in Chapters 3 and 5 that for pattern classification and data compression, the appropriate "distance" is the Kullback-Leibler divergence, or relative entropy, between $Q(\mathbf{h}|\boldsymbol{\xi})$ and $P(\mathbf{h}|\mathbf{v})$:

$$D_{Q\|P} = \sum_{\mathbf{h}} Q(\mathbf{h}|\boldsymbol{\xi}) \log \frac{Q(\mathbf{h}|\boldsymbol{\xi})}{P(\mathbf{h}|\mathbf{v})}. \tag{2.18}$$

Notice that this is not a true distance since it is not symmetric: $D_{Q\|P} \neq D_{P\|Q}$, where

$$D_{P\|Q} = \sum_{\mathbf{h}} P(\mathbf{h}|\mathbf{v}) \log \frac{P(\mathbf{h}|\mathbf{v})}{Q(\mathbf{h}|\boldsymbol{\xi})}. \tag{2.19}$$

(For density functions, the summations are replaced by integrals.)

The choice of whether to use $D_{Q\|P}$ or $D_{P\|Q}$ depends on our objective. The former places emphasis on not inferring unlikely values of $\mathbf{h}$ at the cost of not inferring some of the likely values, whereas the latter places emphasis on inferring all likely values of $\mathbf{h}$ at the cost of inferring some of the unlikely values. For example, consider a real-valued univariate probability density $p(z)$ over z that has two modes, as shown in Figure 2.8. Suppose the variational distribution $q(z|\boldsymbol{\xi})$ is a Gaussian with $\boldsymbol{\xi}$ consisting of a mean and a variance. Figure 2.8a shows the optimum variational distribution that is obtained by minimizing $D_{q\|p}$, whereas Figure 2.8b shows the optimum variational distribution that is obtained by minimizing $D_{p\|q}$.

Notice that in order to compute $D_{Q\|P}$ in (2.18), we need $P(\mathbf{h}|\mathbf{v})$, which is what we were after in the first place. So, in practice, we usually minimize the following *free energy* function:

$$F_{Q\|P} = D_{Q\|P} - \log P(\mathbf{v}) = \sum_{\mathbf{h}} Q(\mathbf{h}|\boldsymbol{\xi}) \log \frac{Q(\mathbf{h}|\boldsymbol{\xi})}{P(\mathbf{h}, \mathbf{v})}. \tag{2.20}$$

Notice that minimizing $F_{Q\|P}$ with respect to $\boldsymbol{\xi}$ gives the same set of parameters as minimizing $D_{Q\|P}$, since $\log P(\mathbf{v})$ does not depend on $\boldsymbol{\xi}$. In order to compute $F_{Q\|P}$, we only need $P(\mathbf{h}, \mathbf{v})$, which is readily available in Bayesian networks. ($P(\mathbf{h}, \mathbf{v})$ is *not* easy to compute in other types of graphical models, such as Markov random fields.)

2.3.2 Choosing the form of the variational distribution

The form of $Q(\mathbf{h}|\boldsymbol{\xi})$ will strongly influence the quality of the variational inference as well as the tractability of computing the distance and its derivatives (which may be needed for the optimization procedure). Exact inference can be achieved in principle by associating one parameter $\xi_\mathbf{h}$ with each state of the hidden variables $\mathbf{h}$, where $\xi_\mathbf{h}$ is meant to be an estimate of $P(\mathbf{h}|\mathbf{v})$. However, computing the distance will require an explicit summation over all possible states of the hidden variables. The number of terms in this sum equals the number of possible configurations of the hidden variables, so this approach will only be tractable when there are not many configurations of the hidden variables. In fact, in most cases the above procedure will not be any more computationally efficient than directly computing $P(\mathbf{h}|\mathbf{v})$ using Bayes' rule.

We would like to choose $Q(\mathbf{h}|\boldsymbol{\xi})$ so that the effect of the hidden variables $\mathbf{h}$ in the distance measure can be integrated out either analytically or using a reasonably small number of computations. In this way, the distance and its gradients can be determined without having to numerically examine each possible state of the hidden variables $\mathbf{h}$.

2.3.3 Variational inference for the burglar alarm problem

In this section, I illustrate variational inference using the burglar alarm network described in Section 2.2.3. One type of variational distribution that is often used is the product form distribution. Under this variational distribution, the hidden variables are independent. For continuous variables, further assumptions may be needed regarding the distributions for each hidden variable (*e.g.*, see Section 4.2). For the binary burglar b and earthquake e variables in the burglar alarm network, we can specify an arbitrary product-form distribution using the parameters ξ_1 and ξ_2 for the probabilities that $b = 1$ and $e = 1$ respectively. That is,

$$Q(b, e|\boldsymbol{\xi}) = Q(b|\boldsymbol{\xi})Q(e|\boldsymbol{\xi}) = \xi_1^b(1 - \xi_1)^{1-b}\xi_2^e(1 - \xi_2)^{1-e}. \qquad (2.21)$$

Inserting this variational distribution into (2.20), and using the simple *binary entropy function* $H(\xi_1) = -\xi_1 \log \xi_1 - (1 - \xi_1) \log(1 - \xi_1)$, we get

$$F_{Q\|P} = \sum_{\substack{b=0,1 \\ e=0,1}} Q(b,e|\boldsymbol{\xi}) \log \frac{Q(b,e|\boldsymbol{\xi})}{P(b,e,a=1)}$$

$$= \sum_{\substack{b=0,1 \\ e=0,1}} Q(b,e|\boldsymbol{\xi})[b \log \xi_1 + (1-b) \log(1-\xi_1) + e \log \xi_2 + (1-e) \log(1-\xi_2)]$$

$$- \sum_{\substack{b=0,1 \\ e=0,1}} Q(b,e|\boldsymbol{\xi}) \log P(b,e,a=1)$$

$$= -H(\xi_1) - H(\xi_2) - \sum_{\substack{b=0,1 \\ e=0,1}} Q(b,e|\boldsymbol{\xi}) \log P(b,e,a=1). \tag{2.22}$$

Notice that the product form of $Q(b,e|\boldsymbol{\xi})$ was used to simplify the first term of the second equality.

At this point, without any further restrictions, we have not gained any computational advantage by using the variational approach. To compute $F_{Q\|P}$ and its derivatives, we must still examine all possible configurations of the hidden variables to compute the expectation of $\log P(b,e,a=1)$. In order to make profitable use of variational inference, $\log P(b,e,a=1)$ must have a form that makes the computation of $F_{Q\|P}$ easy. It turns out that the conditional probabilities (2.7) for the burglar alarm network were obtained from

$$P(a=1|b,e) = \exp[6b + 5e - 4.5be - 7]. \tag{2.23}$$

So, the joint distribution $P(b,e,a=1)$ can be written

$$P(b,e,a=1) = P(a=1|b,e)P(b)P(e)$$

$$= \exp[6b + 5e - 4.5be - 7]0.1^b 0.9^{1-b} 0.1^e 0.9^{1-e}. \tag{2.24}$$

Substituting this into (2.22), we get

$$F_{Q\|P} = -H(\xi_1) - H(\xi_2) - \sum_{\substack{b=0,1 \\ e=0,1}} Q(b,e|\boldsymbol{\xi})[6b + 5e - 4.5be - 7$$

$$+ b \log 0.1 + (1-b) \log 0.9 + e \log 0.1 + (1-e) \log 0.9]$$

$$= -H(\xi_1) - H(\xi_2) - 3.8\xi_1 - 2.8\xi_2 + 4.5\xi_1\xi_2 + 7.21. \tag{2.25}$$

Notice that the hidden variables b and e do not appear in this final expression. Because of the product form of $Q(b,e|\boldsymbol{\xi})$ and the exponential form of $P(b,e,a=1)$, we were able to integrate them out.

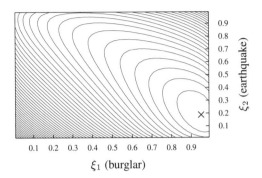

Figure 2.9
The contours of $F_{Q\|P}$ for a variational technique applied to the burglar alarm problem.
The global minimum occurs at $\xi_1 = 0.951$, $\xi_2 = 0.186$.

Figure 2.9 shows a plot of the contours of $F_{Q\|P}$ as a function of ξ_1 and ξ_2. The global minimum occurs at $\xi_1 = 0.951$, $\xi_2 = 0.186$, which means the inference estimates are $\hat{P}(b = 1|a{=}1) = 0.951$ and $\hat{P}(e = 1|a{=}1) = 0.186$. These estimates clearly favor a burglar as the cause of the alarm. Recall that Gibbs sampling allowed us to estimate covariance statistics between the two hidden variables. Variational inference does not readily produce those estimates. However, compared to the marginal probabilities $P(b = 1|a = 1) = 0.751$ and $P(e{=}1|a{=}1) = 0.349$ produced by the probability propagation algorithm, the variational method places more emphasis on the more likely cause b. In this sense, the variational technique produces a product form distribution that reveals covariance better than the marginals, produced, say, by probability propagation. For example, using only the marginal probabilities produced by propagation, we might conclude that the probability that *both* a burglar and an earthquake occurred is $0.751 \times 0.349 = 0.262$. In contrast, using the probabilities produced by the variational method gives $0.951 \times 0.186 = 0.177$, which is closer to the correct value of 0.116 given in (2.8).

In this case, because the burglar alarm network is so small, the analytic form of $F_{Q\|P}$ in (2.25) is not much simpler than the expression that would be obtained if (2.21) were substituted into (2.22) and explicit summation over all values of b and e were performed. However, for larger networks, exponential computational savings may be achieved by using conditional distributions that lead to simple forms of $\log P(\mathbf{h}, \mathbf{v})$.

2.3.4   Bounds and extended representations

In practice, the form of $\log P(\mathbf{h}, \mathbf{v})$ is often not simple, so that a straight-forward variational approach cannot be attempted. In these cases, it may be possible to derive an upper *bound* on the distance that does not depend on $\mathbf{h}$, and then try to minimize the bound instead of the distance itself [Saul, Jaakkola and Jordan 1996]. Effectively, we approximate $\log 1/P(\mathbf{h}, \mathbf{v})$ with an upper bound that *can* be integrated analytically.

Alternatively, we may express each conditional distribution $P(z_k|\mathbf{a}_k)$ in terms of conditional distributions over an extended set of variables [Jaakkola, Saul and Jordan 1996]. For example, $P(z_k|\mathbf{a}_k)$ might be the marginal distribution of $P(z_k, y_k|\mathbf{a}_k)$, where y_k is part of the extended representation. Let $\mathbf{y}^{\mathrm{H}}$ be the extension variables associated with the variables in $\mathbf{h}$. It is sometimes possible to introduce a variational distribution $Q(\mathbf{h}, \mathbf{y}^{\mathrm{H}}|\boldsymbol{\xi})$ over the extended representation for which $\mathbf{h}$ and $\mathbf{y}^{\mathrm{H}}$ *can* be integrated out in the distance measure.

2.4   Helmholtz machines

One of the main drawbacks of Markov chain Monte Carlo inference and variational inference is that for complex networks, each time a set of variables is observed, either a computationally taxing Markov chain must be simulated, or a high-dimensional optimization must be performed to find the best variational distribution. The essential problem, of course, is that the optimal distribution over $\mathbf{h}$ is different for different values $\mathbf{v}$ of the visible variables. A *Helmholtz machine* [Dayan *et al.* 1995; Hinton *et al.* 1995] tackles this problem by coupling the original *generative* network with a *recognition* Bayesian network that is meant to be capable of quickly producing an estimate of, or an approximate sample from, $P(\mathbf{h}|\mathbf{v})$. This recognition network essentially replaces the variational optimization needed for variational inference. It is called a "recognition" network because it is meant to recognize the hidden variable values, or "causes", that are responsible for the values of the visible variables.

As described above, the job of the recognition network is to quickly produce an approximation to $P(\mathbf{h}|\mathbf{v})$. Obviously, the recognition network must be different from the generative network, or the inference could be done directly on the generative network. I will highlight this difference by labeling the recognition distribution with Q. So, the recognition network is used to compute $Q(\mathbf{h}|\mathbf{v})$, which is an approximation to $P(\mathbf{h}|\mathbf{v})$ as given by the generative network. Various types of recognition network are described below, but they all share a common property. Since the recognition network is a Bayesian network, we cannot expect to be able to quickly compute $Q(\mathbf{h}|\mathbf{v})$ for arbitrary

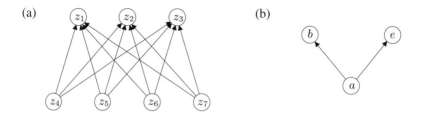

Figure 2.10
(a) An example of a factorial recognition network. (b) A factorial recognition network
for the burglar alarm problem.

sets $\mathbf{h}$ and $\mathbf{v}$. In fact, I will usually assume that the set of visible variables
is the same for each inference case, although, of course, the values for the
visible variables may differ from case to case. This restriction is the main disadvantage of the Helmholtz machine compared to Monte Carlo inference and
variational inference, which usually place no restrictions on which variables
are observed.

2.4.1   Factorial recognition networks

To ensure that the inference process is fast, we ought to design the recognition
network so that the computation of $Q(\mathbf{h}|\mathbf{v})$ can be carried out efficiently. The
simplest recognition network in this sense is one for which each variable in
$\mathbf{h}$ is dependency-separated from each other variable in $\mathbf{h}$ by the visible variables $\mathbf{v}$. In other words, given the visible variables, the hidden variables are
independent. I will refer to such a network as a *factorial* recognition network,
since given the visible variables, the distribution over the hidden variables can
be factored into a product of probabilities:

$$Q(\mathbf{h}|\mathbf{v}) = \prod_{z_k \in \mathbf{h}} Q(z_k|\mathbf{v}). \qquad (2.26)$$

A factorial recognition network with $\mathbf{h} = \{z_1, z_2, z_3\}$ is shown in Figure 2.10a. By condition 2 in Section 1.2.5, variables in $\mathbf{h}$ are dependency-
separated by $\mathbf{v} = \{z_4, z_5, z_6, z_7\}$.

In many cases, the product form approximation given in (2.26) is not very
close to $P(\mathbf{h}|\mathbf{v})$. However, it is the easiest network to design or estimate, and
because the hidden variables are independent given the visible variables, it is
computationally efficient for inference.

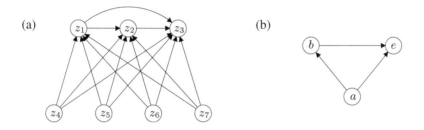

Figure 2.11
(a) An example of a nonfactorial recognition network. (b) A nonfactorial recognition
network for the burglar alarm problem.

Figure 2.10b shows a factorial recognition network for the burglar alarm
problem. The recognition distribution is given by $Q(b, e|a) = Q(b|a)Q(e|a)$,
and so is limited to the sane inference estimates as the variational technique
described in Section 2.3.3. Namely, the factorial recognition network cannot
capture the covariance between the two causes. Can we design a recognition
network that can give better estimates? The answer is "yes", by using a nonfactorial recognition network.

2.4.2   Nonfactorial recognition networks

Although it is easy to imagine situations where a factorial recognition network
will suffice, for the burglar alarm problem discussed above we saw that a factorial recognition network could not capture the covariance between the two
causes of the alarm. In this section, I describe nonfactorial recognition networks that are more powerful than factorial ones.

A *nonfactorial* recognition network can represent a distribution where at
least one variable in **h** is *not* dependency-separated from at least one other
variable in **h** by the visible variables **v**. Of course, there are many ways to
make a network nonfactorial. For example, a nonfactorial recognition network
is obtained by making some hidden variables depend on other ones in addition
to the visible variables. Figure 2.11a shows a fully-connected nonfactorial
recognition network, which can be contrasted with the factorial network in
Figure 2.10a.

Another way to produce a nonfactorial recognition network is through the
use of *auxiliary variables* or *dangling units* [Dayan and Hinton 1996]. These
variables do not influence the output of the generative model, but help facilitate
inference in the recognition network. For example, an auxiliary variable in the
recognition network can be used to choose between two or more modes.

2.4.3   The stochastic Helmholtz machine

Suppose we are interested in only one of the hidden variables, and we would like to obtain its distribution given the visible variables, after marginalizing out the other hidden variables. For a factorial recognition network, each hidden variable is independent given the visible variables. So, the marginal distribution is obtained simply by ignoring the other hidden variables. In fact, the marginal distribution for $z_k \in \mathbf{h}$ in this case is $Q(z_k|\mathbf{v})$, which is part of the recognition network specification.

Such a simple procedure for marginalization is not in general available for nonfactorial recognition networks. In these networks, the hidden variables are not independent given the visible variables. However, Monte Carlo provides an easy way to estimate marginal statistics. If we can obtain a sufficiently large sample from the recognition network, the distribution for z_k can be approximated by constructing a histogram for z_k alone. Of course, we could directly apply Monte Carlo methods such as Gibbs sampling (Section 2.2.2) to the generative network. However, the hope is that we can carefully design the nonfactorial recognition network so that it is better suited to Monte Carlo than the generative network. In fact, we can avoid complicated Markov chain Monte Carlo by using a recognition network for which ancestral simulation (see Section 1.2.4) can be used.

In general, recognition networks can be either factorial or nonfactorial and stochastic or nonstochastic. Here, "nonstochastic" refers to the way the recognition network is used, not to what the network represents. All Bayesian networks represent a stochastic phenomena, but not all networks are used with Monte Carlo. A factorial recognition network can easily be operated stochastically, simply by choosing each hidden variable z_k from its distribution $Q(z_k|\mathbf{h})$. A nonfactorial recognition network can easily be operated nonstochastically, since the joint distribution over the hidden variables factors and the marginal distribution for each hidden variable is readily available. However, a nonfactorial recognition network *usually* cannot be operated nonstochastically. As described above, the dependencies between the hidden variables makes this difficult. However, there are special cases where nonfactorial recognition networks can be operated nonstochastically. In particular, recognition networks that can be viewed as a mixture of factorial networks can be operated nonstochastically with relative ease.

2.4.4   A recognition network that solves the burglar alarm problem

In many cases, a simple nonfactorial recognition network can be used to represent covariances between hidden variables. A nonfactorial recognition network for the burglar alarm problem is shown in Figure 2.11b. The difference between this network and the factorial one in Figure 2.10b, is that e now depends on b as well as a. The conditional distributions for a recognition network that performs exact inference are

$$Q(b=1|a=1) = 0.751, \qquad Q(e|b, a=1) = \begin{cases} 0.154 & \text{if } b = 1, \\ 0.936 & \text{if } b = 0. \end{cases} \qquad (2.27)$$

Sampling hidden variables using ancestral simulation in this network is actually more efficient than using Gibbs sampling in the generative network, as described in Section 2.2.3. (The computational savings are quite low in this case, because there are only two hidden variables.)

The joint distribution over the hidden variables given $a=1$ can be computed from $Q(b, e|a=1) = Q(e|b, a=1)Q(b|a=1)$:

$$Q(b=0, e=0|a=1) = 0.016,$$
$$Q(b=1, e=0|a=1) = 0.635,$$
$$Q(b=0, e=1|a=1) = 0.233,$$
$$Q(b=1, e=1|a=1) = 0.116. \qquad (2.28)$$

These probabilities are identical to the probabilities in (2.8) for exact inference.

3 Pattern Classification

Automated methods for making decisions based on inputs play a very important role both in engineering applications and in helping us understand how biological systems respond to their environments. As many engineers and cognitive scientists will attest, the terms "input" and "decision" for this *pattern classification* problem are not clearly defined in theory. In practice, the problem is usually decomposed through design and analysis. The input to the classifier is provided by a preprocessor that transcribes part of the physical state of the world. Different preprocessors are appropriate for different classifiers, and often an iterative process is used to find the optimal preprocessor-classifier pair for a given problem. In general, the preprocessor uses simple statistical and signal processing techniques, whereas the classifier is left with the "hard" problem of coming up with decisions.

A very simple method for making hard decisions is the *nearest neighbor classifier*. This classifier keeps a database of labeled training patterns. Given a test pattern, the nearest neighbor classifier outputs the class of the pattern in its database that is "closest" to the test pattern. Any distance metric may be used, but typically Euclidean distance or one of its generalizations are used. Figure 3.1 shows a selection of normalized and quantized 8×8 binary images of handwritten digits made available by the US Postal Service Office of Advanced Technology. A database with a total of 7000 patterns was constructed with 700 patterns from each digit class. Using nearest neighbor classification, a misclassification rate of 6.7% was obtained on a test set of 4000 patterns. Slightly better results can be achieved by using the *k-nearest neighbor* method. This method picks the most common class in the k training patterns that are closest to the test pattern.

One interesting property of the k-nearest neighbor method is that it is a *consistent* classifier. That is, as the number of training cases T tends to infinity, the decisions produced by the k-nearest neighbor method (with, *e.g.*, $k = \sqrt{T}$) become Bayes optimal. However, although k-nearest neighbor classification works quite well when a large training set is available, it performs poorly when training data is limited. Figure 3.2 shows a training set consisting of two classes with 30 2-dimensional real-valued patterns in each class. Suppose we wish to classify the indicated test point. The nearest neighbor method will choose class A. In fact, just as our intuition tells us, the test point was drawn from class B. If a k-nearest neighbor classifier is used, class A will consistently be erroneously chosen for sensible values of k.

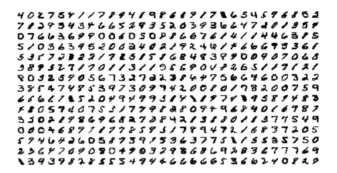

Figure 3.1
450 examples of 8 × 8 binary images of handwritten digits.

The above example illustrates a fundamental flaw with the nearest neighbor approach — namely, that it does not use global structure. Viewing the data from class B with a local (narrow) "window", the test pattern seems very unlikely. However, a more global examination of the data from class B leads us to believe that the data comes from a roughly sinusoidal manifold, and that just by *chance* there isn't any training data for this class in the central region of the figure. Under this view, the test pattern is much more likely. An even more global examination indicates that the two classes of data are probably similar, except for the fact that they lie on manifolds that are relatively inverted. As a result, by inverting one class of data, we actually have 60 points available for estimating the prototypical manifold. In this way, we obtain even more evidence that the test point is from class B.

One way to endow methods with the ability to extract global structure is to use parameterized models that can *generalize* in nontrivial ways. In Bayesian terms, we have prior expectations about certain properties of the data. For example, we expect the probability density function for the data within a given class to be smooth on some scale. The class of distributions that our model can represent should reflect these prior expectations. By fitting the model to the data, this prior knowledge is then modified to obtain a more data-driven set of posterior expectations. In the above example, we decide that a sinusoidal manifold is a reasonable compromise between our prior expectations regarding continuity and the observed data within class B.

Simple parametric models, such as multidimensional Gaussian density functions, can be used to obtain some degree of generalization. However, overly simple models of this sort are inflexible in that they cannot generalize in complex ways. Also, for real-world problems, such inflexible models are often

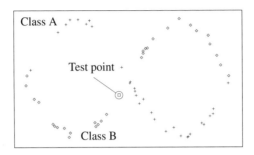

Figure 3.2
Two classes of 2-dimensional training data and a test point.

inconsistent, since they often cannot represent the complexity in natural data sets. In this chapter, I examine the use of more flexible Bayesian network models for pattern classification.

I begin this chapter with a description of how Bayesian networks can be used for pattern classification. Then, in Section 3.2, I present the "autoregressive" network which is quite simple, but performs surprisingly well as a pattern classifier. In Section 3.3, I describe maximum likelihood estimation and "maximum likelihood-bound" estimation for models with latent (hidden) variables. Latent variables are not part of the input pattern, but are meant to represent higher-order structure in the data (*e.g.*, handwriting style). In Section 3.4, I review three techniques for estimating the parameters of sigmoidal Bayesian networks with latent variables: Gibbs sampling, variational inference, and the wake-sleep algorithm. Then, in Section 3.5, all of these models are compared with the k-nearest neighbor classifier and a tree-based classifier when classifying handwritten digits.

An area which is closely related to estimating probability models for pattern classification is unsupervised learning. I view unsupervised learning as the process of estimating a probability model for a class of data. The hope is that some of the latent variables in the model will come to represent interesting features, and that these features can then be automatically extracted for novel input patterns. In Section 4.1 I present results for the Helmholtz machine, when it is given the task of trying to extract structure from noisy 16×16 images of horizontal and vertical bars. Finally, in Section 4.2, I present a new type of parameterized Bayesian network that can be used to simultaneously extract continuous and categorical structure in an unsupervised manner.

3.1   Bayesian networks for pattern classification

Bayesian networks provide a means of producing structured probabilistic models with arbitrary complexity. In this sense, they are *flexible* models. The majority of this chapter is devoted to using Bayesian networks to produce one model for *each* class of training data. A new test pattern is classified by choosing the class of the model that is best suited to the test pattern. In contrast, it is certainly possible to construct a Bayesian network that has one set of pattern variables $\mathbf{v}$, a variable that represents the class j, plus other variables that represent important physical effects. An inference method can then be used to compute $P(j|\mathbf{v})$ using the network. An advantage of this approach is that the model may make efficient use of the similarities and differences between all of the classes. For example, if each class of data in Figure 3.2 is modelled separately, then the similarity between the two classes cannot be exploited as described above. In practice, however, a parameter estimation algorithm may fail to find such similarities and in the process of trying to model both classes fail to properly extract the features from any one class. Another disadvantage of the single-model approach is that a new class of data cannot be introduced without refitting the model. Despite these disadvantages, the single-model approach is seductively interesting. In Chapter 4, I study networks that are estimated from *unlabeled* data, where the hidden variables automatically come to represent data classes.

The multiple-model approach to pattern classification consists of estimating one model for each of the J classes of data. In this sense, each model is conditioned on a class number. For the sake of generality, I will assume that the jth model has a set of features or hidden attributes $\mathbf{h}_j$ that help model the pattern variables $\mathbf{v}$. Network j thus represents a distribution $P(\mathbf{v}, \mathbf{h}_j|j)$. Finally, the class probabilities $P(j)$ must be specified; these are simply determined from the relative sizes of the classes of data and any prior knowledge we have at hand. (For example, even though a training set contains 10 patterns from class 0 and 14 patterns from class 1, if we know ahead of time that the classes are equally likely then we set $P(j = 0) = P(j = 1)$.)

Ideally, the model estimate for class j will yield a distribution that is close to the true distribution $P_{\mathrm{r}}(\mathbf{v}|j)$ of the data from class j:

$$P(\mathbf{v}|j) = \sum_{\mathbf{h}_j} P(\mathbf{v}, \mathbf{h}_j|j) \approx P_{\mathrm{r}}(\mathbf{v}|j). \tag{3.1}$$

However, even if the approximation is good, the sum in the above expression is exponential in the number of feature variables, and so cannot be computed directly. Instead, for a given test pattern $\mathbf{v}$, one of the inference methods described in Chapter 1 can be used to produce class likelihood estimates,

$$\hat{P}(\mathbf{v}|j), \qquad j \in \{0, \ldots, J-1\}. \tag{3.2}$$

Finally, Bayes' rule is used to produce soft classification decisions,

$$\hat{P}(j|\mathbf{v}) = \frac{\hat{P}(\mathbf{v}|j)P(j)}{\sum_{j'} \hat{P}(\mathbf{v}|j')P(j')}, \qquad j \in \{0, \ldots, J-1\}, \tag{3.3}$$

and a hard decision j^* can be made by choosing the best class,

$$j^* = \mathrm{argmax}_j \hat{P}(j|\mathbf{v}). \tag{3.4}$$

The technique used to estimate the class models and the inference method used to estimate $P(j|\mathbf{v})$ depend on the structure of the networks. Before examining intractable models for which inference and parameter estimation must be approximated, I discuss an interesting class of tractable systems. For the sake of notational simplicity, the following sections present models and algorithms for estimating $P(\mathbf{v})$, with the class index j left off. It should be kept in mind that one such density model must be estimated for each class.

3.2   Autoregressive networks

There are a variety of Bayesian network architectures for which inference and parameter estimation can be performed exactly within a reasonable amount of time. An architecture of this type that I discuss here is easy to implement and works surprisingly well on some problems. I define an *autoregressive network* as a fully-connected parameterized Bayesian network without any latent variables. The graph for the network is thus specified completely by an ancestral ordering. Unless I am considering different ancestral orderings of the variables, I will usually assume that the variables are labeled in the ancestral order. Then, the parameterized distribution $P(\mathbf{v}|\boldsymbol{\theta})$ for the data can be written

$$P(\mathbf{v}|\boldsymbol{\theta}) = \prod_{i=1}^{N} P(v_i|\{v_k\}_{k=1}^{i-1}, \boldsymbol{\theta}_i), \tag{3.5}$$

where $\boldsymbol{\theta}$ is the entire set of parameters, and $\boldsymbol{\theta}_i$ is the set of parameters associated with input v_i. Each of the conditional probability distributions in this expression is represented using some sort of parametric or flexible model. Figure 3.3 shows an example of an autoregressive network with five variables.

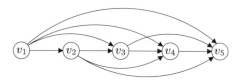

Figure 3.3
An autoregressive network with ancestral ordering v_1, v_2, v_3, v_4, v_5.

3.2.1   The logistic autoregressive network

If the pattern consists of binary variables ($v_i \in \{0, 1\}$) logistic regression [McCullagh and Nelder 1983] (see Section 1.2.7) may be used:

$$P(v_i|\{v_k\}_{k=1}^{i-1}, \boldsymbol{\theta}_i) = v_i g(\textstyle\sum_{k=0}^{i-1}\theta_{ik}v_k) + (1 - v_i)[1 - g(\sum_{k=0}^{i-1}\theta_{ik}v_k)],$$

$$(3.6)$$

where $g(x) = 1/(1 + \exp[-x])$ is the logistic function, and a dummy variable $v_0 = 1$ is used to account for a constant in the arguments of the exponent.

For this *logistic autoregressive network*, $P(\mathbf{v}|\boldsymbol{\theta})$ can be computed in $\mathcal{O}(N^2)$ time in the following way. For each variable v_i, the sum $\sum_{k=0}^{i-1} \theta_{ik}v_k$ is determined from the values of $v_1, \ldots, v_{i-1}$, and then $P(v_i|\{v_k\}_{k=1}^{i-1}, \boldsymbol{\theta}_i)$ is determined from the value of v_i using (3.6). $P(\mathbf{v}|\boldsymbol{\theta})$ is then computed using (3.5).

3.2.2   MAP estimation for autoregressive networks

An autoregressive network can be fit to a set of training patterns $\mathbf{v}^{(1)}, \ldots, \mathbf{v}^{(T)}$ using MAP parameter estimation. To do so, we need to specify both a prior distribution over the parameters $\boldsymbol{\theta}$, and also the training set likelihood given the parameters. Assuming that each training case is independent and identically drawn (i.i.d.), the log-likelihood of the training set is

$$\log P(\{\mathbf{v}^{(t)}\}_{t=1}^{T}|\boldsymbol{\theta}) = \sum_{t=1}^{T} \log P(\mathbf{v}^{(t)}|\boldsymbol{\theta}) = \sum_{t=1}^{T} \log \left[\prod_{i=1}^{N} P(v_i^{(t)}|\{v_k^{(t)}\}_{k=1}^{i-1}, \boldsymbol{\theta}_i) \right]$$

$$= \sum_{i=1}^{N} \left[\sum_{t=1}^{T} \log P(v_i^{(t)}|\{v_k^{(t)}\}_{k=1}^{i-1}, \boldsymbol{\theta}_i) \right]$$

$$= \sum_{i=1}^{N} \log \left[\prod_{t=1}^{T} P(v_i^{(t)}|\{v_k^{(t)}\}_{k=1}^{i-1}, \boldsymbol{\theta}_i) \right]. \qquad (3.7)$$

If the parameters are independent under the prior, then given a training set, the ith term in the sum of the last expression in (3.7) depends on a set of parameters $\boldsymbol{\theta}_i = \{\theta_{i1}, \dots, \theta_{i,i-1}\}$ that are independent of all the other sets of parameters $\boldsymbol{\theta}_{i'}$, $i' \neq i$. So, MAP estimation can be broken down into N subproblems, where subproblem i is to estimate the parameters $\boldsymbol{\theta}_i$ for the model that predicts v_i from $\{v_k\}_{k=1}^{i-1}$.

Here, I derive a gradient-based MAP estimation method for the logistic regression model used in the logistic autoregressive network. Let the data for subproblem i be denoted $\mathcal{D}_i = \{\{v_k^{(t)}\}_{k=1}^{i}\}_{t=1}^{T}$. Up to a constant of proportionality that does not depend on $\boldsymbol{\theta}_i$, the likelihood of the training data for subproblem i is

$$P(\mathcal{D}_i|\boldsymbol{\theta}_i) \propto \prod_{t=1}^{T} P(v_i^{(t)}|\{v_k^{(t)}\}_{k=1}^{i-1}, \boldsymbol{\theta}_i)$$

$$= \prod_{t=1}^{T} [v_i^{(t)} g(\textstyle\sum_{k=0}^{i-1}\theta_{ik}v_k^{(t)}) + (1 - v_i^{(t)})(1 - g(\textstyle\sum_{k=0}^{i-1}\theta_{ik}v_k^{(t)}))],$$

$$(3.8)$$

where the last expression is obtained from (3.6).

I use a prior distribution under which the parameters in $\boldsymbol{\theta}_i$ are independent and normally distributed with mean 0 and a fixed variance σ_i^2:

$$P(\boldsymbol{\theta}_i) = \prod_{k=0}^{i-1} \frac{1}{\sqrt{2\pi\sigma_i^2}} e^{-\theta_{ik}^2/2\sigma_i^2}. \qquad (3.9)$$

Up to a constant of proportionality that is independent of $\boldsymbol{\theta}_i$, the posterior distribution over the model parameters $\boldsymbol{\theta}_i$ given the data $\mathcal{D}_i$ is

$$P(\boldsymbol{\theta}_i|\mathcal{D}_i) \propto P(\boldsymbol{\theta}_i, \mathcal{D}_i) = P(\mathcal{D}_i|\boldsymbol{\theta}_i)P(\boldsymbol{\theta}_i)$$

$$\propto \prod_{t=1}^{T} [v_i^{(t)} g(\textstyle\sum_{k=0}^{i-1}\theta_{ik}v_k^{(t)}) + (1-v_i^{(t)})(1-g(\textstyle\sum_{k=0}^{i-1}\theta_{ik}v_k^{(t)}))] \prod_{k=0}^{i-1} \frac{e^{-\theta_{ik}^2/2\sigma_i^2}}{\sqrt{2\pi\sigma_i^2}}.$$

$$(3.10)$$

Taking the logarithm of this expression and leaving out constants that do not affect the optimization procedure, MAP estimation for subproblem i entails maximizing

$$\mathcal{L}^i = \sum_{t=1}^{T} [v_i^{(t)} \log g(\sum_{k=0}^{i-1} \theta_{ik} v_k^{(t)}) + (1 - v_i^{(t)}) \log(1 - g(\sum_{k=0}^{i-1} \theta_{ik} v_k^{(t)}))]$$

$$-\frac{1}{2\sigma_i^2} \sum_{k=0}^{i-1} \theta_{ik}^2. \tag{3.11}$$

I use the conjugate gradient optimization method [Fletcher 1987] which requires the derivatives of $\mathcal{L}^i$:

$$\frac{\partial \mathcal{L}^i}{\partial \theta_{ik}} = \sum_{t=1}^{T} v_k^{(t)} [v_i^{(t)} - g(\sum_{k'=0}^{i-1} \theta_{ik'} v_{k'}^{(t)})] - \theta_{ik}/\sigma_i^2. \tag{3.12}$$

Both $\mathcal{L}^i$ and its derivatives can be computed in $\mathcal{O}(iT)$ time.

3.2.3 Scaled priors in logistic autoregressive networks

In the prior distribution over the parameters (3.9), how should the variance σ_i^2 of the parameters for the ith input depend on i? That is, before seeing any training data, how do we expect the variance of the parameters for a variable to depend on how many inputs that variable receives?

Assume we don't have prior knowledge of a preferred ordering of the variables. By symmetry, it makes sense to assume a uniform *prior* distribution over the variables; *i.e.*, under the prior each variable is equally likely to have each of the values 0 and 1. The dummy variable $v_0 = 1$ is exempt from this prior, of course. Now, consider the prior probability predictions made for v_i. This prior distribution has two sources of variability: a Gaussian prior over the parameters θ_i, and a uniform distribution over the inputs $\{v_k\}_{k=1}^{i-1}$. By symmetry, this prior distribution over the probability predictions made for v_i should *not* depend on i. As shown below, this restriction determines how to set the variance for the parameters θ_i for each variable v_i.

Since the prediction for v_i is determined by its total input $\sum_{k=0}^{i-1} \theta_{ik} v_k$, the the above restriction can be applied to the total inputs. Averaging over the two sources of variability, we get a mean value of the total input for v_i of

$$\mathrm{E}\left[\sum_{k=0}^{i-1} \theta_{ik} v_k\right] = \sum_{k=0}^{i-1} \mathrm{E}[\theta_{ik} v_k] = \sum_{k=0}^{i-1} \mathrm{E}[\theta_{ik}] E[v_k] = 0. \tag{3.13}$$

We can take $\mathrm{E}[\theta_{ik} v_k] = \mathrm{E}[\theta_{ik}] E[v_k]$, since the parameters and the inputs are independent under the prior. The final step holds since the parameters have mean 0.

Since the mean total input is 0, the variance of the total input for v_i is

$$E\left[\left(\sum_{k=0}^{i-1}\theta_{ik}v_k\right)^2\right] = E\left[\sum_{k=0}^{i-1}\sum_{j=0}^{i-1}\theta_{ik}\theta_{ij}v_kv_j\right]$$

$$= \sum_{k=0}^{i-1}\sum_{j=0}^{i-1}E[\theta_{ik}\theta_{ij}]E[v_kv_j]. \qquad (3.14)$$

Now, since θ_{ik} and θ_{ij}, $k \neq j$ are independent under the prior, $E[\theta_{ik}\theta_{ij}]$ is nonzero only if $j = k$. So, the variance of the total input for v_i is

$$\sum_{k=0}^{i-1}E[\theta_{ik}^2]E[v_k^2] = \sigma_i^2 + \sum_{k=1}^{i-1}\sigma_i^2\frac{1}{2} = \frac{1}{2}(i+1)\sigma_i^2. \qquad (3.15)$$

Under the prior, the probability predictions for v_i should not depend on i. So, the variances of the total inputs for v_1 and v_i should not differ:

$$\sigma_1^2 = \frac{1}{2}(i+1)\sigma_i^2, \quad \text{and so } \sigma_i^2 = \frac{2}{i+1}\sigma_1^2. \qquad (3.16)$$

Note that σ_1^2 is the variance of the total input for v_1, which has no input variables. All of the variances can be set by picking a reasonable value for σ_1^2. In my simulations, I chose $\sigma_1^2 = 4$. This value allows for probabilities near 0 and 1 at the output of the logistic function, without favoring them too much (see Figure 1.10 on page 22).

It may be a good idea to let the biases in the network have a *separate* Gaussian prior, although I have not yet explored this possibility experimentally.

3.2.4 Ensembles of autoregressive networks

An autoregressive network is specified by choosing an order for the variables $v_1, \ldots, v_N$. Leaving computational considerations aside, if the subproblem models $P(v_i|\{v_k\}_{k=1}^{i-1})$ are consistent (*i.e.*, they converge to the correct distribution as the number of training examples tends to infinity) and there is a sufficiently large training set, then the particular ordering chosen is not important. The model for subproblem i will correctly represent the real conditional distribution $P_r(v_i|\{v_k\}_{k=1}^{i-1})$, and so the product of the subproblem distributions will give the true joint distribution. However, the data sets considered here are small, and the parametric subproblem models considered here (*e.g.*, logistic regression) are inconsistent for many distributions of data. In this case, the order of the variables is important in two contrasting ways. Certain orderings may give rise to simpler true conditional distributions $P_r(v_i|\{v_k\}_{k=1}^{i-1})$ that can be more accurately represented by the model distributions $P(v_i|\{v_k\}_{k=1}^{i-1}, \boldsymbol{\theta}_i)$. In contrast, for a given training set, different orderings may lead to different amounts of overfitting.

I do not address here the difficult issue of how to select an ordering that optimally balances these two effects. This problem is difficult both because the discrete ordering cannot be optimized by a gradient-based method and because for the training sets I will consider here, there is not enough data available to get a reliable estimate of which ordering is best. Instead of searching for an optimal ordering, I estimate an *ensemble* of autoregressive networks, where each network uses a randomly selected ordering of the variables. The probability prediction for a given vector $\mathbf{v}$ is then taken to be the average of the predictions over the ensemble of networks.

3.3   Estimating latent variable models using the EM algorithm

The notion of unobserved or hidden variables arises in many model estimation contexts. For example, due to mechanical failure, training data derived from physical measurements may sometimes lack values for some variables in some cases. In contrast, it is often useful to build hidden variables into a model by design. These variables are meant to represent latent causes that influence the visible variables. Several of the Bayesian network models discussed in the remainder of this chapter are latent variable models (*e.g.*, see Section 3.4). For the sake of notational simplicity, I will use $\mathbf{v}$ to refer to the observed variables and $\mathbf{h}$ to refer to the unobserved variables. This is a slight abuse of notation, since it can happen that some visible variables are unobserved. For example, several of the photo-sensors in a digital camera may be burned out, so that some of the variables in the image pattern $\mathbf{v}$ are unobserved.

We would like to estimate a probabilistic model $P(\mathbf{z})$ for a training set consisting of T patterns $\mathbf{v}^{(1)}, \mathbf{v}^{(2)}, \ldots, \mathbf{v}^{(T)}$, where each pattern specifies the values of an observed subset $\mathbf{v}$ of the variables in $\mathbf{z}$. In general, each training case may specify a *different* subset of visible variables.

Let $\mathbf{h}^{(t)} = \mathbf{z} \setminus \mathbf{v}^{(t)}$ be the set of hidden (unobserved) variables for training case t. Assuming that the training cases are i.i.d., the log-likelihood of the training data $\mathcal{D}$ is

$$\log P(\mathcal{D}|\boldsymbol{\theta}) = \log \prod_{t=1}^{T} P(\mathbf{v}^{(t)}|\boldsymbol{\theta}) = \sum_{t=1}^{T} \log P(\mathbf{v}^{(t)}|\boldsymbol{\theta})$$

$$= \sum_{t=1}^{T} \log \left[\sum_{\mathbf{h}^{(t)}} P(\mathbf{v}^{(t)}, \mathbf{h}^{(t)}|\boldsymbol{\theta}) \right]. \tag{3.17}$$

To maximize this log-likelihood, we set its derivative with respect to each parameter θ in $\boldsymbol{\theta}$ to zero:

$$
\begin{aligned}
\frac{\partial \log P(\mathcal{D}|\boldsymbol{\theta})}{\partial \theta} &= \sum_{t=1}^{T} \frac{1}{\sum_{\mathbf{h}^{(t)'}} P(\mathbf{v}^{(t)}, \mathbf{h}^{(t)'}|\boldsymbol{\theta})} \frac{\partial}{\partial \theta} \left[\sum_{\mathbf{h}^{(t)}} P(\mathbf{v}^{(t)}, \mathbf{h}^{(t)}|\boldsymbol{\theta}) \right] \\
&= \sum_{t=1}^{T} \sum_{\mathbf{h}^{(t)}} \frac{1}{\sum_{\mathbf{h}^{(t)'}} P(\mathbf{v}^{(t)}, \mathbf{h}^{(t)'}|\boldsymbol{\theta})} \frac{\partial}{\partial \theta} P(\mathbf{v}^{(t)}, \mathbf{h}^{(t)}|\boldsymbol{\theta}) \\
&= \sum_{t=1}^{T} \sum_{\mathbf{h}^{(t)}} \frac{P(\mathbf{v}^{(t)}, \mathbf{h}^{(t)}|\boldsymbol{\theta})}{\sum_{\mathbf{h}^{(t)'}} P(\mathbf{v}^{(t)}, \mathbf{h}^{(t)'}|\boldsymbol{\theta})} \frac{\partial}{\partial \theta} \log P(\mathbf{v}^{(t)}, \mathbf{h}^{(t)}|\boldsymbol{\theta}) \\
&= \sum_{t=1}^{T} \sum_{\mathbf{h}^{(t)}} P(\mathbf{h}^{(t)}|\mathbf{v}^{(t)}, \boldsymbol{\theta}) \frac{\partial}{\partial \theta} \log P(\mathbf{v}^{(t)}, \mathbf{h}^{(t)}|\boldsymbol{\theta}) = 0, \quad \forall \theta \in \boldsymbol{\theta}.
\end{aligned}
$$

$$(3.18)$$

The relation $\partial \log f(\theta)/\partial \theta = (1/f(\theta))\partial f(\theta)/\partial \theta$ was used in the first and third line of the derivation. Even though $\partial \log P(\mathbf{v}^{(t)}, \mathbf{h}^{(t)}|\boldsymbol{\theta})/\partial \theta$ is quite often easy to compute, in many cases of practical interest the *system of equations* obtained by setting $\partial \log P(\mathcal{D}|\boldsymbol{\theta})/\partial \theta$ to zero for each θ is highly nonlinear and cannot be solved in closed-form. One approach is to perform gradient descent in $\log P(\mathbf{v}^{(t)}, \mathbf{h}^{(t)}|\boldsymbol{\theta})$, while sampling from $P(\mathbf{h}^{(t)}|\mathbf{v}^{(t)}, \boldsymbol{\theta})$ using Markov chain Monte Carlo. This gives a Monte Carlo approximation to gradient descent in $\log P(\mathcal{D}|\boldsymbol{\theta})$ as given in (3.18). Another approach is to solve the system of nonlinear equations iteratively. Although in principle any method for solving a nonlinear system of equations can be used (*e.g.*, Newton's method [Fletcher 1987]), the structure of (3.18) gives rise to a particularly simple two-phase iterative method, called the *expectation maximization* (EM) algorithm [Baum and Petrie 1966; Dempster, Laird and Rubin 1977].

3.3.1 The expectation maximization (EM) algorithm

Often, we have available an efficient method for estimating the model when all of the variables are visible. That is, the system of equations obtained by setting

$$
\sum_{t=1}^{T} \frac{\partial}{\partial \theta} \log P(\mathbf{v}^{(t)}, \mathbf{h}^{(t)}|\boldsymbol{\theta}) = 0, \quad \forall \theta \in \boldsymbol{\theta} \tag{3.19}
$$

for arbitrary $\mathbf{h}^{(t)}$ can be solved quite easily. Notice that it is *essentially* this system of equations that is obtained if the dependence of $P(\mathbf{h}^{(t)}|\mathbf{v}^{(t)}, \boldsymbol{\theta})$ on $\boldsymbol{\theta}$ in (3.18) is ignored. The summation over $\mathbf{h}^{(t)}$ in (3.18) has the effect of replicating training case t once for each configuration of the hidden variables for that case, and weighting each replication by $P(\mathbf{h}^{(t)}|\mathbf{v}^{(t)}, \boldsymbol{\theta})$. This observation leads to the following iterative two-phase EM algorithm:

1. E-step: Compute $P(\mathbf{h}^{(t)}|\mathbf{v}^{(t)}, \boldsymbol{\theta})$ for each configuration $\mathbf{h}^{(t)}$ of the hidden variables for each training case, and set $Q(\mathbf{h}^{(t)}) \leftarrow P(\mathbf{h}^{(t)}|\mathbf{v}^{(t)}, \boldsymbol{\theta})$.

2. M-step: Solve the following system of equations for $\boldsymbol{\theta}$,

$$\sum_{t=1}^{T} \sum_{\mathbf{h}^{(t)}} Q(\mathbf{h}^{(t)}) \frac{\partial}{\partial \theta} \log P(\mathbf{v}^{(t)}, \mathbf{h}^{(t)}|\boldsymbol{\theta}) = 0, \quad \forall \, \theta \in \boldsymbol{\theta}. \qquad (3.20)$$

Stop if a convergence criterion is satisfied; otherwise go to 1.

In practice, the values of $Q(\mathbf{h}^{(t)})$ for each training case are usually not stored during the E-step. Instead, statistics that are sufficient for the M-step are accumulated while processing the training set. There are several proofs that each EM iteration is guaranteed to increase the likelihood of the training data [Baum and Petrie 1966; Dempster, Laird and Rubin 1977; Meng and Rubin 1992; Neal and Hinton 1993]. After presenting a more general algorithm for maximizing *lower bounds* on the data likelihood $P(\mathcal{D}|\boldsymbol{\theta})$, I will show that each iteration of EM is guaranteed to increase the data likelihood.

3.3.2   The generalized expectation maximization algorithm

Neal and Hinton [1993] introduced a new view of the EM algorithm as a method for maximizing a lower bound on the likelihood of a training set. This interpretation opened the door to tractable approximations to EM for models that are clearly intractable. This "generalized expectation maximization algorithm" is an approximation to ML estimation that follows from using the wrong distribution $Q(\mathbf{h}^{(t)})$ in the M-step of the EM algorithm; *i.e.*, $Q(\mathbf{h}^{(t)}) \neq P(\mathbf{h}^{(t)}|\mathbf{v}^{(t)}, \boldsymbol{\theta})$. There are practical reasons for using a suboptimal distribution $Q(\mathbf{h}^{(t)})$, the most obvious being that in some cases it is computationally infeasible to compute $Q(\mathbf{h}^{(t)})$ for *every* configuration of the hidden variables $\mathbf{h}^{(t)}$ for each training case. For example, some of the Bayesian network models discussed below have over one million configurations per training case.

The bound used in generalized EM is obtained using the following form of Jensen's inequality [Cover and Thomas 1991]:

$$\log \sum_i q_i a_i \geq \sum_i q_i \log a_i, \tag{3.21}$$

where $\sum_i q_i = 1$, and a_i are arbitrary scalars. Applying this inequality to the log-likelihood of the training data (3.17), we get

$$\log P(\mathcal{D}|\boldsymbol{\theta}) = \sum_{t=1}^{T} \log \left[\sum_{\mathbf{h}^{(t)}} P(\mathbf{v}^{(t)}, \mathbf{h}^{(t)}|\boldsymbol{\theta}) \right]$$

$$= \sum_{t=1}^{T} \log \left[\sum_{\mathbf{h}^{(t)}} Q(\mathbf{h}^{(t)}) \frac{P(\mathbf{v}^{(t)}, \mathbf{h}^{(t)}|\boldsymbol{\theta})}{Q(\mathbf{h}^{(t)})} \right]$$

$$\geq \sum_{t=1}^{T} \sum_{\mathbf{h}^{(t)}} Q(\mathbf{h}^{(t)}) \log \frac{P(\mathbf{v}^{(t)}, \mathbf{h}^{(t)}|\boldsymbol{\theta})}{Q(\mathbf{h}^{(t)})} = B_{Q\|P}. \tag{3.22}$$

The goal of generalized EM is to jointly estimate a distribution $Q(\mathbf{h}^{(t)})$ (which may or may not be parameterized) and a distribution $P(\mathbf{v}^{(t)}, \mathbf{h}^{(t)}|\boldsymbol{\theta})$, so as to maximize this lower bound on the likelihood. This leads to the following algorithm:

1. Generalized E-step: Increase the bound $B_{Q\|P}$ with respect to a distribution $Q(\mathbf{h}^{(t)})$.

2. Generalized M-step: Increase the bound $B_{Q\|P}$ with respect to $\boldsymbol{\theta}$.

Note that unlike the E-step of the EM algorithm, the generalized E-step may produce a Q-distribution for which $Q(\mathbf{h}^{(t)}) \neq P(\mathbf{h}^{(t)}|\mathbf{v}^{(t)}, \boldsymbol{\theta})$.

The EM algorithm can be viewed as a special case of the generalized EM algorithm, where we alternately maximize the bound $B_{Q\|P}$ with respect to an *unconstrained* distribution $Q(\mathbf{h}^{(t)})$, and then with respect to $P(\mathbf{v}^{(t)}, \mathbf{h}^{(t)}|\boldsymbol{\theta})$ via $\boldsymbol{\theta}$. If the bound is maximized with respect to $Q(\mathbf{h}^{(t)})$ during the generalized E-step, while enforcing $\sum_{\mathbf{h}^{(t)}} Q(\mathbf{h}^{(t)}) = 1$ using a Lagrange multiplier, we obtain $Q(\mathbf{h}^{(t)}) = P(\mathbf{h}^{(t)}|\mathbf{v}^{(t)}, \boldsymbol{\theta})$. This form of the generalized EM algorithm is identical to the standard EM algorithm presented in the previous section. Also, in this case the inequality in (3.22) becomes an equality: $B_{Q\|P} = \log P(\mathcal{D}|\boldsymbol{\theta})$. It follows that the EM algorithm is a maximum likelihood estimation method.

Note that in general, generalized EM *does not* give the same estimates as ML estimation. As a degenerate example, imagine that we use ML estimation to obtain a model $P(\mathbf{v}^{(t)}, \mathbf{h}^{(t)}|\boldsymbol{\theta})$ from a training set, and that we then apply generalized EM with $Q(\mathbf{h}^{(t)})$ fixed at a uniform distribution. In this case, the bound can be increased by moving $P(\mathbf{v}^{(t)}, \mathbf{h}^{(t)}|\boldsymbol{\theta})$ *away* from the ML estimate (unless $P(\mathbf{v}^{(t)}|\mathbf{h}^{(t)}, \boldsymbol{\theta})$ happens to be uniform, in which case a uniform $Q(\mathbf{h}^{(t)})$ makes the bound tight so that $P(\mathbf{v}^{(t)}, \mathbf{h}^{(t)}|\boldsymbol{\theta})$ will not change). However, as long as we are able produce estimates of $Q(\mathbf{h}^{(t)})$ that are "close" to $P(\mathbf{h}^{(t)}|\mathbf{v}^{(t)}, \boldsymbol{\theta})$, generalized EM will be close to ML estimation. Of course, in most cases, if we have the computational resources available to obtain an ML estimate, generalized EM should not be used. In Section 3.4, I introduce a class of Bayesian networks that have many latent (hidden) variables. For these networks, it is computationally intractable to perform EM and so generalized EM is used.

3.4   Multiple-cause networks

In many cases, it makes sense to postulate that a data vector $\mathbf{v}$ naturally arises from the consequences of a set of hidden *causes* $\mathbf{h}$. For example, an image may be nicely described as a two-dimensional rendition of a combination of objects. If h_k is a binary variable indicating the presence of object k in the image, then the model distribution $P(\mathbf{v}|\mathbf{h}, \boldsymbol{\theta}^{\mathrm{V}})$ is the distribution over images given which objects are present. ($\boldsymbol{\theta}^{\mathrm{V}}$ is a set of parameters associated with the distribution over $\mathbf{v}$). This distribution is meant to capture the way in which the objects interact to form the image as well as any inexplicable noise.

The model $P(\mathbf{v}|\mathbf{h}, \boldsymbol{\theta}^{\mathrm{V}})$ may be simplified by assuming that the K causes dependency-separate the image pixels. That is, once we know which causes are present, each pixel is independent of the others. In this case, $P(\mathbf{v}|\mathbf{h}, \boldsymbol{\theta}^{\mathrm{V}}) = \prod_{i=1}^{N} P(v_i|\mathbf{h}, \boldsymbol{\theta}_i^{\mathrm{V}})$. If the visible variables are binary, each conditional distribution can be implemented using, for example, logistic regression. In contrast to the logistic autoregressive network where each visible variable is regressed on a subset of the other visible variables (see (3.5)), in the multiple-cause network each visible variable is regressed on the hidden cause variables $\mathbf{h}$:

$$P(v_i|\mathbf{h}, \boldsymbol{\theta}_i^{\mathrm{V}}) = v_i g(\textstyle\sum_{k=0}^{K} \theta_{ik}^{\mathrm{V}} h_k) + (1 - v_i)(1 - g(\textstyle\sum_{k=0}^{K} \theta_{ik}^{\mathrm{V}} h_k)), \quad (3.23)$$

where $\boldsymbol{\theta}_i^{\mathrm{V}} = \{\theta_{i0}^{\mathrm{V}}, \dots, \theta_{iK}^{\mathrm{V}}\}$, and we take $h_0 = 1$ in order to account for a constant in the summations. Binary Bayesian networks which use logistic regression for the conditional distributions are often called binary sigmoidal

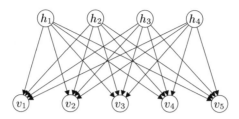

Figure 3.4
A multiple-cause network with five visible variables $\mathbf{v}$ and four hidden cause variables
$\mathbf{h}$.

networks [Neal 1992] and are sometimes called stochastic multi-layer perceptrons.

To complete the model, we provide a distribution $P(\mathbf{h}|\boldsymbol{\theta}^{\mathrm{H}})$ over the set of
causes. Although it seems natural that in many cases the hidden variables h_k
might be interdependent, for the sake of simplicity, I will assume for now that
they are not:

$$P(\mathbf{h}|\boldsymbol{\theta}^{\mathrm{H}}) = \prod_{k=1}^{K} P(h_k|\theta_k^{\mathrm{H}}), \qquad (3.24)$$

where $\boldsymbol{\theta}^{\mathrm{H}} = \{\theta_1^{\mathrm{H}}, \ldots, \theta_K^{\mathrm{H}}\}$. These probabilities can be nicely parameterized
using the logistic function:

$$P(h_k|\theta_k^{\mathrm{H}}) = h_k g(\theta_k^{\mathrm{H}}) + (1 - h_k)(1 - g(\theta_k^{\mathrm{H}})). \qquad (3.25)$$

An example of this type of *multiple-cause* Bayesian network is shown in
Figure 3.4. Notice that the dependency-separation of the variables $\mathbf{v}$ by the set
of hidden variables $\mathbf{h}$ is ensured by condition 2 described in Section 1.2.5.

Supposing that we have somehow obtained an accurate model of the true
causal process for each class of data (*e.g.*, using a method described below), in
order to perform classification we would like to compute the marginal proba-
bility $P(\mathbf{v}|\boldsymbol{\theta})$ for each class model. This can be computed exactly using

$$P(\mathbf{v}|\boldsymbol{\theta}) = \sum_{\mathbf{h}} P(\mathbf{v}|\mathbf{h}, \boldsymbol{\theta}^{\mathrm{V}}) P(\mathbf{h}|\boldsymbol{\theta}^{\mathrm{H}}), \qquad (3.26)$$

where $\boldsymbol{\theta} = \{\boldsymbol{\theta}^{\mathrm{H}}, \boldsymbol{\theta}^{\mathrm{V}}\}$ is the entire set of parameters. However, this sum is
exponential in the number of causes K and so in practice, we must use another
approach. It is obvious from Figure 3.4 that probability propagation cannot

be used to obtain an exact result, since the Bayesian network contains many cycles. In fact, we must use an approximate inference method.

Since exact probabilistic inference is needed for ML and MAP parameter estimation, these estimation methods are also intractable. For example, in order to perform the E-step of the EM algorithm, we must compute $P(\mathbf{h}|\mathbf{v}, \boldsymbol{\theta})$, which has an exponential number (2^K) of terms.

In the next three sections, I show how Gibbs sampling, variational inference, and the stochastic Helmholtz machine can be used to approximate $P(\mathbf{v}|\boldsymbol{\theta})$ and perform generalized EM parameter estimation in multiple-cause networks.

3.4.1   Estimation by iterative probability propagation

For generalized EM by probability propagation, the Q-distribution in the likelihood bound (3.22) can be computed by applying probability propagation in the multiply-connected network. (Since probability propagation is only exact in singly-connected graphical models, propagation in the loopy network will give approximate inference.) Due to the loops in the network, probability propagation will not naturally terminate, but will instead lead to an iterative algorithm. Initially, I frowned upon this approach because modifying the model parameters may cause intermediate stages of iterative inference to become unstable. However, it turns out that variational inference is also susceptible to this effect, so in fact estimation by iterative probability propagation may be an effective learning procedure.

3.4.2   Estimation by Gibbs sampling

In order to estimate a multiple-cause network from a set of training examples $\mathbf{v}^{(1)}, \ldots, \mathbf{v}^{(T)}$, we can perform on-line gradient descent in $\log P(\mathbf{v}, \mathbf{h}|\boldsymbol{\theta})$ while sampling from $P(\mathbf{h}|\mathbf{v}, \boldsymbol{\theta})$ using the Gibbs sampling method described in Section 2.2.2. For the current training case $\mathbf{v}^{(t)}$, we simulate a Markov chain to obtain a configuration $\mathbf{h}^{(t)}$ of the hidden variables. (Notice that in general $\mathbf{h}^{(t)}$ will be different each time $\mathbf{v}^{(t)}$ is processed — ideally, $\mathbf{h}^{(t)}$ will have a distribution $P(\mathbf{h}|\mathbf{v}^{(t)}, \boldsymbol{\theta})$.) In order to perform Gibbs sampling for the logistic multiple-cause network described above, we need to be able to sample from the distribution for each hidden variable h_k given the other cause variables and the visible variables. Since the cause variables are binary, we only need to compute a function that is proportional to $P(h_k|\{h_j\}_{j=1, j \neq k}^K, \mathbf{v}, \boldsymbol{\theta})$. The two values can then be normalized to obtain $P(h_k|\{h_j\}_{j=1, j \neq k}^K, \mathbf{v}, \boldsymbol{\theta})$. Since the total joint probability for $\mathbf{h}$ and $\mathbf{v}$ can be easily computed in $\mathcal{O}(KN)$ time using the ancestral ordering, the joint probability can be used to compute the conditional distribution as follows:

$$P(h_k = 1 | \{h_j\}_{j=1, j \neq k}^{K}, \mathbf{v}, \boldsymbol{\theta})$$

$$= \frac{P(h_k = 1, \{h_j\}_{j=1, j \neq k}^{K}, \mathbf{v} | \boldsymbol{\theta})}{P(h_k = 0, \{h_j\}_{j=1, j \neq k}^{K}, \mathbf{v} | \boldsymbol{\theta}) + P(h_k = 1, \{h_j\}_{j=1, j \neq k}^{K}, \mathbf{v} | \boldsymbol{\theta})}. \quad (3.27)$$

For a given training case $\mathbf{v}^{(t)}$, the latent variables are visited in a specified order while drawing a new value for each variable from its conditional distribution. The entire set of latent variables $\mathbf{h}$ is processed in this fashion for a specified number of times before the Markov chain is terminated and some configuration $\mathbf{h}^{(t)}$ of the latent variables is produced.

The biases for the hidden variables and the parameters connecting the hidden variables to the visible variables are adjusted by following the derivatives of $\log P(\mathbf{v}^{(t)}, \mathbf{h}^{(t)} | \boldsymbol{\theta})$ using a learning rate η as follows:

$$\Delta \theta_k^{\mathrm{H}} = \eta [h_k^{(t)} - g(\theta_k^{\mathrm{H}})], \quad \text{and} \quad (3.28)$$

$$\Delta \theta_{ik}^{\mathrm{V}} = \eta h_k^{(t)} [v_i^{(t)} - g(\sum_{j=0}^{K} \theta_{ij}^{\mathrm{V}} h_j^{(t)})]. \quad (3.29)$$

In order to perform classification, we would like to compute $P(\mathbf{v} | \boldsymbol{\theta})$ for an input vector:

$$P(\mathbf{v} | \boldsymbol{\theta}) = \sum_{\mathbf{h}} P(\mathbf{v}, \mathbf{h} | \boldsymbol{\theta}). \quad (3.30)$$

This problem can be viewed as a form of *free energy estimation* [Sheykhet and Simkin 1990; Neal 1993]. I use a very simple approximation that is quite fast and works well in practice for classification purposes. Since the number of terms in the above sum is exponential in the number of causes, I approximate it by assuming that the majority of the total probability mass is contributed by a small number of clusters in $\mathbf{h}$-space. These clusters are found by simulating a Markov chain as described above. At multiple points in the chain, the configuration of $\mathbf{h}$ and all neighboring configurations (*i.e.*, those configurations within a Hamming distance of 1) are added to a list of "significant terms". Only the neighboring states of $\mathbf{h}$ are considered because once $P(\mathbf{v}, \mathbf{h} | \boldsymbol{\theta})$ has been computed, it is easy to compute the probabilities for configurations that differ from $\mathbf{h}$ by only one bit. After a specified number of clusters have been visited in this manner, the above sum is approximated by adding up the terms for the tabulated configurations. This method for estimating $P(\mathbf{v} | \boldsymbol{\theta})$ will not work well when there is a large number of clusters in $\mathbf{h}$-space that contribute significantly to the sum. However, I have found that in practice the Gibbs sampling learning algorithm tends to favor a small number of clusters, making this approximation reasonable.

3.4.3   Generalized EM using variational inference

In this section, I review the variational method developed by Saul *et al.* [1996] for generalized EM in sigmoidal Bayesian networks. It turns out that a product-form variational distribution leads to an intractable bound, and so the bound itself must be bounded by a tractable function.

For generalized EM by variational inference, the Q-distribution in the likelihood bound (3.22) depends on some variational parameters $\boldsymbol{\xi}$. For the sake of simplicity, consider the bound for *one* training case $\mathbf{v}$:

$$\log P(\mathcal{D}|\boldsymbol{\theta}) \geq B_{Q\|P} = \sum_{\mathbf{h}} Q(\mathbf{h}|\boldsymbol{\xi}) \log \frac{1}{Q(\mathbf{h}|\boldsymbol{\xi})} + \sum_{\mathbf{h}} Q(\mathbf{h}|\boldsymbol{\xi}) \log P(\mathbf{h}, \mathbf{v}|\boldsymbol{\theta}).$$
(3.31)

Generalized EM entails iteratively maximizing this bound, first by varying $\boldsymbol{\xi}$ (the generalized E-step), and second by adjusting the model parameters $\boldsymbol{\theta}$ (the generalized M-step). The first term in this bound is the entropy of the variational distribution $Q(\mathbf{h}|\boldsymbol{\xi})$, and the second term is the expected log-probability of $\mathbf{h}$ and $\mathbf{v}$ under the variational distribution.

Here, I consider a product-form variational distribution over the K latent variables $h_1, \ldots, h_K$ (notice that h_0 is not included since it is fixed to $h_0 = 1$):

$$Q(\mathbf{h}|\boldsymbol{\xi}) = \prod_{k=1}^{K} Q(h_k|\xi_k) = \prod_{k=1}^{K} \xi_k^{h_k} (1 - \xi_k)^{(1-h_k)},$$
(3.32)

where ξ_k is the probability under the variational distribution that $h_k = 1$. Using this variational distribution, the first term in $B_{Q\|P}$ simplifies to

$$\sum_{\mathbf{h}} Q(\mathbf{h}|\boldsymbol{\xi}) \log \frac{1}{Q(\mathbf{h}|\boldsymbol{\xi})} = \sum_{k=1}^{K} \{\xi_k \log \xi_k + (1 - \xi_k) \log(1 - \xi_k)\}.$$
(3.33)

The second term in (3.31) is

$$\sum_{\mathbf{h}} Q(\mathbf{h}|\boldsymbol{\xi}) \log P(\mathbf{h}, \mathbf{v}|\boldsymbol{\theta}) = \sum_{\mathbf{h}} Q(\mathbf{h}|\boldsymbol{\xi}) \log \left[\prod_{k=1}^{K} P(h_k|\theta_k^{\mathrm{H}}) \prod_{i=1}^{N} P(v_i|\mathbf{h}, \boldsymbol{\theta}_i^{\mathrm{V}}) \right]$$

$$= \sum_{k=1}^{K} \sum_{h_k=0}^{1} Q(h_k|\xi_k) \log P(h_k|\theta_k^{\mathrm{H}}) + \sum_{i=1}^{N} \sum_{\mathbf{h}} Q(\mathbf{h}|\boldsymbol{\xi}) \log P(v_i|\mathbf{h}, \boldsymbol{\theta}_i^{\mathrm{V}}).$$
(3.34)

Since the conditional probabilities are given by logistic regression, this term contains many expectations of nonlinear functions. The first step to simplifying these expectations is to express the conditional probability $P(h_k|\theta_k^{\mathrm{H}})$ given in (3.25) in the following way:

$$P(h_k|\theta_k^{\mathrm{H}}) = \frac{\exp(h_k\theta_k^{\mathrm{H}})}{1+\exp(\theta_k^{\mathrm{H}})}. \tag{3.35}$$

The expectation of $\log P(h_k|\theta_k^{\mathrm{H}})$ is

$$\sum_{h_k=0}^{1} Q(h_k|\xi_k) \log P(h_k|\theta_k^{\mathrm{H}}) = \xi_k\theta_k^{\mathrm{H}} - \log\{1+\exp(\theta_k^{\mathrm{H}})\}. \tag{3.36}$$

Similarly, the conditional probability $P(v_i|\mathbf{h},\boldsymbol{\theta}_i^{\mathrm{V}})$ can be written

$$P(v_i|\mathbf{h},\boldsymbol{\theta}_i^{\mathrm{V}}) = \frac{\exp\left(v_i\sum_{k=0}^{K}\theta_{ik}^{\mathrm{V}}h_k\right)}{1+\exp\left(\sum_{k=0}^{K}\theta_{ik}^{\mathrm{V}}h_k\right)}. \tag{3.37}$$

The expectation of $\log P(v_i|\mathbf{h},\boldsymbol{\theta}_i^{\mathrm{V}})$ is then

$$v_i\sum_{k=0}^{K}\theta_{ik}^{\mathrm{V}}\xi_k - \sum_{\mathbf{h}} Q(\mathbf{h}|\boldsymbol{\xi}) \log\{1+\exp\left(\sum_{k=0}^{K}\theta_{ik}^{\mathrm{V}}h_k\right)\}. \tag{3.38}$$

The overall bound for $\mathbf{v}$ is

$$B_{Q\|P} = \sum_{k=1}^{K}\{\xi_k\log\xi_k + (1-\xi_k)\log(1-\xi_k) + \xi_k\theta_k^{\mathrm{H}} - \log\left[1+\exp(\theta_k^{\mathrm{H}})\right]\}$$

$$+ \sum_{i=1}^{N} v_i \sum_{k=0}^{K}\theta_{ik}^{\mathrm{V}}\xi_k - \sum_{\mathbf{h}} Q(\mathbf{h}|\boldsymbol{\xi}) \log\{1+\exp\left(\sum_{k=0}^{K}\theta_{ik}^{\mathrm{V}}h_k\right)\}. \tag{3.39}$$

Except for the last term, the values of these terms and their derivatives can quite easily be computed. The explicit summation over $\mathbf{h}$ in the last term cannot be reduced to a tractable form. However, the last term can be bounded by introducing some extra variational parameters $\boldsymbol{\nu}$. (See Saul, Jaakkola and Jordan [1996] for details.) Generalized EM for the new bound $B'_{Q\|P} \leq B_{Q\|P}$ entails iteratively maximizing this bound, first by varying $\boldsymbol{\xi}$ and $\boldsymbol{\nu}$ (the generalized E-step), and second by adjusting the model parameters $\boldsymbol{\theta}$ (the generalized M-step).

3.4.4 The stochastic Helmholtz machine

A stochastic Helmholtz machine consists of a pair of Bayesian networks that are fit to training data using an algorithm that approximates generalized EM, where the bound on the likelihood may be very complex. In addition to the multiple-cause network that describes $P(\mathbf{v}, \mathbf{h}|\boldsymbol{\theta})$ (the *generative* network), there is a *recognition* network that describes $Q(\mathbf{h}|\mathbf{v}, \phi)$. The stochastic Helmholtz machine requires that the recognition network have an ancestral ordering such that it is easy to draw samples from $Q(\mathbf{h}|\mathbf{v}, \phi)$. The advantage of the stochastic Helmholtz machine over Markov chain Monte Carlo is that each sample from the recognition network is independent, as opposed to dependent on the last sample. The advantage of the stochastic Helmholtz machine over variational inference is that more complicated (*e.g.*, nonfactorial) distributions can be represented by the inference process used for generalized EM. The main disadvantage of the stochastic Helmholtz machine is that a recognition network that is compatible with the generative network must somehow be estimated, and this can be a very difficult task when a complex recognition network is used. An example of inference in the stochastic Helmholtz machine is described in Section 2.4.4. Here, I describe the *wake-sleep algorithm* for on-line estimation of both the generative and recognition parameters ($\boldsymbol{\theta}$ and ϕ) [Hinton *et al.* 1995].

Suppose we have a current generative network (which may or may not be a good model of the data) and a current recognition network. For a parameterized recognition network, the likelihood bound in (3.22) is

$$\log P(\mathcal{D}|\boldsymbol{\theta}) \geq B_{Q\|P} = \sum_{t=1}^{T} \sum_{\mathbf{h}} Q(\mathbf{h}|\mathbf{v}^{(t)}, \phi) \log \frac{P(\mathbf{h}, \mathbf{v}^{(t)}|\boldsymbol{\theta})}{Q(\mathbf{h}|\mathbf{v}^{(t)}, \phi)}. \qquad (3.40)$$

This bound can be estimated by averaging $\log P(\mathbf{h}, \mathbf{v}^{(t)}|\boldsymbol{\theta})/Q(\mathbf{h}|\mathbf{v}^{(t)}, \phi)$ over multiple recognition sweeps for each input pattern. In each recognition sweep, the recognition network is stochastically simulated to obtain a configuration $\mathbf{h}$ of the latent variables.

We would like to maximize $B_{Q\|P}$ with respect to the recognition network parameters ϕ for all $\mathbf{v}$, if possible. As discussed in Section 3.3.2, the unconstrained recognition distribution that maximizes this likelihood bound is

$$Q(\mathbf{h}|\mathbf{v}, \phi) = P(\mathbf{h}|\mathbf{v}, \boldsymbol{\theta}). \qquad (3.41)$$

However, except for very simple recognition networks, this optimization is intractable for the same reason that exact inference is intractable. Instead, we optimize a different function whose global maxima give identical recognition networks in certain limits to those produced by maximizing $B_{Q\|P}$. The limits may not apply in practice, so that the recognition network may be slightly suboptimal.

Assume for the moment that the recognition network is consistent with the distribution $P(\mathbf{h}|\mathbf{v}, \boldsymbol{\theta})$. In this case, the parameters ϕ that maximize

$$B_{P\|Q} = \sum_{\mathbf{h},\mathbf{v}} P(\mathbf{h}, \mathbf{v}|\boldsymbol{\theta}) \log \frac{Q(\mathbf{h}|\mathbf{v}, \phi)}{P(\mathbf{h}, \mathbf{v}|\boldsymbol{\theta})} \qquad (3.42)$$

will also maximize $B_{Q\|P}$ in (3.40). (Note the reversed order of the distributions). So, for a given generative network, the optimum recognition network can be found by maximizing $B_{P\|Q}$ with respect to the recognition parameters ϕ. The derivative of $B_{P\|Q}$ with respect to a recognition network parameter ϕ is

$$\frac{\partial B_{P\|Q}}{\partial \phi} = \sum_{\mathbf{h},\mathbf{v}} P(\mathbf{h}, \mathbf{v}|\boldsymbol{\theta}) \frac{\partial \log Q(\mathbf{h}|\mathbf{v}, \phi)}{\partial \phi}. \qquad (3.43)$$

So, the recognition network can be estimated using stochastic gradient descent by sampling $\mathbf{h}$ and $\mathbf{v}$ from $P(\mathbf{h}, \mathbf{v}|\boldsymbol{\theta})$ using ancestral simulation, and then adjusting the recognition network parameters so as to increase the log-probability of the hidden variables given the visible variables. This procedure is called *sleep-phase* learning, since the recognition network is adjusted to be better suited to the "fantasies" produced by the generative network.

In practice, sleep-phase learning is only an approximation to the generalized E-step described in (Section 3.3.2) for one main reason. An ideal recognition network produces a good approximation to $P(\mathbf{h}|\mathbf{v}, \boldsymbol{\theta})$ even for a vector $\mathbf{v}$ that has a very small probability under $P(\mathbf{h}, \mathbf{v}|\boldsymbol{\theta})$. (This corresponds to a plausible real-world pattern that the generative network has not yet learned.) For sleep-phase learning to produce such a recognition network, an extremely large sample size must be drawn from $P(\mathbf{h}, \mathbf{v}|\boldsymbol{\theta})$ in order to get an example of the unlikely vector. For the sake of tractability, a relatively small sample size must be used, which implies that the ideal recognition network cannot be found. This means that in practice, maximizing $B_{P\|Q}$ does *not* give the same recognition network as would be obtained by maximizing $B_{Q\|P}$. In fact, in order to prevent overfitting of the recognition network, an inconsistent parametric recognition network is used, so that the global maxima of the two functions may not even coincide.

For a given recognition network, the generative network is adjusted in the *wake-phase* using a Monte Carlo implementation of the generalized M-step. That is, on-line stochastic gradient descent in the likelihood bound $B_{Q\|P}$ is performed with respect to the generative network parameters $\boldsymbol{\theta}$. The derivative of the bound with respect to a generative network parameter θ is

$$
\frac{\partial B_{Q\|P}}{\partial \theta} = \frac{\partial}{\partial \theta} \sum_{t=1}^{T} \sum_{\mathbf{h}} Q(\mathbf{h}|\mathbf{v}^{(t)}, \boldsymbol{\theta}) \log \frac{P(\mathbf{h}, \mathbf{v}^{(t)}|\boldsymbol{\theta})}{Q(\mathbf{h}|\mathbf{v}^{(t)}, \boldsymbol{\phi})}
$$

$$
= \sum_{t=1}^{T} \sum_{\mathbf{h}} Q(\mathbf{h}|\mathbf{v}^{(t)}, \boldsymbol{\phi}) \frac{\partial \log P(\mathbf{h}, \mathbf{v}^{(t)}|\boldsymbol{\theta})}{\partial \theta}. \quad (3.44)
$$

For a training vector $\mathbf{v}^{(t)}$, the recognition network is used to sample values for the latent variables $\mathbf{h}$. Then, the generative parameters are adjusted so as to increase the log-probability of the latent variables *and* the visible variables.

The two phases of learning are usually applied in alternation. A training pattern is presented; the recognition network is used to obtain a random $\mathbf{h}$; and the generative network is adjusted. Next, the generative network is used to obtain a random $\mathbf{h}$ and then a random $\mathbf{v}$; and the recognition network is adjusted. The result of this constant mixing of the two phases is that the generative network becomes better at modelling the training data and *at the same time* tries to produce causes for the training data that can be properly inferred by the restricted recognition network. This can be seen mathematically by breaking $B_{Q\|P}$ into two pieces:

$$
B_{Q\|P} = \log P(\mathcal{D}|\boldsymbol{\theta}) - \sum_{t=1}^{T} \sum_{\mathbf{h}} Q(\mathbf{h}|\mathbf{v}^{(t)}, \boldsymbol{\phi}) \log \frac{Q(\mathbf{h}|\mathbf{v}^{(t)}, \boldsymbol{\phi})}{P(\mathbf{h}|\mathbf{v}^{(t)}, \boldsymbol{\theta})}. \quad (3.45)
$$

The first term encourages the generative network to model the data, whereas the second term (a negative Kullback-Leibler pseudo-distance) encourages it to be compatible with the recognition network. As a result of the latter, for a generative network that is estimated using the wake-sleep algorithm, the global maxima of $B_{Q\|P}$ and $B_{P\|Q}$ often *do* coincide.

Assuming that under the recognition distribution, the latent variables are independent given the visible variables, we have:

$$
Q(\mathbf{h}|\mathbf{v}, \boldsymbol{\phi}) = \prod_{k=1}^{K} Q(h_k|\mathbf{v}, \boldsymbol{\phi}_k). \quad (3.46)
$$

Also, consider modelling each of these components using logistic regression:

$$
Q(h_k|\mathbf{v}, \boldsymbol{\phi}_k) = h_k g(\textstyle\sum_{i=0}^{N} \phi_{ki} v_i) + (1 - h_k)(1 - g(\textstyle\sum_{i=0}^{N} \phi_{ki} v_i)), \quad (3.47)
$$

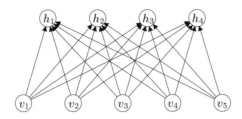

Figure 3.5
A recognition network that implements $Q(\mathbf{h}|\mathbf{v}, \boldsymbol{\phi})$ for the generative network shown in Figure 3.4.

where we take $v_0 = 1$ in order to account for a constant in the exponents. This recognition network is shown in Figure 3.5.

For this logistic recognition network, the recognition parameters are adjusted as follows during the sleep phase, in order to increase $\log Q(\mathbf{h}|\mathbf{v}, \boldsymbol{\phi})$:

$$\Delta\phi_{ki} = v_i(h_k - g(\textstyle\sum_{j=0}^{N}\phi_{kj}v_j)). \tag{3.48}$$

It turns out that in many practical cases this recognition network is sufficient for producing good density estimates. However, if it is estimated in conjunction with a fixed generative network that describes the simple burglar alarm problem (see Section 2.2.3), the likelihood bound $B_{Q\|P}$ may actually *decrease*. Consider how the recognition network is modified for fantasies where the burglar alarm is ringing. We simulate the generative network, obtaining values for b, e, and a, and discard those samples for which $a \neq 1$. For the recognition network parameters ϕ^{BA} and ϕ^{EA} that connect the common consequence a to the two causes b and e, the expected learning updates become

$$\mathrm{E}\big[\Delta\phi^{BA}\big] = \mathrm{E}\big[b - g(\phi^{BA} + \phi^{B0})\big] = P(b = 1|a = 1) - g(\phi^{BA} + \phi^{B0})$$

$$\mathrm{E}\big[\Delta\phi^{EA}\big] = \mathrm{E}\big[e - g(\phi^{EA} + \phi^{E0})\big] = P(e = 1|a = 1) - g(\phi^{EA} + \phi^{E0}),$$
$$\tag{3.49}$$

where ϕ^{B0} and ϕ^{E0} are the recognition biases for b and e. Each connection is modified so as to predict as closely as possible the *marginal* posterior distributions $P(b = 1|a = 1)$ and $P(e = 1|a = 1)$ over the corresponding causes b and e. After training, the recognition distribution over b and e given $a = 1$ will be the product of the marginals. For the configuration $b = 1$, $a = 1$,

$$Q(b = 1, e = 1|a = 1, \phi) = P(b = 1|a = 1)P(e = 1|a = 1)$$
$$= 0.751 \times 0.349 = 0.262, \qquad (3.50)$$

where the values for $P(b = 1|a = 1)$ and $P(e = 1|a = 1)$ were computed from (2.8). This value is quite a bit higher than the correct value of $P(b = 1, e = 1|a = 1) = 0.116$. In fact, if we assume that b and e are independent given $a = 1$, the recognition distribution that maximizes the likelihood bound $B_{Q\|P}$ has $\hat{P}(b = 1, e = 1|a = 1) = 0.177$. This is an example where maximizing $B_{P\|Q}$ is a poor approximation to maximizing $B_{Q\|P}$. Notice, however, that the problem arises because we are using an inconsistent recognition network.

3.4.5 Hierarchical networks

Earlier in this section, I presented multiple-cause networks with the assumption that the causes were independent in the generative network (see (3.24) on page 69). Even with the assumption that the causes are independent, it is still possible to represent quite complex correlations in the visible variables **v**. However, in many cases the causes are certainly interdependent. For example, if the causes variables represent the presence or absence of various objects in facial images, we expect that both a toque and a top-hat are not present simultaneously.

In order to model interdependent causes, we can simply add another layer of "meta-causes" at a higher level in the network. Even if we assume that the "meta-causes" are independent, the network can still represent fairly complex relationships between the causes. Such a *hierarchical* network is shown in Figure 3.6a. We have already seen examples of hierarchical networks, such as the network used in the bars problem example (Figure 1.11).

The parameter estimation methods already described in this chapter are applicable to hierarchical networks with any reasonable depth. Of particular interest, however, is the recognition model for the Helmholtz machine. Figure 3.6b shows a recognition model that is appropriate for the network in Figure 3.6a. Note that the top layer of hidden variables could receive input from the bottom layer of visible variables, not just the middle layer of hidden variables. However, this introduces extra parameters into the Helmholtz machine, which may worsen the effect of overfitting. In my experiments, I use layered generative and recognition networks like the ones shown in Figure 3.6. In some cases, adding extra connections may help.

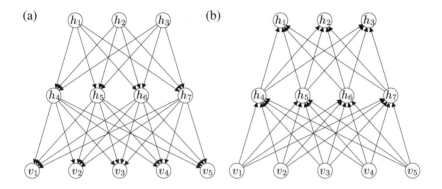

Figure 3.6
(a) A hierarchical network with three extra "meta-cause" variables which produce correlations between the cause variables (middle layer). (b) A recognition network.

3.4.6 Ensembles of networks

According to the Bayesian doctrine for prediction, when using a density model
$P(\mathbf{v}|\boldsymbol{\theta})$ to estimate the probability of $\mathbf{v}$, we ought to integrate out the model
parameters $\boldsymbol{\theta}$. For a prior parameter probability density $p(\boldsymbol{\theta})$ and a training
data likelihood $P(\mathcal{D}|\boldsymbol{\theta})$, we use the posterior $p(\boldsymbol{\theta}|\mathcal{D}) \propto p(\boldsymbol{\theta})P(\mathcal{D}|\boldsymbol{\theta})$ (where
the constant of proportionality does not depend on $\boldsymbol{\theta}$) to obtain an estimate

$$P(\mathbf{v}|\mathcal{D}) = \int_{\boldsymbol{\theta}} P(\mathbf{v}|\boldsymbol{\theta})p(\boldsymbol{\theta}|\mathcal{D})d\boldsymbol{\theta}. \qquad (3.51)$$

For example, this integral can be approximated using Laplace's approximation [Spiegelhalter and Lauritzen 1990], Markov chain Monte Carlo methods
[Neal 1993; Neal 1996] or variational techniques [Jaakkola and Jordan 1997].
Here, I consider an ensemble method that is less sophisticated than the above
approaches, but is also easier to implement and and in practice usually gives a
significant improvement over MAP parameter estimation.

Suppose we perform MAP parameter estimation using multiple restarts (different random initial parameters) so that we have an *ensemble* of M models,
where model m has parameters $\boldsymbol{\theta}_m$. Each model may correspond to a different
local maximum of the posterior $p(\boldsymbol{\theta}|\mathcal{D})$, and we assume that each model is
equally likely in the posterior. We then approximate the above integral by

$$\hat{P}(\mathbf{v}|\mathcal{D}) = \frac{1}{M} \sum_{m=1}^{M} P(\mathbf{v}|\boldsymbol{\theta}_m). \qquad (3.52)$$

If $P(\mathbf{v}|\boldsymbol{\theta})$ does not change much over the width of each mode in the posterior, then as long as the modes are properly represented by the ensemble of models, $\hat{P}(\mathbf{v}|\mathcal{D})$ will be very close to the correct value $P(\mathbf{v}|\mathcal{D})$ given by integration. On the other hand, if there is a mode in the posterior that is so wide that $P(\mathbf{v}|\boldsymbol{\theta})$ *does* vary significantly across the mode, then $\hat{P}(\mathbf{v}|\mathcal{D})$ may be quite different from $P(\mathbf{v}|\mathcal{D})$. This is because only a peak in the posterior is being included in the sum, while the mass surrounding the peak is being ignored, even though the corresponding predictions are quite variable.

Since the Bayesian networks described above are flexible models, we expect that with limited training data they may have multiple data likelihood optima (corresponding to multiple peaks in the posterior, if we assume a uniform prior over network parameters). For this reason, when time permits, a significant classification rate improvement can be obtained by using an ensemble of networks for each class of data. The classification decision is then based on the average probabilities computed from the ensemble for each class.

3.5 Classification of handwritten digits

An interesting and useful pattern classification problem is the classification of handwritten digits. In this section, I present results on the classification of 8×8 binary images of handwritten digits made available by the US Postal Service Office of Advanced Technology. I compare the following Bayesian network methods: logistic autoregressive classifier (LARC-1), a stochastic Helmholtz machine with one hidden layer (SHM-1), a stochastic Helmholtz machine with two hidden layers (SHM-2), and an ensemble of stochastic Helmholtz machines with one hidden layer (ESHM-1). In order to place the performance of these networks in context, I include the following methods: classification and regression trees (CART-1), the naive Bayes classifier (NBAYESC-1), and the k-nearest neighbor method (KNN-CLASS-1). The performances of these classifiers are assessed using 5 different training set sizes (120, 240, 480, 960 and 1920 cases) so that the effect of the number of training cases on each method can be studied. After describing the classifiers and the methods used to estimate them, I present and discuss the performance results.

3.5.1 Logistic autoregressive classifiers: LARC-1,ELARC-1

LARC-1 models each of the 10 classes of data using a logistic autoregressive network (see Section 3.2), where the variables are ordered in a raster-scan fashion. Once each of the 10 networks have been estimated from the training data, a test pattern is classified by outputing the class corresponding to the network that gives the greatest likelihood to the pattern.

Before estimating each network from its respective class of training data, the double precision parameters $\boldsymbol{\theta}$ were initialized to uniformly random values on $[-0.01, 0.01]$. Overfitting was prevented by using MAP estimation with a scaled Gaussian parameter prior. The prior variance of the first input was set to $\sigma_1^2 = 4.0$. A conjugate gradient algorithm was used for MAP estimation.

ELARC-1 uses an ensemble of 8 logistic autoregressive networks, where each element in the ensemble uses a different ordering of the variables in $\mathbf{v}$. One of the elements uses the raster-scan ordering, whereas the other 7 elements use a randomly selected ordering. The probability of a test pattern for a given class is estimated by averaging the probability estimates from each of the 8 networks in the ensemble for that class.

3.5.2 The Gibbs machine: GM-1

GM-1 models the distribution of each of the 10 classes of data using a logistic multiple-cause network of the type shown in Figures 3.4, that is trained using Gibbs sampling. Each network has 64 visible binary (0/1) variables (8×8) and one hidden layer of 16 binary (0/1) variables. Once the 10 networks have been estimated, classification of a test pattern proceeds by estimating the probability of the pattern under each network, using the method described in Section 3.4.2. The class corresponding to the network that gives the highest probability is output as the prediction.

Before estimating a network using Gibbs sampling, all of its double precision parameters were initialized to uniformly random values on $[-0.01, 0.01]$. For each training pattern, a single configuration of the hidden variables was obtained by performing 10 sweeps of Gibbs sampling, while annealing the network from a temperature of 5.0 to 1.0 using a $1/\tau$ schedule, where τ is the sweep count. Then, the network parameters were adjusted using a learning rate of 0.01. For a training set of T patterns, a randomly chosen set of $\lfloor T/3 \rfloor$ cases were set aside as a "validation" set. By monitoring the probability estimate for this validation data, early-stopping was used to prevent overfitting. After every 10 epochs of learning (1 epoch = one sweep through the remaining $\lceil 2T/3 \rceil$ training cases), for each validation pattern, 10 sweeps of Gibbs sampling with annealing were performed as described above, and then 20 sweeps of Gibbs sampling at unity temperature were performed to obtain 20 configurations. Then, the probability of the validation pattern was estimated by computing the probability mass associated with each configuration and its 1-nearest neighbors. Each network was trained for a minimum of 100 epochs (the validation probability estimate was still computed every 10 epochs in this interval). Then, learning was stopped after the current epoch n, if the epoch $n_{\max}$ at which the maximum validation probability estimate occurred took place no less than $n/3$ epochs ago. Also, in order to terminate learning runs where the validation probability estimate continued to increase asymptotically towards a limit, a maximum of 2000 training epochs were performed. In summary, learning was stopped at epoch n if $n \geq 2000$ or if $n_{max} \leq 2n/3$ and $n \geq 100$. (A similar early stopping technique has been used with regression models [Rasmussen 1996].)

3.5.3 The mean field Bayesian network: MFBN-1

MFBN-1 models the distribution of each of the 10 classes of data using a logistic multiple-cause network of the type shown in Figures 3.4. Each network is fit using the variational technique described in Section 3.4.3. Each network has 64 visible binary (0/1) variables (8 × 8) and one hidden layer of 16 binary (0/1) variables. Once the 10 networks have been estimated, classification of a test pattern proceeds by computing the likelihood bound for each network, using the method described in Section 3.4.3. The class corresponding to the network that gives the highest bound is output as the prediction.

Before estimating a network using the variational method, all of its double precision parameters (θ) were initialized to uniformly random values on $[-0.01, 0.01)$. For each training case, the variational parameters were initialized to uniformly random values on $[-0.01, 0.01)$. The variational bound was increased at each generalized E-step using the following iterative method [Saul, Jaakkola and Jordan 1996]. After each iteration, if the bound did not increase by more than 1% then no more iterations were performed for the current training case. A maximum of 10 iterations was performed. These algorithm parameters were suggested by Jaakkola (personal communication). The variational bound was increased at each generalized M-step using batch gradient descent with a learning rate of 0.01.

The validation procedure used to train each network was identical to the one used for GM-1, except that the variational bound was used instead of an estimate of the validation case probability. The validation bound was computed every 5 epochs. No fewer than 100 epochs were performed, and no more than 1000 epochs were performed.

3.5.4 Stochastic Helmholtz machines: SHM-1, SHM-2, ESHM-1

SHM-1 models the distribution of each of the 10 classes of data using a stochastic Helmholtz machine with 64 visible binary (0/1) variables (8 × 8) and one hidden layer of 16 binary (0/1) variables. The generative and recognition networks are of the form shown in Figures 3.4 and 3.5, and logistic regression is used to implement the conditional relationships. The likelihood bound for a given input pattern is estimated using 20 recognition sweeps. Once the 10 machines have been estimated, classification of a test pattern proceeds by estimating the likelihood bound for each machine. The class corresponding to the machine that gives the highest likelihood bound estimate is output as the prediction.

Before estimating a Helmholtz machine using the wake-sleep algorithm, all of its double precision parameters (θ and ϕ) were initialized to uniformly random values on $[-0.01, 0.01)$. A learning rate of 0.01 was used for both phases of learning. The validation procedure used to train each machine was identical to the one used for GM-1, except that instead of obtaining an estimate of the validation set probability as described above, 20 epochs of recognition passes were performed on the validation set to obtain an estimate of the likelihood bound for the validation data.

SHM-2 is similar to SHM-1, except that it uses stochastic Helmholtz machines with a visible layer of 64 binary variables, a middle hidden layer of 16 binary variables, and a top hidden layer of 8 binary variables. The generative and recognition networks are of the form shown in Figure 3.6.

ESHM-1 uses an ensemble of 8 SHM-1 networks to model each class of patterns. Each network in an ensemble is estimated using the above procedure, where a different randomly chosen validation set of $\lfloor T/3 \rfloor$ patterns is set aside for each network. Also, different initial random parameters are chosen for each network. Once 8 networks have been estimated for each of the 10 classes of data, a test pattern is processed by approximating 8 likelihood bounds for each data class. These are averaged together within each class to obtain 10 average likelihood bounds. The final class decision for the test pattern is based on these averages.

3.5.5 The classification and regression tree: CART-1

This tree-based classifier has previously been run on several classification tasks in DELVE [Rasmussen *et al.* 1996]. CART-1 uses a binary decision tree to classify the test patterns, where each node in the tree makes a binary decision based on an axis-aligned decision surface in the input space, and each leaf in the tree has a class label. A test pattern is classified by traversing the tree from the root to a leaf, while following the decisions at each node. That is, decision node d_j looks at a particular input variable v_{i_j} and compares it to a threshold t_j. If $v_{i_j} > t_j$, the right child is chosen, and otherwise the left child is chosen. When a leaf is reached, the class of the leaf node is output by the classifier.

The tree is constructed from a training set using 10-fold cross validation. The details of how the tree is produced can be found in Breiman *et al.* [1984].[1]

---

[1] I used Version 1.1 of the CART software provided by California Statistical Software Inc., 961 Yorkshire Ct. Lafayette, California 94549.

3.5.6 The naive Bayes classifier: NBAYESC-1

The naive Bayes method of modelling can be viewed as a multiple-cause
Bayesian network where there aren't any hidden cause variables. That is, we
assume that each of the inputs is independent given the class identity. For the
binary input case, this model becomes very simple. The naive Bayes model for
each class of data is

$$P(\mathbf{v}|\boldsymbol{\theta}) = \prod_{i=1}^{N} \theta_i^{v_i} (1 - \theta_i)^{1-v_i}, \tag{3.53}$$

where $\theta_i \in [0, 1]$ is the probability that $v_i = 1$ under the model. For a given
class of training data, I use the Bayesian method to obtain a minimum squared-
loss estimate of $P(\mathbf{v})$, assuming a uniform prior for $\boldsymbol{\theta}$:

$$P(\mathbf{v}) = \prod_{i=1}^{N} \left[\frac{f_i + 1}{T + 2}\right]^{v_i} \left[\frac{T - f_i + 1}{T + 2}\right]^{1-v_i}. \tag{3.54}$$

Once one such estimate is obtained for each of the 10 classes of training data,
a test pattern is classified by choosing the class that gives the probability to the
pattern. Notice that if $f_i = 0$ or T, the probability $P(\mathbf{v})$ is not 0 or 1. This
prevents overfitting.

3.5.7 The k-nearest neighbor classifier: KNN-CLASS-1

This is the only nonparametric classifier studied in this section. The software I
used was contributed to DELVE by Michael Revow [Rasmussen *et al.* 1996].
In order to guess the class of an input pattern $\mathbf{v}$, the k-nearest neighbor classifier considers the classes of the k training patterns that are nearest to $\mathbf{v}$ in
Euclidean distance. Let n_j $j = 0, \dots, J - 1$ be the number of such training patterns in class j, so that $\sum_{j=0}^{J-1} n_j = k$. Then, the k-nearest neighbor
classifier outputs the most frequent class:

$$j^* = \operatorname{argmax}_j n_j. \tag{3.55}$$

If two or more classes have the maximum number of k-nearest neighbor training patterns, then the classifier chooses the class whose training patterns are
closest to $\mathbf{v}$ on average in Euclidean distance.

k is chosen using leave-one-out cross validation. If there are T training patterns, T new training sets with $T - 1$ patterns each are produced by leaving
each pattern out once. k is set to 1, and the misclassification rate on the left
out patterns is computed using the k-nearest neighbor classifier. Then, k is in-

creased and this process is repeated until $k = T - 1$. The value for k that gives the lowest leave-one-out cross-validation error is used to make predictions for the test patterns.

In order to estimate the *probability* that $\mathbf{v}$ comes from each class, the k-nearest neighbor method uses

$$p_j = n_j/k. \tag{3.56}$$

In this case, the squared difference between the predicted probability vector and the true class identity vector (a vectors of 0's with a single 1) is used as the cross-validation metric to determine k. See the DELVE manual [Rasmussen *et al.* 1996] for more information.

3.5.8 Results

The performances of the classification methods described above were assessed using the DELVE (data for evaluating learning in valid experiments) system [Rasmussen *et al.* 1996]. Under this system, the digit classification problem that I am interested in is called a *prototask*. A particular choice of training set size (*e.g.*, 120 training patterns) is called a *task*. In order to get an accurate measure of the performances of the methods (with error bars), each method was trained and tested at least 4 times using disjoint training set - test set pairs (each of which is called a *task instance*). An original data set consisting of 10,960 patterns (1096 of each class) was partitioned into a training collection of 7680 patterns and a test collection of 3280 patterns. For each of the tasks with training set sizes 120, 240, 480, and 960, the training collection was partitioned into 8 *disjoint* training sets; for the task with training set size 1920, the training collection was partitioned into 4 disjoint training sets. Notice that for the tasks with training set sizes 960 and 1920, all of the training partition cases were used, whereas for the tasks with training set sizes 120, 240, and 480, not all of the training partition cases were used. For each of the tasks with training set sizes 120, 240, 480, and 960, the test collection was partitioned into 8 *disjoint* test sets with 410 patterns each; for the task with training set size 1920, the test collection was partitioned into 4 disjoint test sets with 820 patterns each. This way of partitioning the data eliminates the dependence between each of the 8 experiments performed to assess the performance of each method on each task instance.

Figure 3.7 shows the losses (fraction of patterns misclassified) for each of the tasks (five boxes). Each horizontal bar gives an estimate of the expected loss for a particular method on a particular task. The methods are ordered (from left to right within each box): CART-1, NBAYESC-1, KNN-CLASS-1, MFBN-1, SHM-1, SHM-2, GM-1, ESHM-1, LARC-1 — this is the same

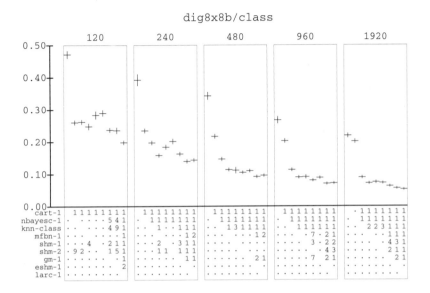

Figure 3.7
Estimates of expected fractions of misclassified patterns for nine methods trained on
five different sizes of training sets.

Table 3.1
Average time in minutes required to train and test the methods from Figure 3.7 for each
of the training set sizes.

	Training set size				
Method	120	240	480	960	1920
CART-1	0.6	1.1	1.9	4.7	5.1
NBAYESC-1	0.0	0.0	0.0	0.0	0.0
KNN-CLASS-1	0.2	1.0	4.6	25.7	192.9
MFBN-1	19.8	64.4	130.5	216.9	344.6
SHM-1	2.3	5.4	11.8	21.8	46.0
SHM-2	3.7	7.8	22.3	41.7	77.6
GM-1	41.7	85.8	176.8	238.0	396.3
ESHM-1	19.4	44.7	95.5	186.7	358.9
LARC-1	0.2	0.5	1.2	3.0	6.5

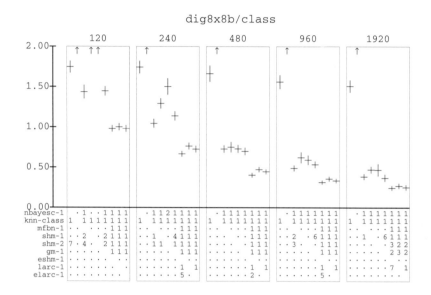

Figure 3.8
Estimates of expected negative log-probability of the true digit identity given by each of eight methods trained on five different sizes of training sets.

ordering as is given top to bottom in the lower-left hand region of the figure. Each vertical bar gives an estimate of the error (one standard deviation) for the corresponding estimate of the expected loss. Numbers in the boxes lying beneath the x-axis are p-values (in percent) for a paired t-test. Choose your favorite method from the list in the lower left-hand corner of the figure and scan from left to right. Whenever you see a number, that means that another method has performed better than your favorite method, *with the given statistical significance*. A low p-value indicates the difference in the misclassification rates is very significant. More precisely, a p-value is an estimate of the probability of obtaining a difference in performance that is equal to or greater than the observed difference, given that we assume the two methods actually perform equally well (the null hypothesis).

The ESHM-1 and LARC-1 methods clearly outperform all other methods for all tasks. If we scan the p-values for these two methods from left to right, we see that there is only a single method that performs significantly better than ESHM-1, and that is LARC-1 on the task with the smallest training set size (120). I found that the performance of ELARC-1 (ensemble of logistic autoregressive networks, not shown) was indistinguishable from plain LARC-1 with respect to classification error. In contrast, ESHM-1 performs significantly better than SHM-1. It is of particular interest that LARC-1, which contains no latent variables, performs slightly better than the methods that contain latent variables.

GM-1 performs the best out of all approximate maximum likelihood methods, including MFBN-1, SHM-1, and SHM-2. However, GM-1 required an order of magnitude more training and validation time than SHM-1. For this reason, an ensemble of logistic multiple cause networks was not considered for the Gibbs sampling estimation method. Table 3.1 shows the average time taken to train and test each method for each training set size on a 195 MHz MIPS R4400 processor. MFBN-1 also required an order of magnitude more training and validation time than SHM-1, and so an ensemble of mean field Bayesian networks was not considered.

Figure 3.8 shows the performance results for soft decisions (the loss is the negative log-probability of the true class under each model). The methods are: NBAYESC-1, KNN-CLASS-1, MFBN-1, SHM-1, SHM-2, GM-1, ESHM-1, LARC-1, ELARC-1. In this case ELARC-1 performs significantly better than LARC-1. Also, in this case ESHM-1 performs slightly better than LARC-1 and ELARC-1.

4 Unsupervised Learning

The Bayesian networks described in the previous chapter are supervised, in the sense that they are trained with pattern - class label pairs. The task in unsupervised learning is for the learning machine to extract "meaningful" hidden causes for the sensory input. Perceptual tasks such as vision and speech recognition can be viewed as inference problems where the goal is to estimate the posterior distribution over the hidden causes (*e.g.*, depth in stereo vision) given the sensory input (c.f. [Hinton and Sejnowski 1986; Hinton *et al.* 1995; Dayan *et al.* 1995]). The recent flurry of research in independent component analysis [Comon, Jutten and Herault 1991; Bell and Sejnowski 1995; Amari, Cichocki and Yang 1996; MacKay 1997b] exemplifies the importance of inferring the continuous-valued latent variables of input data. The latent variables found by this method are linearly related to the input, but perception requires nonlinear inferences such as decision-making and nonlinear continuous inferences, such as depth estimation. In this chapter, I show how the wake-sleep algorithm, slice sampling, and variational techniques can be used to learn networks of binary units and nonlinear continuous units in an unsupervised fashion.

4.1 Extracting structure from images using the wake-sleep algorithm

An interesting problem relevant to vision is that of extracting independent horizontal and vertical bars from an image [Foldiak 1990; Saund 1995; Zemel 1993; Dayan and Zemel 1995; Hinton *et al.* 1995]. Figure 4.1 shows 48 examples of the binary images I am interested in. Each image is produced by randomly choosing between horizontal and vertical orientations with equal probability. Then, each of the 16 possible bars of the chosen orientation is independently instantiated with probability 0.25. Finally, additive noise is introduced by randomly turning on with a probability of 0.25 each pixel that was previously off. The production of these images involves three levels of hierarchy: the first and lowest level represents pixel noise, the second represents bars that consist of groups of 16 pixels each, and the third represents the overall orientation of the bars in the image.

Figure 4.1
Examples of training images whose production involved three levels of hierarchy. First,
an orientation (*i.e.*, horizontal or vertical) is randomly chosen with fair odds. Second,
each bar of the chosen orientation is randomly instantiated with probability 0.25. Third,
additive noise is introduced by randomly turning on with a probability of 0.25 each pixel
that was previously off.

4.1.1 Wake-sleep parameter estimation

Using the wake-sleep algorithm, I trained a stochastic binary Helmholtz machine that has 4 top-layer ("meta-cause") variables, 36 middle-layer variables, and 256 bottom-layer image variables. Each conditional distribution is modelled using logistic regression. Learning is performed through a series of iterations, where each iteration consists of one bottom-up wake phase sweep used to adjust the generative network parameters and one top-down sleep phase sweep used to adjust the recognition network parameters. Every 5000 iterations, the recognition network is used to obtain an estimate (with error bars) of the lower bound on the data log-likelihood under the generative network. To do this, 1000 recognition sweeps are performed without learning. During each recognition sweep, binary values for the hidden variables are obtained for the given training image. The log-probability of the values of *all* the variables under the generative network minus the log-probability of the hidden variable values under the recognition network gives an unbiased estimate of the log-likelihood bound (3.40). In this way, I obtain 1000 i.i.d. noisy unbiased estimates of

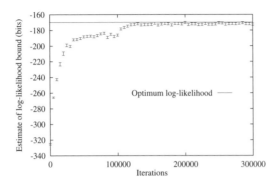

Figure 4.2
Variation of the lower log-likelihood bound with the number of wake-sleep learning
iterations for the stochastic Helmholtz machine.

the log-likelihood bound. The average of these values gives a less noisy unbiased estimate. Also, the variance of this estimate is estimated by dividing the
sample variance by 999.

I am interested in solutions where the generative network can construct the
image by adding features, but cannot remove previously instantiated features.
If the network parameters are in no way constrained to favor this type of solution, perceptually unattractive solutions are found (see Section 4.1.3). So,
I constrain the parameters of the logistic regression model that connects the
middle layer to the bottom layer to be positive by setting to zero any negative
weights every 20th learning iteration. In order to encourage a solution where
each image can be succinctly described by the minimum possible number of
causes in the middle layer, I initialize the middle-layer generative biases to -4.0
which favors most middle-layer variables being inactive (value of 0) on average. All other parameters are initialized to 0.0. For the first 100,000 iterations,
a learning rate of 0.1 is used for the generative parameters of the model feeding
into the bottom layer and for the recognition parameters of the model feeding
into the middle layer; the remaining learning rates are set to 0.001. After this,
learning is accelerated by setting all learning rates to 0.01.

Figure 4.2 shows the learning curve for the first 300,000 iterations of a simulation consisting of a total of 1,000,000 iterations. Aside from several minor
fluctuations, the wake-sleep algorithm maximizes the log-likelihood bound in
this case. Eventually, the bound converges to the optimum value (-170 bits)
shown by the solid line. This value is computed by estimating the average log-

likelihood of the data under the method that was used to produce the data, *i.e.*, the negative entropy of the training data.

By examining the generative parameters after learning, we see that the wake-sleep algorithm has extracted the correct 3-level hierarchical structure. Figure 4.3 shows the parameters for the generative logistic regression models feeding into and out of the middle layer in the network. A black blob indicates a negative parameter and a white blob indicates a positive parameter; the area of each blob is proportional to the magnitude of the parameter (the largest value shown is 7.77 and the smallest value shown is -7.21). There are 36 blocks arranged in a 6×6 grid and each block corresponds to a middle-layer variable. The 4 blobs at the upper-left of a block show the parameters that connect each of the top-layer variables to the corresponding middle-layer variable. The single blob at the upper-right of a block shows the bias for the corresponding middle-layer variable. The 16×16 matrix that forms the bulk of a particular block shows the parameters that connect the corresponding middle-layer variable to the bottom-layer image. These matrices clearly indicate that 32 of the 36 middle-layer variables are used by the network as "feature variables" to represent the 32 possible bars. These feature variables are controlled mainly by the right-most top-layer "orientation" variable – the parameters connecting all the other top-layer variables to the feature variables are nearly zero. If the orientation variable is off, the probability of each feature variable is determined mainly by its bias. Vertical feature variables have significantly negative biases, causing them to remain off if the orientation neuron is off. Horizontal feature variables have only slightly negative biases, causing them to turn on roughly 25% of the time if the orientation variable is off. The parameters connecting the orientation variable to the vertical feature variables are significantly positive, so that when the orientation variable is on the total input to each vertical feature variable is slightly negative, causing the vertical feature variables to turn on roughly 25% of the time. The parameters connecting the orientation variable to the horizontal feature variables are significantly negative, so that when the orientation variable is on the total input to each horizontal feature variable is significantly negative, causing the horizontal feature variables to remain off. Since the parameters connecting the top-layer variable to the 4 middle-layer nonfeature variables are negative, and since the nonfeature variables have large negative biases, the nonfeature variables are usually inactive. Because the bottom-layer biases (not shown) are only slightly negative, a pixel that is not turned on by a feature variable still has a probability of 0.25 of being turned on. This accounts for the additive noise.

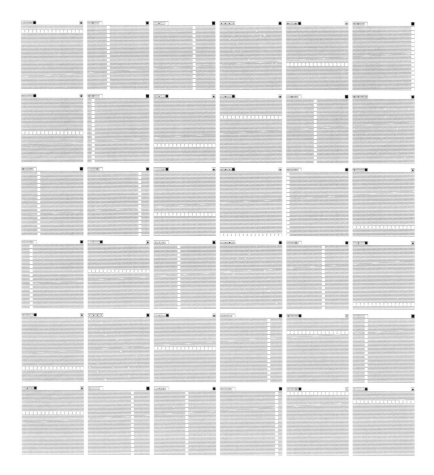

Figure 4.3
Parameters for connections that feed into and out of the middle-layer variables in the
generative network. A black blob indicates a negative parameter and a white blob
indicates a positive parameter; the area of each blob is proportional to the parameter's
magnitude (the largest value shown is 7.77 and the smallest value shown is -7.21).

4.1.2 Automatic clean-up of noisy images

Once learned, the recognition network can nonlinearly filter the noise from a
given image, detect the underlying bars, and determine the orientation of these
bars. To clean up each of the training images shown in Figure 4.1, I apply
the learned recognition network to the image and obtain middle-layer variable

Figure 4.4
Filtered versions of the training examples from Figure 4.1 extracted using the estimated recognition network.

values which reveal an estimate of which bars are on. The results of this procedure are shown in Figure 4.4 and clearly show that the recognition network is capable of filtering out the noise. Usually, the recognition network correctly identifies which bars were instantiated in the original image. Occasionally, a bar is not successfully detected. In two cases a bar is detected that has an orientation that is the opposite of the dominant orientation; however, usually the recognition network chooses a single orientation. Inspection of the original noisy training images for the two incorrect cases shows that aside from the single-orientation constraint, there is significant evidence that the mistakenly detected bars *should* be on. Further training reduces the chance of misdetection.

4.1.3   Wake-sleep estimation without positive parameter constraints

If all the parameters are initialized to 0.0, the parameters that connect the middle layer to the bottom layer are not constrained to be positive, and all the learning rates are set to 0.01, the estimated generative network does not properly extract the bar structure. Figure 4.5 shows the generative network parameters that connect the middle layer to the bottom layer, after 5,000,000 learning iterations. The black bars indicate that some middle-layer variables are capable

Figure 4.5
Parameters for generative connections that feed out of the middle-layer variables after estimation without special initialization of the weights, without different learning rates between layers, and without positive weight constraints in the generative network.

of "uninstantiating" bars that may be instantiated by other variables. Although it is imaginable that such a complex scheme is still capable of modelling the training images, the log-likelihood bound for this trained Helmholtz machine is -190 bits – significantly lower than the optimum value of -170 bits.

4.1.4 How hard *is* the bars problem?

Although this bar extraction problem may seem simple, it must be kept in mind that the network is not given *a priori* topology information – a fixed

Figure 4.6
Training examples from Figure 4.1 after a fixed random rearrangement of the pixels has
been applied. These are indicative of the difficulty of the bars problem in the absence
of a topological prior that favors local intensity coherence.

random rearrangement of the pixels in the training images would not change
the learning performance of the network. Insofar as the network is concerned,
the actual training examples look like those shown in Figure 4.6 which were
produced by applying a fixed random rearrangement to the pixels in the images
from Figure 4.1.

4.2   Simultaneous extraction of continuous and categorical
structure

The Bayesian networks presented so far in this chapter have contained discrete
variables. However, some hidden variables, such as translation or scaling in
images of shapes, are best represented using continuous values. Work done
on continuous-valued Bayesian networks has focused mainly on Gaussian random variables that are linked linearly such that the joint distribution over all
variables is also Gaussian [Pearl 1988; Heckerman and Geiger 1995]. Lauritzen *et al.* [1990] have included discrete random variables within the linear
Gaussian framework. They consider networks that are singly-connected, so

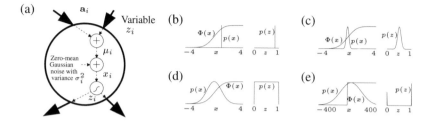

Figure 4.7
(a) schematically shows the dependence of the proposed variable on its parents. (b) to
(e) illustrate four quite different modes of behavior: (b) deterministic mode; (c) stochastic linear mode; (d) stochastic nonlinear mode; and (e) stochastic binary mode (note the
different horizontal scale). For the sake of graphical clarity, the density functions are
normalized to have equal maxima and the subscripts are left off the variables.

that probability propagation can be used. Most work on continuous-valued
Bayesian networks requires that all the conditional distributions represented
by the network can be easily derived using information elicited from experts.
Hofmann and Tresp [1996] consider estimating continuous Bayesian networks
that may be richly connected, but they assume that all variables are observed.
As far as nonlinear continuous networks with latent variables are concerned,
continuous-valued Boltzmann machines have been developed [Movellan and
McClelland 1992], but these suffer from long simulation settling times and the
requirement of a "negative phase" during learning. Tibshirani [1992], MacKay
[1995] and Bishop *et al.* [1997] consider estimating mappings from a continuous latent variable space to a higher-dimensional input space, effectively using
multiple-cause type networks of the form shown in Figure 3.4 on page 69. In
this section, I consider a hierarchical Bayesian network with variables that can
adapt to be continuous or categorical, as needed by the training data [Frey
1997a; Frey 1997b].

4.2.1 Continuous sigmoidal Bayesian networks

The proposed random variable is shown schematically in Figure 4.7a.[1] The
parents $\mathbf{a}_i$ affect z_i via a total input,

$$\mu_i \equiv \sum_{j=0}^{i-1}\theta_{ij}z_j, \tag{4.1}$$

---

[1] Geoffrey Hinton suggested this unit as a way to make factor analysis nonlinear.

where we constrain $\theta_{ij} = 0.0$ if $z_j \notin \mathbf{a}_i$. The probability density over the *presigmoid activity* x_i for variable z_i is

$$p(x_i|\mu_i,\sigma_i^2) \equiv \exp[-(x_i - \mu_i)^2/2\sigma_i^2]/\sqrt{2\pi\sigma_i^2}, \qquad (4.2)$$

where σ_i^2 is a parameter associated with variable z_i (formally, part of $\boldsymbol{\theta}$). The value of z_i (its *postsigmoid activity*) is obtained by passing the presigmoid activity through a sigmoidal cumulative Gaussian squashing function:

$$z_i \equiv \Phi(x_i) \equiv \int_{-\infty}^{x} \frac{1}{\sqrt{2\pi}} e^{-\alpha^2/2} d\alpha. \qquad (4.3)$$

Networks of these variables can *represent* a variety of structures that are brought about by a range of significantly different modes of behavior available to each variable:

Deterministic mode: If the noise variance σ_i^2 is very small, the postsigmoid activity y_i will be a practically deterministic sigmoidal function of the mean (see Figure 4.7b). This mode is useful for representing deterministic nonlinear mappings such as those found in deterministic multilayer perceptrons and mixture of expert models.

Stochastic linear mode: For a given mean, if the squashing function is approximately linear over the span of the added noise, the postsigmoid distribution will be approximately Gaussian with the mean and standard deviation linearly transformed (see Figure 4.7c). This mode is useful for representing Gaussian noise effects such as those found in mixture models, the outputs of mixture of expert models, and factor analysis models.

Stochastic nonlinear mode: If the variance of a variable in the stochastic linear mode is increased so that the squashing function is used in its nonlinear region, a variety of distributions are producible that range from skewed Gaussian to uniform to bimodal (see Figure 4.7d).

Stochastic binary mode: This is an extreme case of the stochastic nonlinear mode. If the variance σ_i^2 is very large, then nearly all of the postsigmoid probability mass will lie near the ends of the interval $(0,1)$ (see Figure 4.7e). *E.g.*, for a standard deviation of 150, less than 1% of the mass lies in $(0.1, 0.9)$. In this mode, the postsigmoid activity z_i appears to be binary with probability of being "on" (*i.e.*, $z_i > 0.5$ or, equivalently, $x_i > 0$):

$$p(i \text{ on}|\mu_i,\sigma_i^2) = \int_0^\infty \frac{\exp[-(x-\mu_i)^2/2\sigma_i^2]}{\sqrt{2\pi\sigma_i^2}} dx$$

$$= \int_{-\infty}^{\mu_i} \frac{\exp[-x^2/2\sigma_i^2]}{\sqrt{2\pi\sigma_i^2}} dx = \Phi\left(\frac{\mu_i}{\sigma_i}\right). \tag{4.4}$$

This sort of stochastic activation is found in binary sigmoidal belief networks [Jaakkola, Saul and Jordan 1996] and in the decision-making components of mixture of expert models and hierarchical mixture of expert models.

4.2.2 Inference using slice sampling

Assuming the variables are labeled in ancestral order, the joint distribution can be written

$$p(\{x_i\}_{i=1}^N) = \prod_{i=1}^N p(x_i|\{x_j\}_{j=0}^{i-1}) \quad \text{or} \quad p(\{z_i\}_{i=1}^N) = \prod_{i=1}^N p(z_i|\{z_j\}_{j=0}^{i-1}),$$
$$\tag{4.5}$$

where N is the number of variables. $p(x_i|\{x_j\}_{j=0}^{i-1})$ and $p(z_i|\{z_j\}_{j=0}^{i-1})$ are the presigmoid and postsigmoid conditional densities for variable z_i. (Recall that the set of parents is represented by parameter constraints.) As usual, I define $z_0 \equiv 1$ to allow for a constant bias.

Even for small networks of these variables, probabilistic inference can be very difficult. Not only is the inference problem combinatorial, but it involves continuous hidden variables whose distribution when conditioned on visible variables may be multimodal with peaks that are broad in some dimensions but narrow in others. I use a Markov chain Monte Carlo procedure, which consists of sweeping a prespecified number of times through the set of hidden variables. A new value is obtained for each hidden variable using slice sampling [Neal 1997] (see Section 2.2.4), based on the distribution for the variable conditioned on all other variables. If an infinite number of slice samples are drawn for each hidden variable before passing on to the next hidden variable, this procedure is equivalent to Gibbs sampling (see Section 2.2.2). In fact, detailed balance still holds if only a fixed number of slice samples are drawn for each variable before passing on to the next variable. In most cases, drawing only one slice sample for each variable before continuing on will be most efficient.

If the parent-child influences cause there to be two very narrow peaks in the conditional distribution $p(z_i|\{z_j\}_{j=0}^{i-1}, \{z_j\}_{j=i+1}^N)$ for a hidden variable (corresponding to a variable in the stochastic binary mode), the slices will almost always consist of two very short line segments and it will be very difficult for the above procedure to switch from one mode to another. To fix this problem, slice sampling is performed in a new domain, $y_i = \Phi(\{x_i - \mu_i\}/\sigma_i)$. In this domain the parent-child distribution $p(y_i|\{z_j\}_{j=0}^{i-1})$ is uniform on $(0, 1)$, and thus $p(y_i|\{z_j\}_{j=0}^{i-1}, \{z_j\}_{j=i+1}^{N}) = p(y_i|\{z_j\}_{j=i+1}^{N})$. It follows that I can use the following function for slice sampling:

$$f(y_i) = \exp\left[-\sum_{k=i+1}^{N}\left\{x_k - \mu_k^{-i} - \theta_{z_k z_i}\Phi\left(\sigma_i\Phi^{-1}(y_i) + \mu_i\right)\right\}^2/2\sigma_k^2\right],$$

(4.6)

where $\mu_k^{-i} = \sum_{j=0,j\neq i}^{i-1}\theta_{z_k z_j}z_j$. Since x_i, y_i and z_i are all deterministically related, sampling from the distribution of y_i will give appropriately distributed values for the other two.[2]

4.2.3   Parameter estimation using slice sampling

I use on-line stochastic gradient ascent to perform generalized EM (see Section 3.3.2). This consists of sweeping through the training set and for each training case following the gradient of $\log p(\{x_i\}_{i=1}^{N})$, while sampling hidden unit values as described above. The parameters are changed as follows:

$$\Delta\theta_{jk} \equiv \eta\,\partial\log p(\{x_i\}_{i=1}^{N})/\partial\theta_{jk} = \eta\left(x_j - \sum_{l=0}^{j-1}\theta_{jl}y_l\right)y_k/\sigma_j^2,$$

$$\Delta\log\sigma_j^2 \equiv \eta\,\partial\log p(\{x_i\})/\partial\log\sigma_j^2 = \eta\left[\left(x_j - \sum_{l=0}^{j-1}\theta_{jl}y_l\right)^2/\sigma_j^2 - 1\right]/2,$$

(4.7)

where η is the learning rate.

I designed two experiments meant to elicit the four modes of operation described above. Both experiments were based on a simple network with one hidden layer **h** containing two variables and one visible layer **v** containing two variables. The training data was obtained by carefully selecting model parameters so as to induce various modes of operation and then generating 10,000 two-dimensional examples. Before training, the log-variances were initialized to 10.0, and the other parameters were initialized to uniformly random values between -0.1 and 0.1. Training consisted of 100 epochs using a learning rate of 0.001 and 20 sweeps of slice sampling to complete each training case. Each task required roughly five minutes on a 195 MHz MIPS R4400 processor.

The distribution of the training cases in visible unit space ($v_1 - v_2$) for the first experiment is shown by the contours in Figure 4.8a. After training the network, I ran the inference algorithm for each of ten representative training cases. The mean postsigmoid activities of the two hidden units are shown beside the cases in Figure 4.8a; clearly, the network has identified four classes

---

[2]Both $\Phi()$ and $\Phi^{-1}()$ do not have closed-form expressions, so I use the C-library erf() function to implement $\Phi()$ and table lookup with quadratic interpolation to implement $\Phi^{-1}()$.

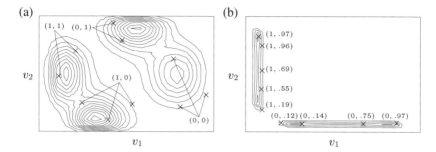

Figure 4.8
For each experiment (a) and (b), contours show the distribution of the 2-dimensional
training cases. The inferred mean postsigmoid activity of the two hidden units after
learning are shown in braces for several training cases, marked by ×.

that it labels $(0, 0)$, $(0, 1)$, $(1, 0)$ and $(1, 1)$. Based on a 30×30 histogram, the
relative entropy between the training set and data generated from the trained
network is 0.02 bits. Figure 4.8b shows a similar picture for the second experiment, using different training data. In this case, the network has identified two
categories that it labels using the first postsigmoid activity. The second postsigmoid activity indicates how far along the respective "ridge" the data point
lies. The relative entropy in this case is 0.04 bits.

The above experiments illustrate how the same network can be used to
model two quite different types of data. In contrast, a Gaussian mixture model
would require many more components for the second task as compared to the
first. Although the methods due to Tibshirani [1992] and Bishop *et al.* [1997]
would nicely model each submanifold in the second task, they would not properly distinguish between categories of data in either task. MacKay's method
may be capable of extracting both the submanifolds and the categories, but I
am not aware of any results on such a dual problem.

It is not difficult to conceive of models for which naive Markov chain Monte
Carlo procedures will become fruitlessly slow. In particular, if two variables
are highly correlated, the procedure of sampling one variable at a time will
converge extremely slowly. Also, the Markov chain method may be prohibitive
for larger networks. One approach to avoiding these problems is to use the
Helmholtz machine or variational methods. In the next section, I present a
general variational method for inference and learning in networks of nonlinear
stochastic units.

4.3   Nonlinear Gaussian Bayesian networks (NLGBNs)

In this section, I present a unifying framework for stochastic neural networks
with nonlinear hidden variables. Nonlinear units are obtained by passing the
outputs of linear Gaussian units through various nonlinearities. The continuous sigmoidal networks described above are a special case of these general
nonlinear networks. A general variational method can be used to maximize a
lower bound on the likelihood of a training set in these networks and the bound
can be used for pattern classification (see Frey and Hinton [1998] for details).

4.3.1   The model

Linear generative models, binary sigmoidal Bayesian networks, continuous
sigmoidal belief networks, and piecewise linear Bayesian networks (such as
the "rectified Gaussian Bayesian networks" in Hinton and Ghahramani [1997])
can all be viewed as networks of Gaussian units that apply various nonlinearities to their Gaussian states. For example, a rectified unit adds Gaussian noise
to the top-down input from its parents, and then outputs this value if it is positive and outputs 0 if the value is negative.

The probability density function over the pre-nonlinearity variables $\mathbf{x} =
(x_1, \ldots, x_N)$ in such a nonlinear Gaussian belief network (NLGBN) is

$$p(\mathbf{x}) = \prod_{i=1}^{N} p(x_i | \{x_j\}_{j \in A_i}) = \prod_{i=1}^{N} \phi\left(x_i; \sum_{j \in A_i} w_{ij} f_j(x_j), s_i^2\right), \qquad (4.8)$$

where A_i is the set of indices for the parents of unit i and $\phi(\cdot)$ is the normal
density function:

$$\phi(y; \mu, \sigma^2) = \frac{1}{\sqrt{2\pi\sigma^2}} e^{-(y-\mu)^2/2\sigma^2}. \qquad (4.9)$$

s_i^2 is the variance of the Gaussian noise for unit i and $f_j(\cdot)$ is the nonlinear function for unit j. For example, some units may use a step function
(making them binary sigmoidal units with a cumulative Gaussian activation
function), whereas other units may use the rectification function (making them
real-valued units that encourage sparse representations). Define $f_0(x_0) = 1$ so
that w_{i0} represents a constant bias for unit i in (4.8).

In the following section, I present a generalization of the variational method
developed by Jaakkola et al. [1996] for networks of binary units and show
that it can be successfully applied to performing approximate inference and
learning in networks with other nonlinearities. The variational method can still
be applied when different types of nonlinearity are used in the same network.

4.3.2 Variational inference and learning

One way to infer the distribution over the hidden variables in an intractable Bayesian network is to postulate a simple parametric *variational distribution* $q(\cdot)$ over the hidden variables. (The variational distribution $q(\cdot)$ is separate from the generative distribution $p(\cdot)$.) A numerical optimization method is then used to adjust the variational parameters to bring $q(\cdot)$ as "close" to the true posterior as possible. See Section 2.3 for a description of this inference technique. In fact, the same variational distribution can be used to perform learning via the generalized EM method described in Section 3.3.2.

Let V be the set of indices of the sensory input variables for the current input pattern, and let H be the set of indices of the hidden variables for the current input pattern, so that $V \cup H = \{1, \dots, N\}$. The variational bound from (3.22) is

$$B_{q\|p} = \langle \log p(\mathbf{x}) \rangle - \langle \log q(\{x_i\}_{i \in H}) \rangle \leq \log p(\{x_i\}_{i \in V}), \qquad (4.10)$$

where $\langle \cdot \rangle$ indicates an expectation over the hidden variables with respect to $q(\cdot)$.

A simple parametric variational distribution is a product of Gaussian distributions:

$$q(\{x_i\}_{i \in H}) = \prod_{i \in H} q(x_i) = \prod_{i \in H} \phi(x_i; \mu_i, \sigma_i^2), \qquad (4.11)$$

where μ_i and σ_i, $i \in H$ are the variational parameters. By adjusting these parameters, we can obtain an axis-aligned Gaussian approximation to the true posterior distribution over the hidden variables.

In the case of NLGBNs and the variational distribution consisting of a product of Gaussians, (4.10) simplifies to

$$B_{q\|p} = -\sum_{i=1}^{N} \frac{1}{2s_i^2} \Big\{ \big[\mu_i - \textstyle\sum_{j \in A_i} w_{ij} M_j(\mu_j, \sigma_j)\big]^2 + \textstyle\sum_{j \in A_i} w_{ij}^2 V_j(\mu_j, \sigma_j) \Big\}$$

$$- \sum_{i=1}^{N} \frac{1}{2} \log 2\pi s_i^2 - \sum_{i \in H} \frac{1}{2}\Big(\frac{\sigma_i^2}{s_i^2} - 1 - \log 2\pi\sigma_i^2\Big). \qquad (4.12)$$

In order to make this formula concise, I have introduced dummy variational parameters for the observed variables: if x_i is observed to have the value x_i^*, we *fix* $\mu_i = x_i^*$ and $\sigma_i = 0$. In (4.12), $M_j(\mu, \sigma)$ is the mean output of unit j

when the input is Gaussian noise with mean μ and variance σ^2:

$$M_j(\mu, \sigma) = \int_x \phi(x; \mu, \sigma^2) f_j(x) dx. \qquad (4.13)$$

$V_j(\mu, \sigma)$ is the variance at the output of unit j when the input is Gaussian noise with mean μ and variance σ^2:

$$V_j(\mu, \sigma) = \int_x \phi(x; \mu, \sigma^2) \{f_j(x) - M_j(\mu, \sigma)\}^2 dx. \qquad (4.14)$$

I assume that these can be easily computed, closely approximated, or in the case of $V_j(\cdot, \cdot)$, bounded from above (the latter will give a new lower bound on $B_{q\|p}$). See Frey and Hinton [1998] for these functions in the case of linear units, binary units, rectified units, and sigmoidal units.

For unit i in (4.12), the term in curly braces measures the mean squared error under $q(\cdot)$ between μ_i and the input to unit i as given by its parents: $\langle\{\mu_i - \sum_{j \in A_i} w_{ij} f_j(x_j)\}^2\rangle$. It is down-weighted by the model noise variance s_i^2, since the importance of the prediction error decreases with noise variance.

Variational inference consists of first fixing $\mu_i = x_i^*$ and $\sigma_i = 0$, $i \in V$ in (4.12) and then maximizing $B_{q\|p}$ with respect to μ_i and $\log \sigma_i^2$, $i \in H$. (The optimization for the variances is performed in the log-domain, since $\log \sigma_i^2$ is allowed to go negative.) I use the conjugate gradient method to perform this optimization, although other techniques could be used (*e.g.*, steepest descent or possibly a covariant method [Amari 1985]). The derivatives of $B_{q\|p}$ with respect to μ_i and $\log \sigma_i^2$, $i \in H$ are given in Frey and Hinton [1998]. After optimization, the means and variances of the variational distribution represent the inference statistics.

For learning, the log-likelihood of the entire training set is bounded from below by a sum of bounds for the individual training patterns. The variational expectation maximization algorithm consists of the following:

- E-Step: Perform variational inference by maximizing the total bound with respect to the multiple sets of variational parameters corresponding to the different input patterns.

- M-Step: Maximize the total bound with respect to the model parameters ($w_{..}$'s and $s_{.}$'s).

Notice that by maintaining sufficient statistics while scanning through the training set in the E-Step, it is not necessary to store the multiple sets of variational parameters.

It turns out that the M-Step can be performed very efficiently. Since the values of the model variances do not affect the values of the weights that maximize $B_{q\|p}$ in (4.12), we can first maximize $B_{q\|p}$ with respect to the weights. As pointed out by Jaakkola *et al.* [1996] for their binary Gaussian belief networks, $B_{q\|p}$ is quadratic in the weights, so we can use singular value decomposition to solve for the weights exactly. Next, the optimal model variances are computed directly.

Software that implements this variational learning algorithm for linear units, binary units, rectified units, and continuous sigmoidal units is available by following pointers at `http://mitpress.mit.edu/book-home.tcl?i sbn=026206202X`.

4.3.3 Results on the continuous stereo disparity problem

In this section, I consider an unsupervised visual feature extraction task, and compare the representations learned by the variational method applied to two types of NLGBN and the representations learned by Gibbs sampling applied to a piece-wise linear NLGBN. If the hidden units all use a piece-wise linear activation function, then Gibbs sampling can be efficiently used for learning, as described in Hinton and Ghahramani [1997]. Zoubin Ghahramani provided the MATLAB software for Gibbs sampling. One of the NLGBNs used for variational learning contains only binary hidden units of the type described by Jaakkola, Saul and Jordan [1996]. So, in this section we see how the variational technique compares to another learning method for continuous hidden units, as well as how the generalization of the variational method from binary to continuous units compares to variational learning in binary networks.

An interesting vision problem where the latent causes are nonlinearly related to the input is the estimation of depth from a stereo pair of sensor images. In the simplified version of this problem presented in Becker and Hinton [1992], the goal is to learn that the visual input consists of randomly placed dots on a surface at one of two depths. These experiments involved 1-dimensional "eyes" that had 12 real-valued sensors each. The eyes viewed a 1-dimensional surface on which 4 dots with intensity drawn uniformly from $[0, 5)$ were randomly positioned. The surface was placed at one of two different depths with equal probability, so that the rays entering the two eyes were relatively shifted leftward or rightward. The 12 sensors in each eye used Gaussian activation filters and added unit-variance Gaussian noise. Twelve examples of the sensory images obtained in this manner are shown in Figure 4.9a, where the 1-dimensional sensory image for the right eye is shown above the image for the left eye.

The stereo disparity problem is much more difficult than the bars problem discussed in Section 4.1, since there is more overlap between the underlying

(a)   (c)

(b)   (d)

Figure 4.9
Learning in NLGBNs using the variational method and Gibbs sampling, for noisy stereo
disparity patterns. (a) shows some training examples. (b) shows the middle-layer to
visible-layer weights learned by the variational method with rectified units. (c) shows
the weights learned by the variational method with binary units. (d) shows the weights
learned by Gibbs sampling with rectified units.

features. To see this, imagine a "multi-eyed" disparity problem in which there
are as many eyes as there are 1-dimensional sensors. We expect the depth
inference to be easier in this case, since there is more evidence for each of the
two possible directions of shift. Imagine stacking the sensory images on top of
each other, so that each resulting square image will contain blurred diagonal
bars that are oriented either up and to the right or up and to the left. Extracting
disparity from this data is roughly equivalent to extracting bar orientation in
the data from the previous section.

100 iterations of variational EM were used to train a three-layer NLGBN with 1 binary top-layer unit, 20 rectified middle-layer units, and 24 linear visible bottom-layer units. The resulting weights projecting from each of the 20 middle-layer units to the two sets of 12 sensors are shown in Figure 4.9b. The algorithm has extracted features that are spatially local and represent each of the two possible depths. Figure 4.9c shows the weights learned by variational EM in a network where all of the hidden units are binary. The lower bound on the likelihood for the trained binary-rectified-linear NLGBN is -43.7 nats, whereas the bound for the trained NLGBN with binary hidden units is -46.1 nats, indicating that the continuous-valued hidden variables give superior likelihood bounds. The Gibbs sampling method with rectified hidden units produced the weight patterns shown in Figure 4.9d. (It is not straightforward to estimate the data likelihood using Gibbs sampling.)

4.3.4 Pattern classification using the variational bound

In contrast to the Monte Carlo method, the variational method provides an easily computed approximation to $\log p(\{x_i\}_{i \in V})$ in the form of the variational bound. If one NLGBN is trained on each class of real-valued data, a test pattern can be classified by selecting the class whose corresponding NLGBN gives the highest bound. This method is used in [Frey and Hinton 1998] to show that multi-layer NLGBNs with rectified units are competitive at classifying grey-level images of handwritten digits.

5 Data Compression

The goal of data compression is to exploit the redundancy in input patterns so as to represent individual patterns concisely on average. In this book, I focus on lossless data compression, in which the original pattern can be completely recovered from the concise representation. A *source code* maps each input pattern **v** to a codeword, such that for each valid codeword there is a unique input pattern. I will consider sources where the patterns are i.i.d. (independent and identically drawn) from a distribution $P_r(\mathbf{v})$.

Shannon's noiseless source coding theorem [Shannon 1948] states that the average codeword length cannot be less than the entropy of the source:

$$E[\ell(\mathbf{v})] \geq \mathcal{H}, \tag{5.1}$$

where $\ell(\mathbf{v})$ is the length in bits of the codeword for input pattern **v**, and $\mathcal{H}$ is the entropy of the source:

$$\mathcal{H} = -\sum_{\mathbf{v}} P_r(\mathbf{v}) \log_2 P_r(\mathbf{v}). \tag{5.2}$$

Traditional approaches to data compression have focused on producing source codes whose codeword lengths are nearly optimal, where the optimal length of the codeword for **v** is $\log_2 P_r(\mathbf{v})$.

Arithmetic coding [Rissanen and Langdon 1976; Witten, Neal and Cleary 1987] is a practical algorithm for producing near-optimal codewords when the source distribution $P_r(\mathbf{v})$ is known. If **v** is binary-valued, $P_r(\mathbf{v})$ can be easily estimated and arithmetic coding can be used to produce near-optimal "fractional bit" codewords. If **v** is high-dimensional and the distribution is quite complex (*e.g.*, images of faces), it may be desirable to estimate a more sophisticated flexible probability model $P(\mathbf{v})$. Unfortunately, even if such a model can be estimated so that $P(\mathbf{v}) \approx P_r(\mathbf{v})$, there may not be a practical way to encode **v** using the model. For example, an arithmetic encoder requires a table of the probabilities for all possible inputs. For a 16×16 binary image, this table would have 2^{256} entries! Not only do we need a model that provides a probability $P(\mathbf{v})$, but we also need a model that somehow decomposes $P(\mathbf{v})$ in a way that allows the encoder to encode the variables one at a time (or in small groups).

Graphical models provide a structured description of $P(\mathbf{v})$, and so they seem like a good place to look for the source models described above. However, it turns out that Markov random fields do not provide the right type of structure. For example, the Boltzmann machine [Hinton and Sejnowski 1986] (a Markov random field that learns) is poorly suited to data compression, because it does not decompose $P(\mathbf{v})$ in a way that is suitable for efficient piecewise compression. (A method such as Markov chain Monte Carlo must be used to estimate the partition function, which normalizes the probabilities.) On the other hand, Bayesian networks *do* provide an ideal structure for data compression.

In Section 5.1, I show how Bayesian network source models that do not have latent variables can be used very efficiently to compress data. Then, in Section 5.2, I go on to discuss source models that have many latent variables. Values can be chosen for the latent variables and the entire configuration can be encoded. In this way, a "multi-valued source code" with many codewords for each input pattern is obtained. In many cases, these codewords cannot be mixed together in a tractable way. To remedy this problem, I show how extra information can ride "piggyback" on the choice of codeword and derive the communication rate for this "bits-back" procedure. In Section 5.3, we see that a broad class of approximations to maximum likelihood parameter estimation actually minimizes this communication rate. In Section 5.4, I outline the "bits-back coding" algorithm, which is a practical implementation of the "bits-back" idea. It turns out that by using an arithmetic decoder in the bits-back encoder and an arithmetic encoder in the bits-back decoder, we can achieve a practical communication rate that is nearly optimal. Finally, in Section 5.5, I present compression results for Helmholtz machine source models that are adapted using the wake-sleep algorithm.

5.1   Fast compression with Bayesian networks

Suppose we have at hand a Bayesian network for the binary variables in $\mathbf{v}$, such that $P(\mathbf{v}) \approx P_{\mathrm{r}}(\mathbf{v})$. As discussed in Section 1.2.3, the joint distribution for a Bayesian network can be written

$$P(\mathbf{v}) = \prod_{k=1}^{N} P(v_k|\mathbf{a}_k), \qquad (5.3)$$

where N is the number of variables in $\mathbf{v}$, and $\mathbf{a}_k$ are the parents of v_k. This decomposition is very well-suited to arithmetic coding.

In order to encode $\mathbf{v}$, we pick an ancestral order for the variables. I will assume without loss of generality that $v_1, \ldots, v_N$ is such an ordering. Compression begins with v_1, whose observed value is fed into the arithmetic encoder, along with its distribution $\{P(v_1 = 0), P(v_1 = 1)\}$, which is part of the network specification. Next, we compute $\{P(v_2 = 0|\mathbf{a}_2), P(v_2 = 1|\mathbf{a}_2)\}$ using the conditional probability given in the network specification as well as the values of v_2's parents (*i.e.*, either $\{v_1\}$ or $\varnothing$) which have already been encoded. We feed the observed value of v_2 into the arithmetic encoder, along with its distribution. Encoding continues in this fashion until all network variables have been encoded.

For this procedure to work as described, the Bayesian network must be fully visible. That is, all network variables are part of the input pattern. Suppose there are some latent variables $\mathbf{h}$ that are not part of the input. Then, the Bayesian network models $P(\mathbf{v}, \mathbf{h})$. These variables may be important for representing higher-order structure in the input $\mathbf{v}$, as discussed extensively in Chapter 3. Now, the decomposition in (5.3) cannot be used.

If there aren't many latent variables, we can use a procedure that is similar to the one described above. We pick an ancestral order and proceed as described above, encoding only the observed variables. Whenever we encounter an observed variable that is not dependency-separated from an unobserved variable by the variables that have been encoded so far, the unobserved variable must be integrated out, by summing over its values. The complexity of this encoding procedure is usually exponential in the number of unobserved variables. Sometimes, the graphical structure of the network permits this procedure to be done in a very efficient way. For example, the latent variables in a hidden Markov model [Rabiner 1989] with a fixed state space size can be integrated out in a way so that the encoding complexity is linear in the number of latent variables (number of time steps).

5.2 Communicating extra information through the codeword choice

In general, when the latent variables in a Bayesian network cannot summed away to compute $P(\mathbf{v})$ in a tractable way, we are left with the option of *picking* values for them. Then, the entire set of variables $\{\mathbf{v}, \mathbf{h}\}$ can be encoded using the procedure described above, as if all values were observed. This can be viewed as a *multi-valued source code*, where there are many codewords for each input $\mathbf{v}$. The codeword depends on which values are chosen for the latent variables. Often, as with the hidden Markov model, these codewords can be mixed in an efficient way. However, there is an interesting class of multi-valued source codes (*e.g.*, Bayesian networks with latent variables) for which the multiple codewords *cannot* be mixed in a tractable manner.

Figure 5.1
A scheme in which auxiliary data is communicated along with the symbol in order to achieve optimal compression when the source code is multi-valued.

The approach I take to solve this problem [Frey and Hinton 1996; Frey and Hinton 1997] is motivated by the "bits-back" argument of Hinton and Zemel [1994], which they used to develop a Lyapunov function for machine learning. It turns out that Wallace [1990] devised a similar argument to construct minimum-length integer-length messages for use in minimum-message-length inference. By selecting codewords through the use of extra *auxiliary* data, the auxiliary data can ride "piggyback" on the codewords for the symbols that we are encoding. Compared to the optimal single-valued source code obtained by mixing together the codewords for an input pattern, the bits communicated in the auxiliary data will make up for the lengths of the suboptimal codewords that are sent. In particular, the communication rate will be *less* than the rate that would be obtained by always picking the shortest codeword. A block diagram for this communication scheme is shown in Figure 5.1. A simple example will help illustrate this procedure.

5.2.1   Example: A simple mixture model

Consider a source that outputs real numbers that are distributed according to a mixture of two Gaussians. These numbers are rounded to some precision to form a set of symbols. The component distributions and the output distribution are shown in Figure 5.2a, where the rounding effect is left out for the sake of graphical simplicity.

The most natural source code to use in this case is one that requires one bit to specify from which Gaussian a given symbol was produced plus however many bits are needed to code the symbol using that Gaussian. However, the identity of the Gaussian that produced a given symbol is often ambiguous. In particular, a number near v_0 could well have come from either Gaussian. In these cases the source model maps each symbol to two codewords — one for each Gaussian — producing a multi-valued source code. If we were to always pick the shorter of the two codewords, we would effectively be assuming the symbols were distributed as in Figure 5.2b. However, this distribution is obviously incorrect — it is not even normalized — and will lead to suboptimal compression.

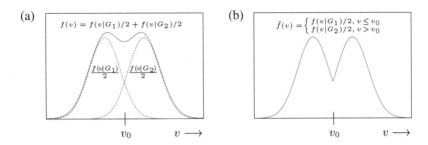

(a) $f(v) = f(v|G_1)/2 + f(v|G_2)/2$

$\frac{f(v|G_1)}{2}$ $\frac{f(v|G_2)}{2}$

v_0 $v \longrightarrow$

(b) $\tilde{f}(v) = \begin{cases} f(v|G_1)/2, v \le v_0 \\ f(v|G_2)/2, v > v_0 \end{cases}$

v_0 $v \longrightarrow$

Figure 5.2
The most natural source model may produce multiple codewords for a given symbol. (a) shows a source with a single binary hidden variable which identifies from which Gaussian, G_1 or G_2, the symbol value v is sampled. Values of v near v_0 are likely to have come from either Gaussian. (b) shows the resulting coding density effectively used if we were to always pick the shorter codeword. This density wastes coding space because it is wrongly shaped and has an area significantly less than unity.

The obvious way around this problem is to use a single-valued code that is based on a summation of the mixture component probabilities. That is, we assign a new codeword to each symbol based on its total probability mass, obtained by summing the contributions from each Gaussian. Although this procedure is obviously computationally feasible for this example, there are more complicated models where it is not (see Section 5.5). In fact, the same rate can be achieved by using the original multi-valued source code and communicating extra information through the *choice* of codeword. This may seem surprising, since for a given symbol both codewords in the multi-valued source code are longer than the codeword in the single-valued source code.

Consider a sender that wishes to encode a rounded value v' that requires 2 bits if encoded using G_1 and requires 3 bits if encoded using G_2 (*i.e.*, v' is twice as likely under G_1 as it is under G_2). Including the single bit required to specify which Gaussian is being used, an optimal source code (where the Gaussian identity is explicit) will thus have codewords with lengths $\ell_1 = 3$ bits and $\ell_2 = 4$ bits. If the sender always picks the shorter codeword, the average codeword length is 3 bits.

Suppose instead that whenever the sender must communicate the particular symbol v', the sender chooses between the two codewords with equal probability. (In general, the ratio of choices will depend on v'.) It appears the average codeword length in this case is $(\ell_1 + \ell_2)/2 = 3.5$ bits, which is higher than that obtained by always choosing the shortest codeword. However, this cost is effectively lowered because the receiver can recover information from the choice of codeword in the following manner. Say the sender has high-entropy auxiliary data available in the form of a queued bit stream with 0 and 1 having equal frequency. When encoding v', the sender uses the next bit in the auxiliary data queue to choose between G_1 and G_2. The sender then produces a codeword that will have an average length of 3.5 bits (it is important to note that this codeword specifies which of G_1 and G_2 is being used).

When decoding, the receiver reads off the bit that says which Gaussian was used and then determines the rounded value v' from the codeword. Given the decoded value, the receiver can run the same encoding algorithm that the sender used, and determine that a choice of equal probability was made between G_1 and G_2. Since the receiver also knows which Gaussian was selected, the receiver can recover the queued auxiliary data bit that was used to make the choice. In this way, on average 1 bit of the auxiliary data is communicated at no extra cost. I refer to these recovered bits as *bits-back*.

If the auxiliary data is useful, the average effective codeword length is reduced by 1 bit due to the savings, giving an effective average length of 2.5 bits — less than the 3 bits required by the shortest codeword. I refer to this method of source coding as *bits-back coding*. It is important to note that the ratio of choices between G_1 and G_2 depends on the symbol being encoded. For example, if the rounded value is far to the right of v_0 in Figure 5.2a, then picking the codewords equally often would be very inefficient, since the codeword under G_1 would be extremely long, making the benefit of the single recovered bit negligible. In this case the sender should pick G_1 much less often and as a result the sender will read off only "part" of a bit from the auxiliary data queue to determine which codeword to use. As we will see below, choosing between the two codewords with equal probability is not optimal in the above example.

5.2.2   The optimal bits-back coding rate

The rate for bits-back coding can be determined by defining a distribution that is used to select codewords for a given input symbol (pattern), $\mathbf{v}$:

$$Q(\mathbf{h}|\mathbf{v}), \qquad\qquad (5.4)$$

where $\mathbf{h}$ is a binary vector representing the index of the selected codeword for input $\mathbf{v}$. (It is represented as a vector, since it too must be encoded.) Letting $\ell(\mathbf{v}, \mathbf{h})$ be the length of the $\mathbf{h}$th codeword[1] for a specific pattern $\mathbf{v}$, the expected length of the two-part codeword for $\mathbf{v}$ is

---

[1]The codewords may have fractional lengths produced, say, by arithmetic coding

$$\mathcal{E}(\mathbf{v}) \equiv \sum_{\mathbf{h}} Q(\mathbf{h}|\mathbf{v})\ell(\mathbf{v}, \mathbf{h}). \tag{5.5}$$

The expected bits-back for $\mathbf{v}$ is the information content (entropy) of the distribution used to select codewords:

$$\mathcal{H}(\mathbf{v}) \equiv -\sum_{\mathbf{h}} Q(\mathbf{h}|\mathbf{v}) \log_2 Q(\mathbf{h}|\mathbf{v}). \tag{5.6}$$

The difference between (5.5) and (5.6) gives the communication cost for $\mathbf{v}$:

$$\mathcal{F}(\mathbf{v}) \equiv \mathcal{E}(\mathbf{v}) - \mathcal{H}(\mathbf{v}) = \sum_{\mathbf{h}} Q(\mathbf{h}|\mathbf{v}) \log_2 \frac{Q(\mathbf{h}|\mathbf{v})}{2^{-\ell(\mathbf{v},\mathbf{h})}}. \tag{5.7}$$

The overall rate $\mathcal{F}$ for bits-back coding is given by averaging this cost over the source distribution, $P_\mathrm{r}(\mathbf{v})$:

$$\mathcal{F} \equiv \sum_{\mathbf{v}} P_\mathrm{r}(\mathbf{v})\mathcal{F}(\mathbf{v}) = \sum_{\mathbf{v}} P_\mathrm{r}(\mathbf{v}) \sum_{\mathbf{h}} Q(\mathbf{h}|\mathbf{v}) \log_2 \frac{Q(\mathbf{h}|\mathbf{v})}{2^{-\ell(\mathbf{v},\mathbf{h})}}. \tag{5.8}$$

It is easily proven from (5.8) that for each $\mathbf{v}$ the codeword selection distribution which minimizes the bits-back coding rate is the Boltzmann distribution:

$$Q^*(\mathbf{h}|\mathbf{v}) \equiv 2^{-\ell(\mathbf{v},\mathbf{h})} / \sum_{\mathbf{h}'} 2^{-\ell(\mathbf{v},\mathbf{h}')}. \tag{5.9}$$

I denote by * those quantities determined from the Boltzmann distribution. Note that this distribution depends on the input symbol, $\mathbf{v}$. The optimal rate for a given multi-valued source code is achieved if for each input symbol a codeword is selected using the corresponding Boltzmann distribution. By substituting (5.9) into (5.8), we find that the optimal bits-back coding rate is

$$\mathcal{F}^* = -\sum_{\mathbf{v}} P_\mathrm{r}(\mathbf{v}) \log_2 \left[\sum_{\mathbf{h}} 2^{-\ell(\mathbf{v},\mathbf{h})} \right]. \tag{5.10}$$

This rate is the same as the rate for a single-valued source code that has codeword lengths which properly reflect the total codeword space associated with each symbol in the multi-valued source code.

In the mixture of Gaussians example, where for symbol v' we had $\ell_1 = 3$ bits and $\ell_2 = 4$ bits,

$$Q^*(G_1|v') = 2^{-3}/(2^{-3} + 2^{-4}) = 2/3,$$

$$Q^*(G_2|v') = 2^{-4}/(2^{-3} + 2^{-4}) = 1/3,$$

$$\mathcal{E}^*(v') = \frac{2}{3}(3 \text{ bits}) + \frac{1}{3}(4 \text{ bits}) = 3.333 \text{ bits},$$

$$\mathcal{H}^*(v') = -\frac{2}{3}\log_2\left(\frac{2}{3}\right) - \frac{1}{3}\log_2\left(\frac{1}{3}\right) = 0.918 \text{ bits},$$

$$\mathcal{F}^*(v') = 3.333 \text{ bits} - 0.918 \text{ bits} = 2.415 \text{ bits}. \tag{5.11}$$

This is the minimum $\mathcal{F}(v')$ for the given example. A slightly higher than optimal $\mathcal{F}(v')$ of 2.5 bits was obtained above using $\hat{Q}(G_1|v') = \hat{Q}(G_2|v') = 0.5$.

5.2.3   Suboptimal bits-back coding

For complex source models, the summation in the denominator of (5.9) is usually intractable; in these cases, it is not possible to obtain the exact Boltzmann distribution. When it *is* possible to obtain the exact Boltzmann distribution, the denominator in (5.9) can often be directly used to create a single-valued source code. The advantage of bits-back coding is that when the multi-valued source code is unmixable, an approximation to the Boltzmann distribution can be used. There are a variety of practical algorithms for obtaining such an approximation, including Markov chain Monte Carlo methods [Geman and Geman 1984; Hinton and Sejnowski 1986; Ripley 1987; Potamianos and Goutsias 1993], variational methods [Chandler 1987; Peterson and Anderson 1987; Zhang 1993; Saul, Jaakkola and Jordan 1996], and inverse model methods [Hinton *et al.* 1995; Dayan *et al.* 1995] (see Section 5.5). The rate for an arbitrary codeword selection distribution $Q(\mathbf{h}|\mathbf{v})$ can be compared to the optimal rate given by the Boltzmann distribution:

$$\mathcal{F} - \mathcal{F}^* = \sum_{\mathbf{v}} P_{\mathrm{r}}(\mathbf{v}) \sum_{\mathbf{h}} Q(\mathbf{h}|\mathbf{v}) \log_2 \frac{Q(\mathbf{h}|\mathbf{v})}{Q^*(\mathbf{h}|\mathbf{v})}. \tag{5.12}$$

This is the information divergence (a.k.a. relative entropy) between the codeword selection distribution and the Boltzmann distribution, averaged over the source distribution. It is always non-negative and yields the increase in coding rate caused by the approximation to the Boltzmann codeword selection distribution.

A suboptimal selection distribution of particular interest is $Q^{\mathrm{short}}(\mathbf{h}|\mathbf{v})$, which always picks the shortest codeword, $\mathbf{h}^{\mathrm{short}}(\mathbf{v})$. (This is analogous to the two-part codes discussed by Rissanen [1989].) In this case, the rate increase compared to the optimal rate is

$$\mathcal{F}^{\text{short}} - \mathcal{F}^* = \sum_{\mathbf{v}} P_{\text{r}}(\mathbf{v}) \sum_{\mathbf{h}} Q^{\text{short}}(\mathbf{h}|\mathbf{v}) \log_2 \frac{Q^{\text{short}}(\mathbf{h}|\mathbf{v})}{Q^*(\mathbf{h}|\mathbf{v})}$$

$$= \sum_{\mathbf{v}} P_{\text{r}}(\mathbf{v}) \log_2 \frac{1}{Q^*(\mathbf{h}^{\text{short}}(\mathbf{v})|\mathbf{v})}. \qquad (5.13)$$

Bits-back coding makes gains over shortest codeword selection by approximately taking into account the entire codeword space associated with an input symbol, as opposed to just the codeword space associated with the shortest codeword. If several of the shortest codewords have roughly equal lengths, or if there are a large number of codewords with lengths somewhat larger than the shortest, then $Q^*(\mathbf{h}^{\text{short}}(\mathbf{v})|\mathbf{v})$ is significantly less than unity indicating that picking the shortest codeword is far from optimal. Relative to Rissanen's work, bits-back coding provides a tractable way to approximate the stochastic complexity [Rissanen 1989] and furthermore *communicate* at this rate.

5.3   Relationship to maximum likelihood estimation

The whole idea of a multi-valued source code may seem absurd. Why waste codeword space by associating multiple codewords with each symbol? An answer to this question must be closely related to the structure of the source model. In addition to the input pattern being encoded, it is often useful and natural to consider extra *latent* variables whose purpose is to capture high-order structure. For example, when modelling grey-scale images, it may help to create a latent variable that measures overall image contrast. The codeword for a particular image will include a binary representation of this contrast value. However, there may be several quite different contrast values that are equally plausible, leading to several different codewords.

A *generative* model of the type described above typically provides a parameterized distribution $P(\mathbf{h}|\boldsymbol{\theta}^{\text{H}})$ that can be used for encoding the set of latent variables $\mathbf{h}$, as well as a distribution $P(\mathbf{v}|\mathbf{h}, \boldsymbol{\theta}^{\text{V}})$ to be used for encoding the input symbol $\mathbf{v}$ for a given setting of the latent variables. Such a codeword will have an optimal length (*e.g.*, obtained using arithmetic coding) given by

$$\ell(\mathbf{v}, \mathbf{h}) \equiv -\log_2 P(\mathbf{h}|\boldsymbol{\theta}^{\text{H}}) - \log_2 P(\mathbf{v}|\mathbf{h}, \boldsymbol{\theta}^{\text{V}}). \qquad (5.14)$$

Note that the generative structure implies that $P(\mathbf{v}|\mathbf{h}, \boldsymbol{\theta}^{\mathrm{V}})$ is easy to compute. (Rissanen [1989] refers to this type of code as a *two-part code*.)

The set of parameters $\boldsymbol{\theta} = \{\boldsymbol{\theta}^{\mathrm{H}}, \boldsymbol{\theta}^{\mathrm{V}}\}$ must be fixed by hand, estimated using a stored data set, or adapted on-line. Estimating these parameters is a difficult task when there are latent variables. The popular technique of maximum likelihood estimation minimizes the following cost:

$$\mathcal{C} = -\sum_{\mathbf{v}} P_{\mathrm{r}}(\mathbf{v}) \log_2 P(\mathbf{v}|\boldsymbol{\theta}) = -\sum_{\mathbf{v}} P_{\mathrm{r}}(\mathbf{v}) \log_2 \left[\sum_{\mathbf{h}} P(\mathbf{h}|\boldsymbol{\theta}^{\mathrm{H}}) P(\mathbf{v}|\mathbf{h}, \boldsymbol{\theta}^{\mathrm{V}})\right].$$

$$(5.15)$$

Combining (5.14) and (5.15), we find that maximum likelihood estimation minimizes

$$\mathcal{C} = -\sum_{\mathbf{v}} P_{\mathrm{r}}(\mathbf{v}) \log_2 \left[\sum_{\mathbf{h}} 2^{-\ell(\mathbf{v},\mathbf{h})}\right], \qquad (5.16)$$

which is equal to the optimal bits-back coding rate (5.10). In contrast, maximum likelihood estimation *does not* minimize the rate for an encoder that always picks the shortest codeword.

Often, maximum likelihood estimation is not tractable when the generative model is overly complex. In these cases, it is possible to use various approximations to maximum likelihood estimation. A common approach [Peterson and Anderson 1987; Neal and Hinton 1993; Zhang 1993; Hinton *et al.* 1995; Dayan *et al.* 1995; Saul, Jaakkola and Jordan 1996] is to minimize an *upper bound* on $\mathcal{C}$, thus guaranteeing that the cost is lower than a certain value. (This is described in Section 3.3, where it is called *maximum likelihood-bound estimation*.) The logarithmic term in (5.16) is first bounded by introducing an extra distribution $Q(\mathbf{h}|\mathbf{v})$ and using Jensen's inequality:

$$\log_2 \left[\sum_{\mathbf{h}} 2^{-\ell(\mathbf{v},\mathbf{h})}\right] = \log_2 \left[\sum_{\mathbf{h}} Q(\mathbf{h}|\mathbf{v}) \frac{2^{-\ell(\mathbf{v},\mathbf{h})}}{Q(\mathbf{h}|\mathbf{v})}\right]$$

$$\geq \sum_{\mathbf{h}} Q(\mathbf{h}|\mathbf{v}) \log_2 \frac{2^{-\ell(\mathbf{v},\mathbf{h})}}{Q(\mathbf{h}|\mathbf{v})}. \qquad (5.17)$$

Inserting this bound into (5.16), we get an upper bound on $\mathcal{C}$:

$$\mathcal{C} \leq \sum_{\mathbf{v}} P_{\mathrm{r}}(\mathbf{v}) \sum_{\mathbf{h}} Q(\mathbf{h}|\mathbf{v}) \log_2 \frac{Q(\mathbf{h}|\mathbf{v})}{2^{-\ell(\mathbf{v},\mathbf{h})}}, \qquad (5.18)$$

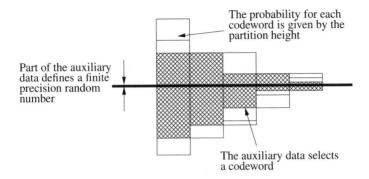

The probability for each codeword is given by the partition height

Part of the auxiliary data defines a finite precision random number

The auxiliary data selects a codeword

Figure 5.3
Feeding a random number into an arithmetic decoder with appropriate probabilities (shown by the partition heights within a column) selects codewords (shaded partitions), while at the same time conserving information.

which is equal to the suboptimal bits-back coding rate (5.8). So, these methods — including the algorithms presented in Section 3.4 — minimize the suboptimal bits-back coding rate. As with exact maximum likelihood estimation, these methods *do not* minimize the rate for an encoder that always picks the shortest codeword.

5.4 The "bits-back" coding algorithm

To implement the communication scheme shown in Figure 5.1, we need a general method of recovering the auxiliary data bits from the codeword choices. In the mixture of Gaussians example, we considered a specific input symbol for which there were two codewords. These codewords were selected equally often so that a single bit could be used for bits-back. If the codeword selection distribution is dyadic[2], Huffman *decoding* [Huffman 1952] can be used to pick codewords. In this section, I consider the case of an arbitrary codeword selection distribution. Software that implements this bits-back coding algorithm can be found by following the pointers given at http://mitpress.mit.edu/book-home.tcl?isbn=026206202X.

In the case of an arbitrary codeword selection distribution, it is not obvious how random codeword choices can be made without losing auxiliary data information. To address this problem, consider the operation of an arithmetic

---

[2]*i.e.*, each probability is an integral power of 2.

(a)

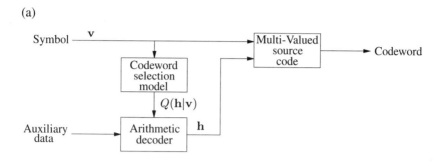

(b)

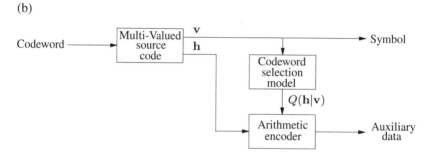

Figure 5.4
The block diagrams for (a) the bits-back encoder and (b) the bits-back decoder.

decoder [Rissanen and Langdon 1976; Witten, Neal and Cleary 1987]. It
receives a finite-precision number on $[0, 1)$ and extracts from it a series of
decisions according to a table of probabilities. If a collection of uniformly
distributed finite-precision numbers on $[0, 1)$ is decoded in parallel, we will
obtain a collection of decisions whose distribution exactly matches the table
of probabilities. Figure 5.3 shows how an arithmetic decoder can be used to
conserve the information in the auxiliary data when making random codeword
choices. The probabilities associated with the decisions form the table of the
arithmetic decoder, while the auxiliary data defines a random number to be
decoded. Each column of the figure corresponds to a single codeword choice
and is partitioned into several possible outcomes with the height of each partition proportional to the probability of the corresponding outcome. It is easy to
see that if the random number defined by the auxiliary data is uniform, codeword choices will be made according to the codeword selection distribution
(as shown for a particular case by the shaded partitions). It is also easy to see

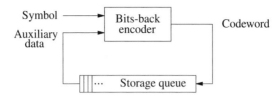

Figure 5.5
The need for extra auxiliary data is eliminated by feeding the codeword bits back into
the bits-back encoder as auxiliary data.

that by applying an arithmetic encoder to the sequence of decisions, we can
regenerate the random number.

Figures 5.4a and 5.4b show block diagrams for the bits-back encoder and
decoder respectively. When the bits-back encoder acquires a symbol $\mathbf{v}$, it
uses the codeword selection distribution $Q(\mathbf{h}|\mathbf{v})$ with an arithmetic decoder
to choose codeword $\mathbf{h}$, while consuming some auxiliary data bits. The multi-
valued source code is then used to produce a codeword of length $\ell(\mathbf{v}, \mathbf{h})$. (For
the experiments described in the next section, the multi-valued source code is
implemented using an arithmetic encoder in conjunction with a source model
distribution $P(\mathbf{h}|\theta)P(\mathbf{v}|\mathbf{h}, \theta)$ as described in Section 5.3). When the bits-back
decoder receives the codeword, it first decodes $\mathbf{v}$ and $\mathbf{h}$ using the multi-valued
source code. It then uses the codeword selection distribution $Q(\mathbf{h}|\mathbf{v})$ with
an arithmetic encoder to recover auxiliary data bits back from the codeword
choice $\mathbf{h}$.

Insofar as algorithm complexity goes, for an arbitrary codeword selection
distribution, the codeword selection procedure described above requires an
arithmetic encoder/decoder pair. If codewords are produced using arithmetic
coding, the incremental cost of the codeword selection procedure is not over-
whelming. In a hardware implementation, the codeword selection procedure
can run in parallel with codeword production.

5.4.1 The bits-back coding algorithm with feedback

In practice, when encoding a block of symbols, extra auxiliary data is often
not readily available. One solution to this problem is to use the binary form
of a portion of the block of symbols for auxiliary data. However, so that the
bits-back are efficiently utilized, this portion of symbols should first be source
coded. Figure 5.5 shows a scheme for using the *same* multi-valued source
code for doing just this, when the codewords have integer lengths. In order
to encode a block of symbols, some initial *primer* bits (*e.g.*, a few unencoded

source symbols) are first placed in the queue. When the next symbol is bits-back encoded, some of the bits in the storage queue are used for auxiliary data. The resulting codeword is fed back into the storage queue so that it can (possibly) be used as auxiliary data later on. Once the entire block of symbols is encoded, the bits-back decoder proceeds to remove the codewords from the storage queue *in reverse order*. Since the decoder has no way of knowing *a priori* how long each codeword is, it is essential that the *encoder* reverse the bits within each codeword before feeding the codeword into the storage queue. The source symbols are decoded in reverse order compared to the order in which they were encoded. As decoding proceeds, the recovered bits-back are fed into the opposite end of the storage queue and will later be used as codeword bits or primer.

This method is inherently block-oriented, since each block must be decoded in the opposite order in which it was encoded. As a consequence, a block delay is introduced, which is often undesirable. Shorter block lengths will lead to extra overhead due to the primer and also due to framing information (such as a codeword used to indicate the end of the block). However, if the block delay is tolerable, this scheme nicely eliminates the need for extra auxiliary data.

When the multi-valued source code is implemented using arithmetic coding, the above feedback procedure cannot be used as defined. An arithmetic encoder produces a sequence of codeword bits and in general there is no way to break apart this sequence into pieces of integer length such that each piece corresponds to one symbol. This problem is easily solved by dividing the block of symbols into sub-blocks. The arithmetic encoder used to produce codeword bits is halted after each sub-block of symbols is processed. The resulting series of codeword bits is reversed and fed into the storage queue as described above. Practical arithmetic encoders usually waste only a few bits (2 in the implementation described in Witten, Neal and Cleary [1987]) when encoding is terminated. The sub-block size should be chosen so as to minimize the effect of this wastage. For example, if the optimal bits-back coding rate is 1 bit/symbol, then choosing a sub-block size of 1000 symbols/sub-block will lead to a rate increase of only 0.2%. On the other hand, if the optimal bits-back coding rate is 1000 bits/symbol, arithmetic encoding can be terminated after each symbol (*i.e.*, the sub-block size is 1 symbol/sub-block) and the rate will increase by only 0.2%.

5.4.2 Queue drought in feedback encoders

At first sight, it may appear that queue drought is a serious problem. This can occur if the arithmetic decoder in the bits-back encoder uses up all of the bits in the storage queue and still can't make a codeword choice. In fact, this is usually not a problem because practical arithmetic decoders/encoders [Witten, Neal and Cleary 1987] use a coding value with a restricted size (32 bits in my implementation). Consequently, in my implementation no more than 32 auxiliary data bits will ever be drawn from the storage queue when making a codeword choice. In degenerate cases where the codeword selection distribution places very little mass on one or more short codewords, it is possible for a queue drought to occur when a sequence of very short codewords are chosen that consistently draw a large number of bits each from the storage queue. However, even in such degenerate cases, the sequence of events that leads to a queue drought is highly atypical. I have found that in practice queue drought is not a problem, as long as a reasonable amount of primer (say 20 patterns) is used.

5.5 Experimental results

In this section, I present two sets of results for bits-back data compression. The source models are Helmholtz machines trained using the wake-sleep algorithm (see Section 3.4). The first data set consists of simple patterns of horizontal and vertical bars. The second data set consists of binary images of handwritten digits.

5.5.1 Bits-back coding with a multiple-cause model

In this section, I describe how bits-back coding can be applied to a binary Bayesian network source model, that has one layer of hidden binary variables. Then, I present compression results when the model is fit to images of horizontal and vertical bars using the wake-sleep algorithm described in Section 3.4.4. I compare the compression efficiency of the one-to-many bits-back source coding algorithm with the one-to-one source code obtained using approximate shortest codeword selection, and also with the UNIX `gzip` utility. The multi-valued source code has over 68 billion codewords for each input symbol, and there is no tractable way to mix them, as there is with a hidden Markov model. For a given symbol, most of these codewords are extremely long and therefore play a negligible role in the source code. However, it turns out that the rate for an algorithm that uses a tractable approximation to shortest codeword selection is significantly higher than the suboptimal bits-back coding rate. This indicates that multiple codewords should in some way be accounted for.

It turns out that there isn't an efficient way to convert the multi-valued source code for the sigmoidal Bayesian network into a single-valued source code that achieves a rate that is comparable to the bits-back coding rate. To perform such a conversion, we must compute most of the probability mass corresponding to the codewords for a given data vector. Because of the combinatorial way in which the latent variables $\mathbf{h}$ interact to produce $P(\mathbf{v}|\mathbf{h})$, the marginal probability mass $P(\mathbf{v})$ cannot be computed in a tractable manner. $\mathbf{v}$ could be encoded bit by bit using Gibbs sampling to collect statistics. However, this procedure would require the computationally taxing simulation of a Markov chain for each element in $\mathbf{v}$.

In order to use bits-back coding, we need a codeword selection distribution that is close to $P(\mathbf{h}|\mathbf{v}, \boldsymbol{\theta})$. The Helmholtz machine with the wake-sleep learning algorithm provides an estimate of the optimal codeword selection distribution. The learning algorithm jointly estimates the generative network $P(\mathbf{v}, \mathbf{h}|\boldsymbol{\theta})$ and a recognition network $Q(\mathbf{h}|\mathbf{v}, \boldsymbol{\phi}) \approx P(\mathbf{h}|\mathbf{v}, \boldsymbol{\theta})$. So, an input pattern can be encoded as follows. The sender first uses an ancestral order for the recognition network to compute the probability for the first latent variable (in the ancestral order). This probability and some auxiliary data are then fed into an arithmetic *decoder* which outputs a value for the first latent variable. Given the input pattern and the value for the first latent variable, the sender then computes the probability for the second latent variable, and so on. Once $\mathbf{h}$ has been chosen in this manner, the entire configuration for $\{\mathbf{v}, \mathbf{h}\}$ is arithmetically *encoded* using the method described in Section 5.1.

The receiver decodes the entire configuration for $\{\mathbf{v}, \mathbf{h}\}$ and then computes the probability for the first latent variable using the same ancestral order that was used by the sender. This probability and the value for the variable are fed into an arithmetic *encoder*. While this process is repeated for the remaining latent variables, the arithmetic encoder will output auxiliary data bits.

So that we can compare the performance of bits-back coding with the actual entropy rate of the source, I used a synthetic source to produce 6×6 binary images. The images are iid., and each image is produced by turning on each of the 12 possible horizontal and vertical bars with probability 0.2. (Both types of bars may appear in the same image.) The entropy rate of this source is 8.6 bits/image.

The multiple-cause network had a single hidden layer containing 36 binary variables, in addition to the visible layer containing 36 binary variables. In order to avoid the need for extra auxiliary data, bits-back coding with feedback was used (see Section 5.4.1). The images were grouped into sub-blocks of size 20 images/sub-block and a block size of 200 sub-blocks/block was used. Before each block was encoded, the first sub-block of binary images was used to prime the storage queue. After each block of images was communicated, both the encoding model and the decoding model were adapted using the wake-sleep algorithm with a gradient descent step size of 0.01. The parameters for both the generative network and the recognition network were initialized to 0.0 before any images were processed. I also approximated short-

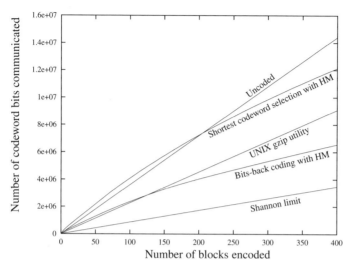

Figure 5.6
Experimental results for a Helmholtz machine with one hidden layer of binary units applied to binary synthetic images.

est codeword selection by picking for each image $\mathbf{v}$ the configuration $\mathbf{h}$ that maximized $Q(\mathbf{h}|\mathbf{v}, \phi)$. (The quality of this approximation is discussed below.) Choosing the configuration $\mathbf{h}$ that maximizes $Q(\mathbf{h}|\mathbf{v}, \phi)$ can be done efficiently by considering one latent variable at a time. Figure 5.6 shows the number of codeword bits communicated as a function of the number of blocks encoded for both of these methods. The curves for the uncoded binary image data and the Shannon limit given by the entropy rate of the source are also given. The curve for the UNIX gzip utility with the "-best" option is shown for comparison. (Although the UNIX gzip utility is not really meant for image compression, I include it as a reference point for the reader.) It is evident that if we were to compare the Helmholtz machine with gzip, we would arrive at different conclusions depending on whether we used approximate shortest codeword selection or bits-back coding. The bits-back coding curve is clearly superior to the curve for approximate shortest codeword selection.

Table 5.1 gives a comparison of the rates obtained for the next block after 400 blocks of images were processed. The rate for approximate shortest codeword selection is significantly higher than the rate for bits-back coding, indicating that a significant practical savings can be made by using the new algorithm as opposed to shortest codeword selection. However, the communication rate for a logistic autoregressive network that was trained on-line (using

Table 5.1
Rate comparisons of software-implemented codes for synthetic images.

	Rate (bits/image)
Uncoded binary images	36.0
UNIX gzip utility (with "-best" option)	22.7
Approximate shortest codeword selection (Helmholtz machine)	21.0
Bits-back coding (Helmholtz machine)	12.3
Logistic autoregressive network	10.7
Shannon limit	8.6

a learning rate of 0.01) is also given in Table 5.1, and is significantly lower than the rate for the Helmholtz machine. It appears that although bits-back coding opens the door to new multi-valued source codes, the ones studied in this section are not yet competitive with simpler compression methods.

How close does the approximation to shortest codeword selection come to actually picking the shortest codeword for each data vector? Since there are over 68 billion codewords for each image in the above example, we cannot make a direct comparison by actually searching for the shortest codeword. However, consider the same type of multiple-cause network, except with 9 hidden variables and 9 visible variables, applied to similar synthetic data, except with an image size of 3×3 and a bar probability of 0.1. This network is small enough that an exhaustive codeword search is possible. After processing 400 blocks of 1000 images each, I found that the approximation to shortest codeword selection gave a rate of 5.92 bits/image and exact shortest codeword selection gave a rate of 5.87 bits/image. These two rates are indistinguishable in the first decimal place. I expect that the results for the approximation used for the larger network are also close to the results that would have been obtained if an exhaustive search had been performed.

5.5.2 Compressing handwritten digits

The first step in efficient document compression is to segment the document into text components and nontext components. The text components may then be further segmented into isolated characters and then compressed using a model of the characters. Here, I consider modelling handwritten digits using a hierarchical Helmholtz machine and then compressing them using bits-back coding. Figure 5.7 shows 50 examples of the binary images that were used in this experiment. The binary Bayesian network source model had three hidden

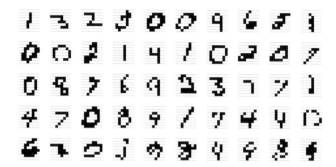

Figure 5.7
Examples of 8 × 8 binary images of handwritten digits.

Table 5.2
Rate comparisons for software-implemented source codes on the binary digit data.

	Rate (bits/image)
Original binary file	64
Approximate shortest codeword selection	
(Helmholtz machine)	60
`gzip -best`	39
Bits-back coding (Helmholtz machine)	33

layers of binary variables and one bottom layer of 64 visible variables. From top to bottom, the three layers of causes had 16 variables, 20 variables, and 24 variables, giving a total of 60 latent variables (2^{60} codewords for each input pattern). Both the top-down and the bottom-up networks were fully-connected from layer to layer, but had no connections within each layer. The Helmholtz machine was fit to a training set of 100,000 images, using the wake-sleep algorithm.

A comparison of the average rates obtained on the training set using approximate shortest codeword selection and bits-back coding with the estimated binary Bayesian network, as well as the rates obtained by the UNIX `gzip` utility with the `-best` option, are given in Table 5.2. The rate for shortest codeword selection is again significantly higher than the rate for bits-back coding, indicating that a significant practical savings can be made by using bits-back coding.

5.6   Integrating over model parameters using bits-back coding

As noted in Section 5.3, bits-back coding is closely related to statistical inference. In fact, the optimal bits-back coding rate is equivalent to Rissanen's *stochastic complexity* [Rissanen 1989] if we interpret the choice of codeword as a model parameter. Also, if the codewords are constructed by choosing a prior over codeword identities ($P(\mathbf{h}|\boldsymbol{\theta}^{\mathrm{H}})$ in (5.14)), bits-back coding effectively integrates over a discrete set of models.

Both of these relationships lead to an interesting application for bits-back coding. Suppose we are interested in encoding blocks of source symbols and that the source changes from block to block, but not within any single block. Given a model with a continuous parameter vector $\boldsymbol{\theta}$, there is a single block codeword with length $-\log_2 P(\mathcal{D}|\boldsymbol{\theta})$ for each block of source symbols, $\mathcal{D}$. According to the principles of Bayesian analysis, we ought to encode $\mathcal{D}$ by integrating over the entire continuum of models, giving a codeword of length $-\log_2 P(\mathcal{D}) = -\log_2 \int_{\boldsymbol{\theta}} P(\mathcal{D}|\boldsymbol{\theta})P(\boldsymbol{\theta})d\boldsymbol{\theta}$. In practice, this integral is usually impossible to compute and an approximation must be used. One approximation is to use the maximum *a posteriori* (MAP) model (*i.e.*, $\hat{\boldsymbol{\theta}} = \mathrm{argmax}_{\boldsymbol{\theta}} P(\mathcal{D}|\boldsymbol{\theta})P(\boldsymbol{\theta})$), for which the parameters $\hat{\boldsymbol{\theta}}$ are communicated using some (hard to determine) precision.

In fact, bits-back coding can be used to communicate each block of symbols using the entire continuum of models, as long as a good approximation to the posterior distribution, $Q(\boldsymbol{\theta}|\mathcal{D})$, is available. This distribution is used as the *model* selection distribution (in place of the *codeword* selection distribution) and the model parameters are communicated to an *arbitrary* precision. Whereas with the MAP approach, greater precision eventually leads to an *increase* in coding rate, with the bits-back coding approach, greater precision usually leads to a *decrease* in coding rate. Intuitively, this can be seen as an interaction of two processes. First, the extra codeword length caused by greater precision is partly recovered as bits-back. Second, greater precision usually leads to a more accurate approximation to the posterior distribution, and therefore shorter codewords on average. The latter process dominates except in the unusual case when the quantized version of $Q(\boldsymbol{\theta}|\mathcal{D})$ has a lower entropy relative to $P(\boldsymbol{\theta}|\mathcal{D})$ than the unquantized version. I am currently exploring the use of bits-back coding for integrating over continuous parameter spaces.

6 Channel Coding

Our increasingly wired world demands efficient methods for communicating discrete messages over physical channels that introduce errors. Examples of real-world channels include twisted-pair telephone wires, shielded cable-TV wire, fibre-optic cable, deep-space radio, terrestrial radio, and indoor radio. Each of these channels is subject to information-theoretic limitations, physical degradation, and governmental regulation. The prime information-theoretic limitation is Shannon's limit, which gives the maximum average number of information bits that can be communicated per second over a specific channel for a given set of transmitter constraints (*e.g.*, transmission power). Examples of physical degradation include attenuation, thermal noise, self-interference (inter-symbol-interference), multiple-user interference, multiple-path radio reflections, and power limitations in practical circuits. Examples of governmental regulations include transmission power limits, bandwidth usage, and information packet sizes. Together, all of these restrictions and many more define the practical channel coding problem of how to communicate discrete messages reliably.

Despite the multi-faceted nature of the practical channel coding problem, the bottom line is nonetheless quite straightforward. (See MacKay [1998] for an excellent introduction to information theory and its connections with probabilistic inference.) In order to communicate, the transmitter sends a finite-duration real-valued *signalling waveform*. This waveform is determined by a binary information sequence, which we usually assume is uniformly distributed over all possible information sequences. The duration of this waveform may correspond to a relatively short block of information or an infinite-length limiting-case block of information. Once the transmitter has produced a signalling waveform, it is transformed stochastically by the channel and a *received waveform* or *channel output waveform* is obtained at the output of the channel. The receiver then uses the received waveform to make a guess at the information sequence.

Physical channels are usually *band-limited*, meaning that for practical purposes the channel output waveform will not have any frequency components above some limit W Hz. Many channels are also linear (or we assume they are), so that the frequency components of the signalling waveform that are above W Hz will not influence the channel output. Because of this, we need only consider signalling waveforms that are also band-limited to W Hz. Using Nyquist sampling at a rate of $1/\Delta t = 2W$ samples/second, a signalling waveform defined on $[0, N\Delta t]$ can be represented *exactly* by the discrete-time sequence $\mathbf{a} = \{a_i\}_{i=0}^{N-1}$. The transmission of each sample a_i is called a *channel usage*. Similarly, the channel output waveform can be represented exactly by the discrete-time sequence $\mathbf{y} = \{y_i\}_{i=0}^{N-1}$.

Since the information sequence is effectively random, for multiple trials different signalling sequences will be produced according to some (usually discrete) distribution $p(\mathbf{a})$. The channel output sequence is probabilistically related to this sequence by a channel model $p(\mathbf{y}|\mathbf{a})$.

For a fixed level of additive noise, the transmitter can communicate in an error-free fashion simply by using a very powerful signalling waveform. However, this is an uninteresting and practically expensive solution to the channel coding problem. In practice, a limit is placed on the average transmission power:

$$\int_{\mathbf{a}} p(\mathbf{a})\left[\frac{1}{N}\sum_{i=0}^{N-1} a_i^2\right] d\mathbf{a} \le P. \tag{6.1}$$

It turns out that the information rate (in bits/channel usage) that can be communicated with arbitrarily low probability of bit error, is bounded from above by the *capacity* C of the channel:

$$C = \max_{\substack{p(\mathbf{a}) \\ \text{subject to (6.1)}}} \frac{1}{N} \int_{\mathbf{a},\mathbf{y}} p(\mathbf{a})p(\mathbf{y}|\mathbf{a}) \log_2 \frac{p(\mathbf{y}|\mathbf{a})}{p(\mathbf{y})} d\mathbf{a} d\mathbf{y}, \tag{6.2}$$

where the power constraint in (6.1) is enforced during the maximization. This optimal information rate was introduced by Shannon [1948], and is just the mutual information between the channel input sequence and the channel output sequence. (As a practical note, to lower the bit error rate or to use an information rate that is closer to C, we must generally use longer signalling waveforms.)

The channel coding design game essentially consists of devising *encoders* (ways to map information sequences to signalling sequences) and *decoders* (ways to guess at what the information sequence is for a given received sequence). In this book, I am mainly interested in conveying to the reader the insight and breadth of application offered by describing channel coding problems using Bayesian networks and using the probabilistic inference algorithms presented in Chapter 2 to perform decoding. For this reason, I begin this chapter by distilling out the essence of the channel coding problem and presenting a simple prototypical problem that will be the focus for the remainder of the chapter. In the prototypical problem, the transmitter sends a discrete-time binary sequence of $+1$'s and -1's (this is called *binary signalling*), and each of these values is corrupted by additive Gaussian noise. So, the encoder maps each information sequence to a binary signalling sequence, and given a received noisy sequence, the decoder makes a guess at the binary information sequence. It turns out that the solution to this problem has far-reaching consequences in multi-level (nonbinary) coding [Imai and Hirakawa 1977], mainly due to recent proofs by Wachsmann and Huber [1995] and Forney [1997].

In Section 6.2, I show how Bayesian networks and probability propagation can be used to describe and decode Hamming codes, convolutional codes, turbocodes, serially-concatenated convolutional codes, and low-density parity-check codes. In Section 6.4, I introduce "trellis-constrained codes", which are a trellis-based generalization of all of the above codes. In Section 6.7, I present a method for speeding up iterative decoders that are implemented on serial machines.

6.1 Review: Simplifying the playing field

The real-valued signalling sequences described above are the price to pay for an efficient description of digital communication in the real world, where signal amplitudes are usually real-valued. The channel coding problem would be much simpler to pose and implement if (1) signal levels were discrete, (2) the channel model was simple, and (3) the mapping from information sequences to channel inputs was assumed to be of a relatively simple form. While this approach can simplify the problem, it can also lead to a communication rate that is far below the general capacity given in (6.2). In this section, I simplify the coding problem in the ways described above, while attempting to argue that if done properly, the simplification will lead to a communication rate that is practically very close to capacity.

6.1.1 Additive white Gaussian noise (AWGN)

A channel model that is simple and works well in practice is the AWGN channel. Additive white Gaussian noise with single-sided spectral density N_0 is added to the signalling waveform to obtain the channel output waveform. Assuming the channel is bandlimited to W Hz (as described above), the decoder can apply a low-pass filter with bandwidth W Hz and sample the noisy waveform at the Nyquist rate to get a discrete-time sequence $\{y_i\}_{i=0}^{N-1}$. It turns out that an AWGN channel simply adds independent Gaussian noise to each input value a_i, where the variance of the noise is related to N_0 by $\sigma^2 = N_0/2$:

$$p(\mathbf{y}|\mathbf{a}) = \prod_{i=0}^{N-1} p(y_i|\mathbf{a}) = \prod_{i=0}^{N-1} p(y_i|a_i)$$

$$p(y_i|a_i) = \frac{1}{\sqrt{2\pi\sigma^2}} e^{-(y_i - a_i)^2/2\sigma^2}, \quad i = 0, 1, \ldots, N-1. \qquad (6.3)$$

If the decoder applies a low-pass filter with a higher bandwidth, then frequency components of the AWGN that are above W Hz will increase the effective noise on the sequence $\{y_i\}_{i=0}^{N-1}$.

The AWGN channel leads to an appealing formulation of maximum likelihood (ML) signal detection. The log-probability density of the received sequence given the signalling sequence is

$$\log p(\mathbf{y}|\mathbf{a}) = \log \prod_{i=0}^{N-1} p(y_i|a_i) = -\frac{1}{2\sigma^2} \sum_{i=0}^{N-1} (y_i - a_i)^2 - N \log \sqrt{2\pi\sigma^2}.$$

$$(6.4)$$

So, ML signal detection for the AWGN channel consists of finding the allowed signalling sequence $\mathbf{a}$ that is closest to $\mathbf{y}$ in *Euclidean distance*.

6.1.2   Capacity of an AWGN channel

For the AWGN channel, each channel output y_i depends only on a_i, and not any a_j, $j \neq i$. Consequently, the signalling distribution $p(\mathbf{a})$ that will give the highest mutual information is of product form:

$$p(\mathbf{a}) = \prod_{i=0}^{N-1} p(a_i). \qquad (6.5)$$

(This distribution allows us to stuff as much information into each a_i as possible.) In this case, the capacity in (6.2) simplifies to

$$C = \max_{\substack{p(a_i) \\ \mathrm{VAR}[a_i] \leq P}} \int_{a_i, y_i} p(a_i) p(y_i|a_i) \log_2 \frac{p(y_i|a_i)}{p(y_i)} \, da_i dy_i \qquad (6.6)$$

bits per channel usage. Note that for a product-form signalling distribution, the power limit in (6.1) becomes $\mathrm{VAR}[a_i] = \int_{a_i} p(a_i) a_i^2 da_i \leq P$.

It turns out that the maximum in (6.6) is obtained by a Gaussian signalling distribution with variance P (Cover and Thomas [1991]), and the capacity is

$$C = \frac{1}{2}\log_2\left(1 + \frac{P}{\sigma^2}\right). \qquad (6.7)$$

For example, if $P = 3\sigma^2$, then $C = 1$ bit/channel usage. For reasonable power levels, it is not possible to deterministically map C bits of information to a value a_i that will have a Gaussian distribution (or even close to Gaussian). For example, try mapping 1 bit of information to a variable whose distribution is close to Gaussian!

The optimality of a Gaussian signalling distribution leads to a new type of coding concept called *shaping*. A signalling technique has good shape if the marginal signalling distributions are nearly Gaussian. If the signalling shape is poor, then the capacity given in (6.7) cannot be achieved no matter how good a code is used. For example, if binary signalling is used ($a_i \in \{-\sqrt{P}, +\sqrt{P}\}$), then the channel capacity cannot be achieved, as shown in Section 6.1.6 and Figure 6.2.

The interplay between shaping and coding is very important. As another example, here is a method that has an excellent signalling shape, but uses a poor code. We first construct a table that maps each information vector **u** to a real value $c_{\mathbf{u}}$ in a way so that a uniform distribution over information vectors induces a nearly Gaussian distribution over $c_{\mathbf{u}}$. For a given information vector **u**, the transmitter simply sends a constant waveform, $a_i = c_{\mathbf{u}}$, $i = 0, \ldots, N - 1$. Using this method, each marginal distribution $p(a_i)$ can be made to be as close to Gaussian as desired, by increasing N and refining the map from **u** to $c_{\mathbf{u}}$. However, because the waveform is constant there is no way to introduce a good code. A fruitful structure that leads to a nice mix between coding and shaping is the *signal constellation*.

6.1.3 Signal constellations

Since the information sequence is discrete and the signalling sequence is determined from the information sequence, the allowable set of signalling sequences is also discrete. How should we specify the set of allowed signalling sequences? One way is to require that the signalling variable at each time step be a member of a fixed signal set. Figure 6.1a shows the signalling points for two signalling variables a_0 and a_1, where each variable can take on one of eight values. Even if a good code is used with these signalling points, the marginal signalling distributions are quite far from Gaussian and so the rate will be below capacity. Instead, consider breaking the signalling sequence into a series of groups (*i.e.*, subspaces) containing n values each. A discrete set of values (called a *constellation*) is then judiciously chosen within each n-dimensional subspace in a way that leads to marginal signalling distributions that are close to Gaussian.

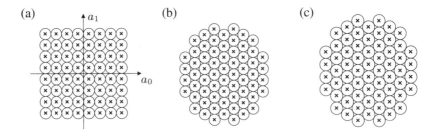

Figure 6.1
Signal constellations can be used to increase the Euclidean distance between signalling points (indicated by crosses). (a) A naive constellation for an $n = 2$ signalling set with 64 points. (b) The same 64 points can be rearranged in order to reduce the transmission power. (c) The constellation from (b) scaled up so that its transmission power is the same as the power for (a) — notice that the nearest-neighbor distance has increased.

Another way to understand signal constellations is through a sphere-packing argument. Consider the 2-dimensional constellation shown in Figure 6.1a that corresponds to the naive approach described above. For a fixed noise level in an AWGN channel, detection error falls off with distance between nearest-neighbor signals. Imagine centering a 2-dimensional sphere on each signal point as shown. Now, by trying to pack the spheres as tightly as possible, we obtain the constellation shown in Figure 6.1b. The nearest-neighbor distance has not changed, but the transmission power has decreased (since the sum of squared distances to signalling points is lower). In order to use the same power as the naive approach uses, we can now increase the Euclidean distance between nearest-neighbors as shown in Figure 6.1c. This will increase the noise-tolerance of the system, and so increase the communication rate relative to the naive approach. For higher-dimensional constellations, this sphere-packing gain becomes more valuable. (This simple example ignores the increase in the number of nearest neighbors from 4 to 6. See Lee and Messerschmitt [1994] for more details.)

6.1.4 Linear binary codes can get us to capacity

Although the design of optimal high-dimensional constellations is straightforward in theory, it is very difficult to implement practical encoders and decoders that use these constellations. Consequently, we must approximate optimal constellations by practical ones. Ways of doing this include trellis codes (a.k.a. coset codes) [Ungerboeck 1982; Calderbank and Sloane 1987; Forney 1988], which your telephone modem probably uses. Alternatively, Wachsmann and Huber [1995] and Forney [1997] have shown that by using a technique called *multilevel coding* [Imai and Hirakawa 1977], we can achieve the capacity in (6.2) by combining several relatively simple *linear binary codes*. That is, optimal constellations can be well approximated if we can design appropriate linear binary codes. I refer to these new proofs to justify my focus on linear binary codes in this book.

A *binary code* maps each binary information vector $\mathbf{u}$ of length K to a binary codeword vector $\mathbf{x}$ of length N. The *rate* R of such a binary code is defined as

$$R = K/N. \tag{6.8}$$

I will sometimes highlight the mapping by writing the codeword for $\mathbf{u}$ as $\mathbf{x}(\mathbf{u})$. A binary code is *linear* if for any $\mathbf{u}_1$ and $\mathbf{u}_2$, $\mathbf{x}(\mathbf{u}_1 \oplus \mathbf{u}_2) = \mathbf{x}(\mathbf{u}_1) \oplus \mathbf{x}(\mathbf{u}_2)$, where, "$\oplus$" indicates component-wise modulo 2 addition ($0 \oplus 0 = 0, 0 \oplus 1 = 1$, $1 \oplus 0 = 1$, and $1 \oplus 1 = 0$). Note that this form of linearity is highly nonlinear in the sense of continuous algebra (where $1 + 1 = 2$). In general, linear codes are easier to analyze than nonlinear ones.

Each bit in the codeword can be transmitted using *binary signalling*, also called *binary antipodal signalling*. (If the binary signal is modulated by a carrier so that it is a passband signal, it is sometimes called *binary phase-shift keying* (BPSK).) For $x_i = 1$ we transmit $a_i = \sqrt{P}$ and for $x_i = 0$ we transmit $a_i = -\sqrt{P}$. In this way, the average transmitted power is P. For an AWGN channel, we can write the probability density of channel output y_i directly in terms of x_i (bypassing a_i):

$$p(y_i|x_i) = \begin{cases} \frac{1}{\sqrt{2\pi\sigma^2}} e^{-(y_i - \sqrt{P})^2/2\sigma^2} & \text{if } x_i = 1 \\ \frac{1}{\sqrt{2\pi\sigma^2}} e^{-(y_i + \sqrt{P})^2/2\sigma^2} & \text{if } x_i = 0. \end{cases} \tag{6.9}$$

A simple linear binary code is the repetition code. Each information bit is transmitted m times, so that $R = K/mK = 1/m$. Using (6.9), the probability density of channel outputs $y_0, \ldots, y_{m-1}$ given x_0 is

$$p(y_0, \ldots, y_{m-1}|x_0) = \prod_{i=0}^{m-1} p(y_i|x_0)$$

$$\propto \begin{cases} e^{-(\frac{1}{m}\sum_{i=0}^{m-1} y_i - \sqrt{P})^2/2(\sigma^2/m)} & \text{if } x_0 = 1 \\ e^{-(\frac{1}{m}\sum_{i=0}^{m-1} y_i + \sqrt{P})^2/2(\sigma^2/m)} & \text{if } x_0 = 0, \end{cases} \tag{6.10}$$

where the constant of proportionality does not depend on x_0. By basing the decoding decision on $\frac{1}{m}\sum_{i=0}^{m-1} y_i$, the receiver effectively reduces the noise variance by a factor of $1/m$. It turns out that this is a very poor code, because the suppression of noise comes at too high a cost in terms of decreasing the code rate.

6.1.5   Bit error rate (BER) and signal-to-noise ratio (E_b/N_0)

For many engineering applications, the distortion value of interest is the probability p_b that an information bit will be guessed incorrectly by the decoder. When analytic methods are not available for computing p_b, we must resort to simulation. Often the simulation results are summarized as a point estimate called the bit error rate (BER). The BER is usually simply the observed fraction of information bit errors. When it is not possible to simulate the transmission of enough words to accurately pin down the probability of bit error, techniques such as the one described in Frey and MacKay [1998b] can be used to produce a confidence interval.

To compare the BERs of different coding schemes, we need a relatively robust measure of the noise level that each system is being exposed to. Simply stating the noise variance for an AWGN channel is not sufficient, since one system may be transmitting at a much higher power than another. Also, as shown above, performance can be improved in a trivial fashion simply by repeating signals. A reasonably robust measure of the noise level is

$$E_b/N_0 = \frac{P}{N_0 R} = \frac{P}{2\sigma^2 R}, \qquad (6.11)$$

where P is the transmitter power, N_0 is the single-sided spectral density of the AWGN, σ^2 is the AWGN variance, and R is the rate of the code. E_b/N_0 is the ratio between the power that is transmitted per information bit, and the AWGN power. It is usually given in units of decibels (dB),

$$10 \log_{10} E_b/N_0. \qquad (6.12)$$

Notice that although dividing by R in (6.11) does cancel the effect of the improvement obtained trivially by repeating signals, it does not take into account the increased bandwidth needed for lower rate codes. In fact, in the next section we see that the minimum E_b/N_0 needed for error-free communication depends on the rate. So, when comparing one coding system to another that uses a lower rate, we must keep in mind that there is usually some way to modify the former system so as to lower its rate and at the same time lower the E_b/N_0 it needs to achieve error-free communication at that rate.

6.1.6   Capacity of an AWGN channel with binary signalling

Engineering bandwidth restrictions aside, what are the communication limits for an AWGN channel when we use binary $+1/-1$ signalling (binary antipodal signalling with $P = 1$)? (Without loss of generality, we will assume that $P = 1$.) The answer to this question depends on whether we are willing to tolerate a certain non-vanishing BER. Before considering the non-vanishing BER case in the next section, I will address the simpler case of a vanishing BER. More specifically, what is the minimum E_b/N_0 needed to communicate error-free using a rate R code on an AWGN channel with binary signalling?

The mutual information between the channel input a_i and the channel output y_i at time step i gives the number of bits that can be communicated per channel usage on average. For an AWGN channel with binary signalling, the mutual information as a function of the noise variance is

$$M(\sigma^2) = \sum_{a_i=-1,+1} \int_{y_i} p(a_i, y_i) \log_2 \frac{p(a_i, y_i)}{p(a_i)p(y_i)} dy_i$$

$$= \sum_{a_i=-1,+1} \int_{y_i} p(a_i, y_i) \log_2 p(y_i|a_i) da_i dy_i - \int_{y_i} p(y_i) \log_2 p(y_i) dy_i$$

$$(6.13)$$

The first term is the entropy of y_i given a_i, which is just the entropy of a Gaussian distribution, $0.5 \log_2(2\pi\sigma^2 e)$. Since $p(y_i)$ is a mixture of two Gaussians, the second term is

$$\int_{y_i} \left[\frac{e^{-(y_i-1)^2/2\sigma^2}}{2\sqrt{2\pi\sigma^2}} + \frac{e^{-(y_i+1)^2/2\sigma^2}}{2\sqrt{2\pi\sigma^2}} \right] \log_2 \left[\frac{e^{-(y_i-1)^2/2\sigma^2}}{2\sqrt{2\pi\sigma^2}} + \frac{e^{-(y_i+1)^2/2\sigma^2}}{2\sqrt{2\pi\sigma^2}} \right] dy_i,$$

$$(6.14)$$

which can be approximated quite well using a Monte Carlo method. In this fashion, it is possible to obtain a good estimate of $M(\sigma^2)$.

To communicate error-free, the rate of the code must be less than the mutual information between the channel input and the channel output: $R < M(\sigma^2)$ [Shannon 1948]. Inserting $\sigma^2 = 1/(2RE_b/N_0)$ (see (6.11)) into this inequality, we get $R < M(\frac{1}{2RE_b/N_0})$. After rearrangement, we have

$$E_b/N_0 > \frac{1}{2RM^{-1}(R)}.$$

$$(6.15)$$

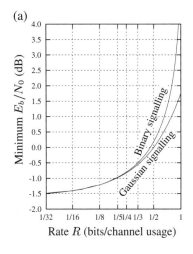
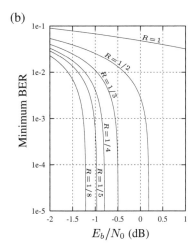

Figure 6.2
(a) The minimum E_b/N_0 needed for error-free communication with a rate R code, over an AWGN channel using binary signalling and optimal (Gaussian) signalling. (b) The minimum achievable BER as a function of E_b/N_0 for several different code rates using binary signalling.

This bound (based on an interpolated inverse of a Monte Carlo estimate of $M(\sigma^2)$) is shown in Figure 6.2a, along with the minimum E_b/N_0 required by optimal (Gaussian) signalling (see Section 6.1.2).

For example, an $R = 1/2$ code requires $E_b/N_0 > 0.2$ dB. To communicate error-free without coding ($R = 1$), an infinite E_b/N_0 is needed.

A standard result from information theory is that regardless of rate, an E_b/N_0 of at *least* $\log_e 2 = -1.5917$ dB) is required for error-free communication [Cover and Thomas 1991]. This limit is apparent from the convergence of the curve as $R \to 0$.

6.1.7   Achievable BER for an AWGN channel with binary signalling

If we are willing to tolerate a certain non-vanishing BER while using a rate R code, it turns out we can use a lower E_b/N_0 than described in the previous section. One way to pose the problem for this scenario is: For an optimal code with rate R and a specified BER, what is the minimum required E_b/N_0? We can think of this as a two-stage problem. First, we find a shorter representation for the information vector. This representation will obviously be lossy, since a uniformly random vector of information bits cannot be represented losslessly on average by a shorter binary vector. Second, we use a new optimal code to communicate this shorter representation error-free over the channel with the largest tolerable noise variance. Since the representation is shorter than the information vector, the new code rate R' will be lower than the old one: $R' < R$. So, the tolerable noise variance for error-free communication of the lossy representation will be higher than the tolerable noise variance for error-free communication of the information vector.

We would like to use a representation that is as short as possible, so that R' will be as low as possible and the tolerable noise variance will be as large as possible. However, shorter representations are also more lossy and will lead to higher BERs. What is the minimum ratio between the length of the representation and the length of the information vector, such that the error rate does not rise above the specified BER? It turns out that the minimum ratio is just the mutual information between a uniformly random bit and its noisy duplicate, where the probability that the value of the duplicate is flipped is BER. (This can be viewed as a result of rate-distortion theory applied to a Bernoulli source [Cover and Thomas 1991].) This mutual information is

$$1 + \text{BER} \log_2(\text{BER}) + (1 - \text{BER}) \log_2(1 - \text{BER}). \qquad (6.16)$$

The new code rate is

$$R' = R\left[1 + \text{BER} \log_2(\text{BER}) + (1 - \text{BER}) \log_2(1 - \text{BER})\right]. \qquad (6.17)$$

For a specified R and BER, we can compute R', determine the maximum tolerable noise variance $\sigma^2 = M^{-1}(R')$, and compute the minimum $E_b/N_0 = 1/(2\sigma^2 R)$ (to compute E_b/N_0, we use the original R, not R'). Figure 6.2b shows the achievable BER as a function of E_b/N_0 for several different rates. For each rate, the value for E_b/N_0 at which the BER converges to zero is the same as the value shown in Figure 6.2a. These achievable BER curves are used as guides for ascertaining the performances of codes and decoders later in this chapter.

6.2 Graphical models for error correction: Turbocodes, low-density parity-check codes and more

A critical component of a channel coding system is the decoder. Even if the code gives excellent performance when optimal decoding is used, if there is no way to implement a practical decoder that gives similar performance, it is not clear that the code is of any use. Channel decoders can be broken into two classes: algebraic and probabilistic. Algebraic decoders for binary codes usually quantize the channel output to two or three levels. The received vector

y is interpreted as a copy of the binary codeword vector **x**, with some of the bits flipped. Alternatively, received values that are highly ambiguous (*e.g.*, the value 0.1 when $+1/-1$ binary signalling is used) are considered as *erasures* — *i.e.*, the corresponding bit in **y** is assumed to be unknown. In both cases, decoding is a matter of using linear algebra (in a finite field) to find the binary codeword vector **x** that is closest to **y** in Hamming distance (dimensions that are erased are ignored). There are many techniques for algebraic decoding [Lin and Costello 1983; Blahut 1990; Wicker 1995] and algebraic decoders usually take advantage of special structure that is built into the code to make decoding easier. However, it is obvious that by using such a coarsely quantized form of the channel output, these decoders are suboptimal. For example, the value 0.1 from above does provide *some* evidence that a signal value of +1 was sent.

Probabilistic decoders are designed to make as much use as is practically possible of the real-valued unquantized channel output. The goal of probabilistic decoding is either maximum likelihood (ML) information sequence detection, or maximum *a posteriori* (MAP) information bit detection:

$$\mathbf{u}^{\mathrm{ML}} = \mathrm{argmax}_{\mathbf{u}} \ p(\mathbf{y}|\mathbf{u}),$$

$$u_k^{\mathrm{MAP}} = \mathrm{argmax}_{u_k} \ p(u_k|\mathbf{y}) \ \ 0 \leq k \leq K - 1. \tag{6.18}$$

Obviously, ML sequence detection minimizes the word error rate (we usually assume that all words are equally likely *a priori*), while MAP bit detection minimizes the BER. So, by definition, optimal probabilistic decoders are superior to optimal algebraic decoders. However, can we implement useful probabilistic decoders? The success of algebraic decoders is due to the way they take advantage of the algebraic structure of a code. Is there an analogous structure that probabilistic decoders can use? In this section, I show how graphical models can be used to describe probabilistic structure for channel codes and how the inference algorithms that make use of this structure can be used for probabilistic decoding.

6.2.1 Hamming codes

Hamming codes are an extension of the notion of adding a single parity-check bit to a vector of information bits. Instead of adding a single bit, multiple bits are added and each of these parity-check bits depends on a different subset of the information bits. Hamming developed these codes with a special algebraic structure in mind. Consequently, they are really meant for binary channels where the noise consists of randomly flipping bits. However, Hamming codes are short and easy to describe, so they make a nice toy example for the purpose of illustrating probabilistic decoding.

An (N, K) Hamming code takes a binary information vector of length K and produces a binary codeword of length N. For an integer $m \geq 2$, N and K must satisfy $N = 2^m - 1$ and $K = 2^m - m - 1$. The Bayesian network for a $K = 4$, $N = 7$ rate $4/7$ Hamming code is shown in Figure 6.3a. The algebraic structure of this code can be cast in the form of the conditional probabilities that specify the Bayesian network. Assuming the information bits are uniformly random, we have $P(u_k = 1) = P(u_k = 0) = 0.5$, $k = 0, 1, 2, 3$. Codeword bits 0 to 3 are direct copies of the information bits: $P(x_k|u_k) = \delta(x_k, u_k)$, $k = 0, 1, 2, 3$. Codeword bits 4 to 6 are parity-check bits:

$$P(x_4|u_0, u_1, u_2) = \delta(x_4, u_0 \oplus u_1 \oplus u_2),$$
$$P(x_5|u_0, u_1, u_3) = \delta(x_5, u_0 \oplus u_1 \oplus u_3),$$
$$P(x_6|u_1, u_2, u_3) = \delta(x_6, u_1 \oplus u_2 \oplus u_3). \tag{6.19}$$

Assuming binary antipodal signalling with power P over an AWGN channel, the conditional channel probabilities $p(y_i|x_i)$, $i = 0, 1, 2, 3, 4, 5, 6$ are given by (6.9), where σ^2 is related to E_b/N_0 by (6.11).

This code is small enough that we can compute the MAP bit values in (6.18) exactly using Bayes' rule. The BER-E_b/N_0 curve for MAP bit decoding and the achievable BER (see Section 6.1.7) at rate $4/7$ are shown in Figure 6.3b. Although there is an 8 dB gap between these curves at a BER of 10^{-6}, the MAP decoder gives a significant improvement of 2 dB over uncoded transmission.

By making hard decisions for the channel outputs (calling a value below 0 a "0" and calling a value above 0 a "1"), an algebraic decoder can be used. This decoder applies a *parity-check matrix* to the received binary word in order to try to locate any errors. (See Lin and Costello [1983] for details.) In this fashion, it can correct up to one bit error per codeword. The curve for algebraic decoding is also shown in Figure 6.3b. Algebraic decoding gives an improvement of only 0.5 dB over uncoded transmission at a BER of 10^{-6}. Although this may seem surprising, keep in mind that the receiver for the uncoded transmission is allowed to *average* the channel output to reduce the effective noise (see Section 6.1.4) $7/4$ times longer than the receiver for the algebraic decoder.

One way to approximate the probabilities $P(u_k|\mathbf{y})$ used for MAP bit decoding is to apply the probability propagation inference algorithm (Section 2.1) to the Bayesian network shown in Figure 6.3a [Frey and MacKay 1998a]. Probability propagation is only approximate in this case because the network is multiply-connected or "loopy" (*e.g.*, u_0-x_4-u_1-x_5-u_0). Once a channel output vector $\mathbf{y}$ is observed, propagation begins by sending a message from y_k

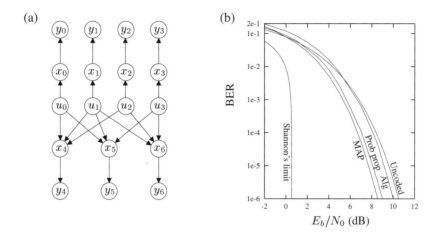

Figure 6.3
(a) The Bayesian network for a $K = 4$, $N = 7$ Hamming code. (b) BER performance
for the maximum *a priori* decoder, an iterative probability propagation decoder, the
optimal algebraic decoder, and uncoded transmission.

to x_k for $k = 0, 1, 2, 3, 4, 5, 6$. Then, a message is sent from x_k to u_k for
$k = 0, 1, 2, 3$. An *iteration* now begins by sending messages from the information variables u_0, u_1, u_2, u_3 to the parity-check variables x_4, x_5, x_6
in parallel. The iteration finishes by sending messages from the parity-check
variables back to the information variables in parallel. Each time an iteration
is completed, new estimates of $P(u_k|\mathbf{y})$ for $k = 0, 1, 2, 3$ are obtained. The
curve for probability propagation decoding using 5 iterations is shown in Figure 6.3b. It is quite close to the MAP decoder, and significantly superior to the
algebraic decoder.

For this simple Hamming code, the complexities of the probability propagation decoder and the MAP decoder are comparable. However, the similarity in
performance between these two decoders raises the question: "Can probability
propagation decoders or other approximate decoder give performances comparable to MAP decoding in cases where MAP decoding is computationally
intractable?" Before exploring a variety of systems where probability propagation in multiply-connected networks gives surprisingly good results, I will
review convolutional codes, whose graphical models are essentially singly-
connected chains. For these networks, the probability propagation algorithm
is exact and it reduces to the well-known forward-backward algorithm [Baum
and Petrie 1966] (a.k.a. BCJR algorithm [Bahl *et al.* 1974]). (For more on this
connection, see Smyth, Heckerman and Jordan [1997].)

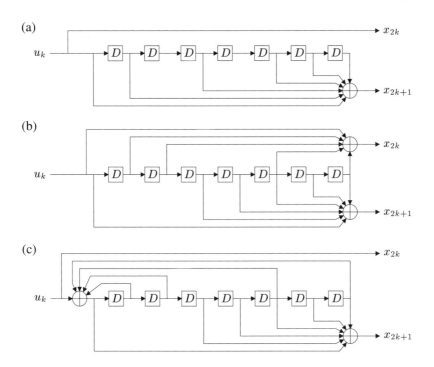

Figure 6.4
The linear feedback shift register (LFSR) configurations for rate 1/2 convolutional codes with maximum $d_{\min}$. (a) A systematic nonrecursive convolutional code ($d_{\min} = 7$). (b) A nonsystematic nonrecursive convolutional code ($d_{\min} = 10$). (c) A systematic recursive convolutional code ($d_{\min} = 10$).

6.2.2 Convolutional codes

Convolutional codes are produced by driving a finite state machine with information bits. The outputs of the finite state machine (which may include copies of the inputs) are then used as codeword bits. A code for which each information bit appears as a codeword bit is called *systematic*. Typically, linear convolutional codes are used, and any code in this class can be represented by a *linear feedback shift register* (LFSR). An example of a systematic code of this type with a memory of 7 bits is shown in Figure 6.4a. Each box represents a 1-bit memory element and D is a delay operator: $D^n u_k = u_{k-n}$. In this example, there is no feedback from the shift register to its input; a convolutional code of this type is called *nonrecursive*. An output is produced by adding (modulo 2) values "tapped" from the memory chain. The output taps for this rate 1/2 systematic nonrecursive convolutional code were chosen to maximize the minimum distance $d_{\min}$ between codewords [Lin and Costello 1983]. For this code, $d_{\min} = 7$, meaning that the codeword vectors for *any* two information vectors will differ in at least 7 places. Using the delay operator, this code can be described by the following two equations:

$$x_{2k} = u_k, \quad x_{2k+1} = G(D)u_k = (1 + D + D^3 + D^5 + D^6 + D^7)u_k, \quad (6.20)$$

where $G(D)$ is called the *generator polynomial*. This polynomial is often expressed in octal form by letting the coefficient of D^0 be the least significant bit and the coefficient of D^7 be the most significant bit. In this case the octal representation is 353_8.

Since $d_{\min}$ plays the central role in determining the error-correcting capabilities of a code at high signal-to-noise ratio E_b/N_0, we would like to use codes that have large $d_{\min}$. One way to obtain a greater $d_{\min}$ for convolutional codes is to use a larger memory. However, it turns out that decoding complexity increases exponentially with the size of the memory. In fact, it is possible to increase the minimum distance of any systematic nonrecursive convolutional code without using more memory. Figure 6.4b shows a rate 1/2 nonsystematic nonrecursive convolutional code that has $d_{\min} = 10$. (The two sets of output taps that maximize $d_{\min}$ were found using a method described in Lin and Costello [1983].) This code can be described as follows:

$$x_{2k} = G_1(D)u_k = (1 + D + D^2 + D^5 + D^7)u_k,$$
$$x_{2k+1} = G_2(D)u_k = (1 + D^3 + D^4 + D^5 + D^6 + D^7)u_k. \quad (6.21)$$

For a nonsystematic convolutional code, there are two generator polynomials corresponding to the two sets of output taps. For this code, the octal representation is $(247_8, 371_8)$.

Although the performance of the nonsystematic code described above is better than the systematic one at high E_b/N_0, it is the other way around for values of E_b/N_0 near the Shannon limit. Berrou and Glavieux [1996] have argued that a nice compromise between these codes is a systematic recursive convolutional code. The code in Figure 6.4b can be converted to a systematic code by taking one set of the output taps (either one will do) and using them as *feedback* to the input of the shift register, making a LFSR. If we do this with the upper set of taps, we obtain the rate 1/2 systematic recursive convolutional code shown in Figure 6.4c. This code can be described by the following two equations:

$$x_{2k} = u_k,$$

$$x_{2k+1} = G(D)u_k = \frac{1 + D^3 + D^4 + D^5 + D^6 + D^7}{1 + D + D^2 + D^5 + D^7} u_k. \qquad (6.22)$$

The second equation is to be interpreted as

$$(1 + D + D^2 + D^5 + D^7)x_{2k+1} = (1 + D^3 + D^4 + D^5 + D^6 + D^7)u_k, \qquad (6.23)$$

which can be derived from the figure.[1] The former expression allows us to retain the G(D) notation, which in this case is $247_8/371_8$. From the point of view of linear algebra, we have obtained this new code simply by dividing $G_1(D)$ and $G_2(D)$ from above by $G_1(D)$. It can be shown that this operation does not change the algebraic structure of the code. For example, the new code has $d_{\min} = 10$ as before. However, as we saw in the previous section, there is more to channel coding than algebraic structure. It turns out that this systematic recursive code performs better than the above nonsystematic nonrecursive code at low E_b/N_0.

6.2.3 Decoding convolutional codes by probability propagation

Bayesian networks for nonsystematic and systematic convolutional codes are shown in Figures 6.5a and 6.5d. In the former case, both codeword bits at stage k depend on the encoder state as well as the information bit, whereas in the latter case, one codeword bit is simply a direct copy of the information bit. Notice that because of the dependency of at least one codeword bit at stage k on the encoder state *and* the information bit, these networks are not singly-connected. However, they can be converted to singly-connected networks in the following way. By *duplicating* the information bits, we obtain the networks shown in Figures 6.5b and 6.5e (see Section 2.1.4). By *grouping* each state variable with one of these duplicates as shown by dashed loops, we obtain the singly-connected networks shown in Figures 6.5c and 6.5f (see Section 2.1.4).

In the new networks, each state variable actually contains a copy of the current information bit. We can interpret each state variable as a binary number whose least significant bit (LSB) is a copy of the current information bit and whose most significant bit (MSB) is the oldest value in the LFSR (*i.e.*, the value in the memory element that appears on the far right in the LFSRs shown

---

[1]In fact, this representation is algebraically consistent. We can, for example, multiply the numerator and the denominator in (6.22) by a polynomial in D without changing the set of output sequences that the LFSR can produce. See Wicker [1995] for a textbook treatment.

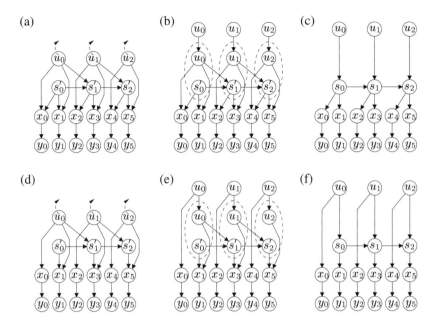

Figure 6.5
The multiply-connected Bayesian network (a) for a nonsystematic convolutional code
can be converted to a singly-connected network by duplicating the information variables (b) and then grouping together information variables and state variables (c). The
multiply-connected network for a systematic convolutional code can be converted to a
singly connected one (d) — (f).

in Figure 6.4). Let $s_k/2$ be the binary number obtained by cutting off the LSB
of s_k, and let $s_k\%2$ be the value of the LSB of s_k. Let $f(s_{k-1})$ be the binary
number obtained by cutting off the MSB of s_{k-1} and replacing the LSB of
s_{k-1} with the value of the LFSR feedback bit obtained by adding (modulo 2)
the values of the bits in $s_{k-1}/2$ that correspond to the LFSR feedback taps.
So, $f(s_{k-1})$ is the value of the new state at stage k, *excluding* information bit
u_k. Finally, let $g(s_k)$ be the bit obtained by adding (modulo 2) the values of
the bits in s_k that correspond to the LFSR output taps. If there are two sets of
taps, then there will be two output functions $g_1(s_k)$ and $g_2(s_k)$.

Now, we can specify the conditional probabilities for the convolutional code
Bayesian networks. For the sake of brevity, I will consider only the systematic
code shown in Figure 6.5f. Assuming the information bits are uniformly random, we have $P(u_k = 1) = P(u_k = 0) = 0.5$, $k = 0, \dots, K - 1$. The state
transition probabilities are

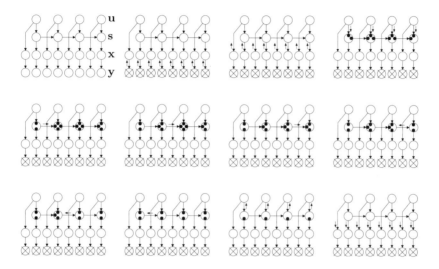

Figure 6.6
The computation of $P(u_k|\mathbf{y})$, $P(s_k|\mathbf{y})$, and $P(x_i|\mathbf{y})$ by probability propagation using the *forward-backward message-passing schedule*, which minimizes the total number of messages passed. Arrows represent messages in transit, whereas solid dots represent messages waiting to be sent.

$$P(s_k|s_{k-1}, u_k) = \delta(s_k/2, f(s_{k-1}))\delta(s_k\%2, u_k), \quad k = 0, \ldots, K-1,$$

$$(6.24)$$

where we assume $s_{-1} = 0$ to initialize the chain. The codeword bit probabilities are

$$P(x_{2k}|u_k) = \delta(x_{2k}, u_k), \quad k = 0, \ldots, K-1,$$
$$P(x_{2k+1}|s_k) = \delta(x_{2k+1}, g(s_k)), \quad k = 0, \ldots, K-1. \qquad (6.25)$$

Assuming binary antipodal signalling with power P over an AWGN channel, the conditional channel probabilities $p(y_i|x_i)$, $i = 0, \ldots, 2K-1$ are given by (6.9), where σ^2 is related to E_b/N_0 by (6.11).

Probability propagation in the singly-connected Bayesian networks for convolutional codes can be used to compute the *a posteriori* bit probabilities $P(u_k|\mathbf{y})$ exactly. The MAP values u_k^{MAP} can be obtained by applying a threshold of 0.5 to these probabilities. Although the probability messages can be passed in any order, the *forward-backward message-passing schedule* gives the lowest number of total messages passed, and so it is most appropriate for

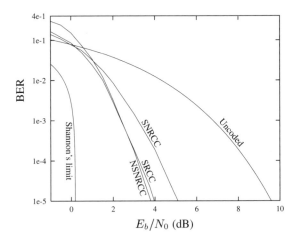

Figure 6.7
Performances of the following 7-bit memory LFSR convolutional codes with maximum $d_{\min}$: systematic nonrecursive convolutional code (SNRCC), systematic recursive convolutional code (SRCC), nonsystematic nonrecursive convolutional code (NSNRCC).

decoding on a serial machine. Figure 6.6 shows how messages are passed according to this schedule in the Bayesian network for a simple systematic convolutional code. First, probability messages are propagated from the observed channel output variables (crossed vertices) to the "backbone" of the chain (the state variables). Then, the messages are buffered as shown. (See Section 2.1.3 for an explanation of buffered messages in probability propagation.) Pictorially, when a message arrives at a vertex on an edge, but is buffered and not propagated on to the other neighbors, I draw a small dot adjacent to each of the other edges. Each of these dots can be turned into an arrow (indicating a message is being passed) at any time. Next messages are passed forward along the chain, and then backward along the chain. Finally, messages are propagated to the information bits and to the codeword bits. (It is not necessary to propagate probabilities to the observed variables, since $P(y_i|\mathbf{y})$ is trivial to compute.) Notice that this algorithm computes $P(u_k|\mathbf{y})$, $P(s_k|\mathbf{y})$, *and* $P(x_i|\mathbf{y})$. If all we need are the information bit probabilities $P(u_k|\mathbf{y})$, then it is not necessary to propagate the last set of messages shown in the figure.

Figure 6.7 shows the performances of the three convolutional codes described above. The systematic nonrecursive convolutional code has a BER that is significantly higher than the BERs for the other two codes at reasonably high E_b/N_0. The nonsystematic nonrecursive convolutional code and the systematic recursive convolutional codes have similar BERs, except for at low

E_b/N_0, where the systematic code has a significantly lower BER. The software used to obtain these results is available by following pointers at http: //mitpress.mit.edu/book-home.tcl?isbn=026206202X.

6.2.4 Turbocodes: parallel concatenated convolutional codes

Although the convolutional codes and decoder described above give roughly a 5.7 dB improvement over uncoded transmission at a BER of 10^{-5}, they are still roughly 3.7 dB from Shannon's limit at this BER. Up until the last few years, a serially-concatenated Reed-Solomon convolutional code [Lin and Costello 1983] was considered to be the state of the art. At a BER of 10^{-5}, this system is roughly 2.3 dB from Shannon's limit. However, in 1993, Berrou, Glavieux, and Thitimajshima introduced the *turbocode* and the practical iterative *turbodecoding* algorithm. Their system was roughly 0.5 dB from Shannon's limit at a BER of 10^{-5}. Also, these binary codes have been successfully combined with multi-level coding to obtain bandwidth-efficient coding within 0.7 dB of Shannon's limit [Wachsmann and Huber 1995].

The original presentation of turbocodes lacked a principled framework. For example, it was not at all clear how decoding should proceed when there were three or more constituent convolutional codes instead of two [Divsalar and Pollara 1995]. However, it turns out that the turbocode can be concisely described as a multiply-connected graphical model, and that the turbodecoding algorithm is just probability propagation in this model [Frey and Kschischang 1997; Frey and MacKay 1998a; Kschischang and Frey 1998; McEliece, MacKay and Cheng 1998]. This general graphical model framework makes it easier to describe new codes and their corresponding iterative decoding algorithms. For example, decoding a turbocode that has three constituent convolutional codes is just a matter of propagating probabilities in the corresponding graphical model.

Figure 6.8a shows the Bayesian network for a rate 1/2 turbocode. For a given information vector, the codeword consists of the concatenation of two constituent convolutional codewords, each of which is based based on a different permutation in the order of the information bits. The subnetwork indicated by a dashed loop is essentially the same as the network for the systematic convolutional code described above. The only difference is that every second LFSR output is left off, for a reason given below. The information bits are also fed into the upper convolutional encoder, but in permuted order. Every second LFSR output of the upper code is also left off. By leaving off every second LFSR output in both constituent codes, the total number of codeword bits is twice the number of information bits, so the rate is 1/2.

Once the channel output **y** for an encoded information vector is observed, an approximate inference method can be used to approximate $P(u_k|\mathbf{y})$ and

(a)   (b)

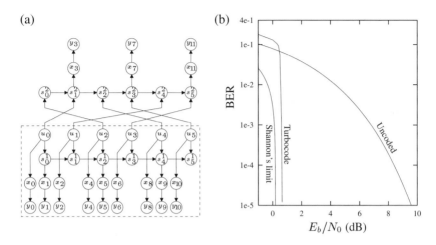

Figure 6.8
(a) The Bayesian network for a $K = 6$, $N = 12$ rate 1/2 turbocode. (b) The performance of a $K = 65,536$ rate 1/2 turbocode using 18 iterations of turbodecoding.

perform approximate MAP bit decoding. Variational inference has been used to decode a similar class of "low-density parity-check" codes [MacKay 1997a] (see Section 6.2.5), but there it was found that probability propagation in the multiply-connected graphical model gave better results. Here, I focus on decoding by probability propagation. Figure 6.8b shows the performance of the probability propagation decoder for a $K = 65,536$ rate 1/2 turbocode with a randomly drawn permuter. The software used to obtain these results is available by following pointers at http://mitpress.mit.edu/book-home .tcl?isbn=026206202X.

Each (identical) constituent convolutional code uses a 4-bit LFSR with polynomials $(21/37)_8$. Although at low E_b/N_0 the turbocode gives a BER that is significantly higher than the BER for uncoded transmission, the turbocode curve drops below a BER of 10^{-5} at less than 0.5 dB from Shannon's limit. Berrou and Glavieux suggest that for very low BER performance (say 10^{-10}), the permuter should be designed to maximize $d_{\min}$ [Berrou and Glavieux 1996]. I have found that for BERs at or above 10^{-5}, a randomly drawn permuter typically works fine.

Since the turbocode network is multiply-connected (there are cycles when the edge directions are ignored), we must specify a message-passing schedule in order to decode by probability propagation. That is, the order in which messages are passed can affect the final result as well as the rate of convergence

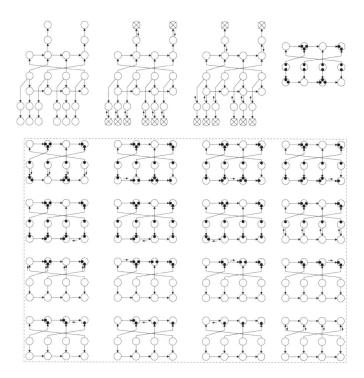

Figure 6.9
The message-passing schedule corresponding to the standard turbodecoding algorithm.

to a good decoding solution. Since the network is multiply-connected, we must also specify when to stop passing messages, since otherwise they would propagate indefinitely. Figure 6.9 shows how messages are passed up to the end of the first *iteration* of turbodecoding. First, messages are passed from the channel output variables (crossed vertices) to the state variables of both constituent codes. Assuming we are only interested in estimating $P(u_k|\mathbf{y})$, we can now ignore the channel output variables and the codeword variables. The simplified network with buffered messages waiting to be sent is shown in the upper-right picture in Figure 6.9.

Next, messages are passed from the information variables to the state variables of one of the constituent codes. This chain is processed in the forward-backward manner and then messages are propagated to the information variables. Messages are then passed to the state variables of the other constituent code (these are called "extrinsic information" in Berrou and Glavieux [1996]).

Once the second chain has been processed in the forward-backward manner, messages are propagated back to the information variables, as shown in the lower-right picture in Figure 6.9. This completes the first *iteration* of turbodecoding. Messages are then propagated from the information variables back to the first constituent code chain, and so on. The series of 16 pictures outlined by a dashed rectangle in Figure 6.9 shows how messages are passed during one complete iteration of turbodecoding. (Note that after the first iteration, there aren't any buffered messages in the first picture within the dashed rectangle. The buffered messages in this picture are due to the initial observations.)

6.2.5 Serially-concatenated convolutional codes, low-density parity-check codes, and product codes

It turns out that many of the iterative decoding algorithms for a variety of codes can be viewed as probability propagation in the corresponding graphical models for the codes [Frey and Kschischang 1997]. Figure 6.10a shows the Bayesian network for a serially-concatenated convolutional code [Benedetto and Montorsi 1996b]. The information bits are first encoded using the upper convolutional code. The generated codeword bits x^1 are then permuted and fed into a second convolutional encoder, whose output bits x^2 are transmitted over the channel. The iterative decoding algorithm introduced by Benedetto and Montorsi [1996a] was presented without reference to any of the literature on probability propagation. However, their iterative decoding algorithm is in fact probability propagation in the corresponding Bayesian network. After observing the channel output y, the decoder propagates messages from y to the lower chain. Then, messages are propagated forward and backward along the lower chain before being passed to the upper chain. The upper chain is processed and then messages are passed back to the lower chain, and so on.

The analytic upper bounds on the error rate for maximum-likelihood decoded serially-concatenated convolutional codes are superior to those for turbocodes [Benedetto *et al.* 1997]. However, it is not clear that these theoretical bounds are of any practical value. First, the bounds are based on the average performance over all possible permuters. Suppose that on average 1 in every 1000 permuters gives a very poor code that when ML-decoded gives a BER of 0.1. Further, suppose that the other permuters give codes that when ML-decoded give BERs of 10^{-10}. If we randomly pick a permuter, we are very likely to get a code that gives a BER of 10^{-10}. However, the average performance over all permuters is $0.001 \cdot 0.1 + 0.999 \cdot 10^{-10} \approx 10^{-4}$. In this way, the average performance over permuters can be misleading. Second, since ML decoding is intractable, in practice we must use a suboptimal decoder, such as probability propagation. Even if the ML-curve for one code is superior to

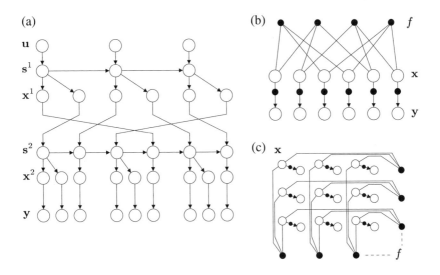

Figure 6.10
The Bayesian networks for (a) a $K = 3$, $N = 9$ rate 1/3 serially-concatenated convolutional code; (b) a $K = 2$, $N = 6$ rate 1/3 low-density parity-check code; and (c) a $K = 3$, $N = 9$ rate 1/3 product code. In the latter two figures, the channel output variables have been left out for visual clarity.

that of another code, the performance of the practical iterative decoder may be inferior.

It is suggested by Benedetto *et al.* [1997] that for short block lengths (say, $K = 200$) serially-concatenated convolutional codes give better performance than turbocodes, when iterative decoding is used. However, for short block lengths, it is not at all clear that either of these codes performs better than sequential decoding [Lin and Costello 1983] with a convolutional code with large memory.

Figure 6.10b shows the factor graph for a low-density parity-check code [Gallager 1963; Tanner 1981; MacKay and Neal 1996]. Unlike convolutional codes, turbocodes, and serially-concatenated convolutional codes, these codes do not have a simple directed generative structure that maps information bits to codeword bits. So, the factor graph is a more suitable graphical model for describing low-density parity-check codes. Notice that the relationship between the codeword bits **x** and the channel output signals **y** can still be signified with directed edges. Low-density parity-check codes were largely forgotten in the channel coding community for roughly 35 years, probably due to the computationally intensive encoder and decoder that Gallager proposed. However, it turns out that these codes have excellent theoretical performance [MacKay 1997a] and that the iterative decoder proposed by Gallager is in fact equivalent to probability propagation in the network shown above. In these codes, each parity-check function $f_i(\cdot)$ evaluates to 1 if the codeword bits $\{x_j\}_{j \in Q_i}$ to which $f_i(\cdot)$ is connected have even parity:

$$f_i(\{x_j\}_{j \in Q_i}) = \delta\left(0, \bigoplus_{j \in Q_i} x_j\right), \qquad (6.26)$$

where $\oplus$ is addition modulo 2 (XOR). The term "low-density" refers to the fact that each parity-check function is connected to very few codeword bits (a vanishing fraction, as $N \to \infty$). (Notice that since this network is parity-check oriented and does not show how an information vector leads to a codeword, it appears an encoder must use a pre-derived generator matrix and encode the K information bits in $\mathcal{O}(K^2)$ time.) The iterative decoder passes messages between the parity-check functions and the codeword bit variables. In fact, each parity-check function can be represented by a simple convolutional code network with one bit of memory. As a result, the decoder is simpler than the iterative decoder for turbocodes. However, it appears they do not come as close to Shannon's limit as do turbocodes for rates of 1/3 and 1/2 [MacKay and Neal 1996].

Figure 6.10c shows the factor graph for a product code. In this graph, the parity-check functions check rows and columns of codeword bits. Recently proposed iterative decoders for product codes [Lodge *et al.* 1993; Hagenauer, Offer and Papke 1996] can be viewed as probability propagation in the corresponding networks. As with the low-density parity-check code, the decoder iteratively passes messages between the parity-check functions and the codeword bit variables.

6.3   "A code by any other network would not decode as sweetly"

In the previous section, I presented the graphical models for a variety of codes whose iterative decoding algorithms can be viewed as probability propagation in the corresponding graphical models. Can we use this perspective to propose new codes and derive new iterative decoders? Partly, the answer is "yes". However, we cannot expect to obtain good results simply by tossing the ingredients of a graphical model into a bag and shaking. First, we want the resulting code to give excellent performance if ML decoding is used. Second, we want the resulting code to give good results when decoded by probability propagation, which is only an approximation to maximum likelihood decoding.

For example, since any linear binary code can be described by a set of parity-check equations, it may seem that a fruitful approach to getting closer to capacity is to simply find a good code (*e.g.*, a random linear code), write down its parity-check equations, construct the corresponding graphical model, and then decode it using probability propagation. However, in general the parity-check network will be multiply-connected. Since probability propagation is only approximate in such networks, the performance of the decoder will depend heavily on which set of linearly independent equations is used. Graphical operations, such as grouping parity-check functions together, will also heavily influence the decoder's performance.

In order to obtain a good coding system, we need to simultaneously find a good code and a corresponding graphical model that gives good performance when decoded by probability propagation. Keeping these issues in mind, a wise approach to proposing new code networks is to incrementally generalize previous work.

6.4   Trellis-constrained codes (TCCs)

In this section, I present "trellis-constrained" codes [Frey and MacKay 1998b] that can be viewed as a trellis-based generalization of turbocodes, serially-concatenated convolutional codes, low-density parity-check codes, and product codes.

The term *trellis* was introduced by Forney [1973] and refers to a diagram that explicitly shows the values of a discrete state variable at each time step and the allowed state transitions. A trellis is more general than a LFSR, since in a trellis the state transitions and even the number of states may vary with time. (Also, a trellis can represent a nonlinear code.) Figure 6.11a shows the trellis for the first 4 time steps of a rate 1/2 systematic recursive convolutional code with LFSR polynomials $(5/7)_8$, *i.e.*, $x_{2k} = u_k$ and $x_{2k+1} = (1 + D^2)u_k/(1 + D + D^2)$. The number of levels of the state variables (black discs) corresponds to the memory of the LFSR, and in this case there are 2 bits of memory. Each branch in the trellis indicates an allowed state transition, and the corresponding branch variable values (in this case the LFSR outputs x_{2k}, x_{2k+1}) are written beside each branch. Figure 6.11b shows the corresponding Bayesian network. In the Bayesian network, the branch variables are functions of the state alone, so each state variable has 8 levels instead of the 4 levels used in the trellis.

Figure 6.12a shows the factor graph for a trellis with 6 segments. For linear codes, any two adjacent state variables (large white discs) and the corresponding codeword bits (small white discs) must satisfy a linear set of equations, so the local transition function is represented by the small black discs with a

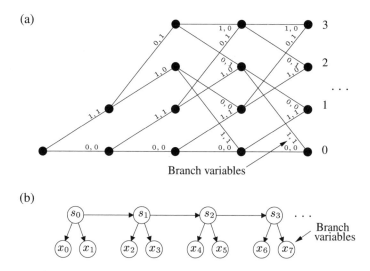

Figure 6.11
(a) shows the trellis for a simple rate 1/2 systematic recursive convolutional code. Each branch indicates an allowed state transition, and the corresponding pair of output bits are written beside the branch. (b) shows the corresponding Bayesian network, which requires one extra bit of state so that the outputs can be determined directly from the state variables.

"+" inside. Each function evaluates to 1 if its neighboring variables satisfy the local set of linear equations, and to 0 otherwise. The global function is equal to the product of the local functions. A given configuration of the codeword bits is a codeword if the global function evaluates to 1 for some configuration of the state variables.

Figures 6.12b and c show the factor graphs for a simple turbocode and a low-density parity-check code. In the latter case, each of the six trellises is a simple parity-check trellis that enforces even parity on its six codeword bits. These codes can be viewed as a set of codeword bits that must satisfy multiple trellis constraints. A codeword in a *trellis-constrained code* (TCC) must simultaneously be a codeword of multiple constituent trellises. If $f_t(\mathbf{x})$ is the constituent codeword indicator function for *trellis* $t \in \{1, \dots, T\}$, the global codeword indicator function is

$$f(\mathbf{x}) = \prod_{t=1}^{T} f_t(\mathbf{x}).$$

(6.27)

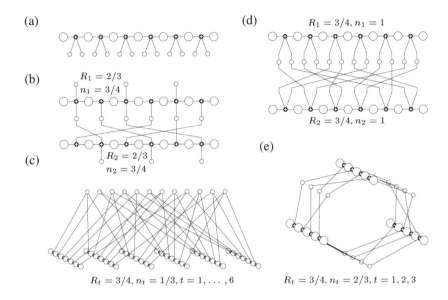

(a)

(b) $R_1 = 2/3$
     $n_1 = 3/4$

(c) $R_2 = 2/3$
     $n_2 = 3/4$

(d) $R_1 = 3/4, n_1 = 1$

     $R_2 = 3/4, n_2 = 1$

(e)

$R_t = 3/4, n_t = 1/3, t = 1, \ldots, 6$ $R_t = 3/4, n_t = 2/3, t = 1, 2, 3$

Figure 6.12
A codeword in a *trellis-constrained code* must simultaneously be a codeword of all the
constituent trellises, with the codeword bits reordered. The factor graphs are shown for
(a) a single convolutional code; (b) a turbocode, where each parity bit is a codeword
bit of only one trellis; (c) a low-density parity-check code; (d) a homogeneous trellis-
constrained code; and (e) a ring-connected trellis-constrained code. The small unfilled
discs represent codeword bits.

Each constituent indicator function is given by a product of the local functions
within the corresponding trellis. Usually, the codeword bits interact with the
constituent trellises through permuters that rearrange the order of the codeword
bits. Figure 6.13 pictorially depicts this scheme.

For the turbocode in Figure 6.12b, there are two constituent functions, $f_1(\cdot)$
and $f_2(\cdot)$. $f_1(\cdot)$ indicates that the upper row of codeword bits are valid output
from a convolutional encoder with the middle row of codeword bits as input.
$f_1(\cdot)$ does *not* directly place any restrictions on the lower row of codeword
bits, so it effectively only checks 3/4 of the codeword bits. $f_2(\cdot)$ indicates that
the lower row of codeword bits are valid output from a convolutional encoder
with the middle row of codeword bits as input. In contrast to $f_1(\cdot)$, $f_2(\cdot)$ does
not place any restrictions on the *upper* row of codeword bits.

The rate R of a TCC is related to the rates of the constituent trellises R_t,
$t = 1, \ldots, T$ in a simple way. If n_t is the fraction of codeword bits that

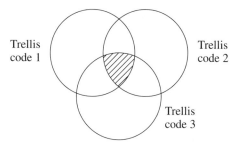

Figure 6.13
A *trellis-constrained code* is the intersection of the codes for multiple trellises, where
the codeword symbols of each constituent trellis code are permuted.

trellis t checks, then trellis t removes at most $(1 - R_t)n_t N$ binary degrees
of freedom from the code. It may remove a small number less if some of its
constraint equations are linearly dependent on those given by other constituent
trellises. For large, randomly generated permuters this effect is quite small,
so it can be ignored when computing rates in the remainder of this section.
(As a result, the actual rates may be slightly *higher* than the given rates.) The
total number of binary degrees of freedom left after all trellis constraints are
satisfied is $N - \sum_{t=1}^{T}(1 - R_t)n_t N$, so the rate of the TCC is

$$R = 1 - \sum_{t=1}^{T}(1 - R_t)n_t. \qquad (6.28)$$

From this equation, it is easy to verify that the turbocode in Figure 6.12b has
rate 1/2 and that the low-density parity-check code in Figure 6.12c also has
rate 1/2. (Note that a k-bit parity-check trellis has rate $(k - 1)/k$.)

Unlike encoding turbocodes and serially-concatenated convolutional codes,
encoding a general TCC takes quadratic time in N. In a general TCC, we can
designate a subset of the codeword bits as the systematic bits of the entire code
and then use Gaussian elimination to compute a generator matrix (once only).
Using this method for encoding requires $R(1 - R)N^2$ binary operations.

Decoding a TCC involves performing the forward-backward algorithm for
each trellis and exchanging information between trellises in the fashion specified by the probability propagation algorithm. The constituent trellises may be
processed in parallel or sequentially.

Next, I present two new families of TCCs and show that they perform in the
same regime as do turbocodes and low-density parity-check codes.

6.4.1   Homogeneous trellis-constrained codes

In a turbocode, the constituent trellises share only a systematic subset of their
codeword bits. The other parity bits of each constituent encoder are not constrained by the other encoders. Figure 6.12d shows the factor graph for a simple *homogeneous TCC* with $T = 2$, in which *all* of the bits are constrained by
each constituent trellis. From the general rate formula in (6.28), we see that
the rate for a homogeneous turbocode is

$$R = 1 - T(1 - R_{\text{avg}}), \qquad (6.29)$$

where $R_{\text{avg}} = \left(\sum_{t=1}^{T} R_t \right) / T$.

One difference between the homogeneous TCC and the turbocode is that the
rate of a homogeneous TCC decreases directly with the number of trellises T.
In the simulations discussed below, I used $T = 2$ and $R_1 = R_2 = R_{\text{avg}} = 3/4$
to get $R = 1/2$. To obtain the same rate with $T = 3$ would require $R_{\text{avg}} = 5/6$. In contrast, the rate for a turbocode varies roughly inversely with T. A
rate 1/2 turbocode with $T = 3$ can be obtained with $R_1 = R_2 = R_3 = 3/4$.
Another difference is that the permuter length of a homogeneous TCC is N,
whereas for a turbocode, the permuter length is RN.

The trellises in a homogeneous TCC share all their bits, so we can't simply
encode by dividing the bits in each constituent trellis into a systematic set and
a parity set and running a linear-time encoding method for each trellis, as is
possible in a turbocode. Instead, a previously computed generator matrix is
applied to a previously selected systematic subset of codeword bits, which
takes $R(1 - R)N^2$ binary operations.

The iterative decoder processes each constituent trellis using the forward-
backward algorithm, and passes "extrinsic information" between the trellises
in the manner specified by the probability propagation algorithm. For two trellises, the decoding schedule is straightforward. For $T > 2$, different decoding
schedules are possible. The trellises may be processed sequentially, in which
case the current trellis uses the most recently computed probabilities produced
by the other trellises. Alternatively, the trellises may be processed in parallel,
in which case the current trellis uses the probabilities produced by the other
trellises in the previous decoding iteration.

For the sake of gaining insight into these new compound codes and the behavior of their iterative decoders, decoding continues until a codeword is found
or a large number of iterations have been performed. After each decoding iteration, the current bit-wise MAP estimates are used to determine whether a
valid codeword has been found, in which case the iterative procedure is terminated. If 100 iterations are completed without finding a codeword, the block is

labeled a decoding failure. Notice that given the factor graph of a code, determining that a codeword is valid is simply a matter of checking that all the local functions evaluate to 1.

Using Monte Carlo, I estimated the performance of an $N = 131,072, T = 2$ homogeneous TCC with $R_1 = R_2 = 3/4$, giving $R = 1/2$. (See Frey and MacKay [1998b] for a description of how the BER confidence intervals were computed.) Each rate 3/4 trellis was obtained by shortening every fifth bit of a rate 4/5 nonsystematic convolutional code with maximum $d_{\min}$. (The generator polynomials for this code are given in Daut, Modestino and Wismer [1982] and are $(32, 4, 22, 15, 17)_{\text{octal}}$.) Figure 6.14 shows the performance of this homogeneous TCC, relative to the turbocode introduced by Berrou *et al.* [1993] and the best rate 1/2, $N = 65,389$ low-density parity-check code published to date [MacKay and Neal 1996]. Although it does not perform as well as the turbocode, it performs significantly better than the low-density parity-check code. It seems likely that there is room for improvement here, since the set of generator polynomials that gave maximum $d_{\min}$ were used and this is probably not the best choice. (Keep in mind, however, that the performance of a homogeneous TCC is not necessarily governed by the same constituent trellis properties that govern the performance of a turbocode.) Of significant importance compared to turbocodes, I have observed that this homogeneous TCC has higher-weight low-weight codewords.

6.4.2   Ring-connected trellis-constrained codes

Figure 6.12e shows the factor graph for a simple *ring-connected TCC* with $T = 3$. This code can be viewed as a serially-concatenated convolutional code [Benedetto and Montorsi 1996b; Benedetto and Montorsi 1996a] in which some of the output bits are constrained to be equal to some of the input bits. The factor graph thus forms a ring of connected trellises. In the ring-connected TCC shown, each constituent trellis checks exactly $2/T$ of the codeword bits. From the general rate formula in (6.28), the rate for such a ring-connected turbocode is

$$R = 2(R_{\text{avg}} - 1/2). \qquad (6.30)$$

Unlike turbocodes and homogeneous TCCs, for such a ring-connected TCC the rate does not depend on the number of constituent trellises T. However, the permuter lengths are $1/T$ relative to the block length.

For ring-connected TCCs, we cannot use the same type of encoding procedure that is used for serially-concatenated convolutional codes, since some of the "output" bits must match some of the "input" bits. As with the homogeneous TCC, we can encode with approximately $R(1-R)N^2$ binary operations

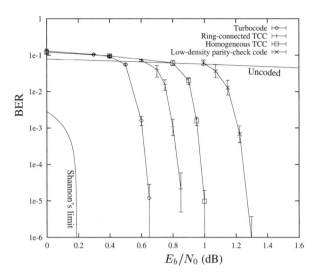

Figure 6.14
The performances of a homogeneous TCC and a ring-connected TCC compared to the best rate 1/2 turbocode and low-density parity-check code performances published to date.

by applying a previously computed generator matrix to a previously selected systematic subset of codeword bits. However, if $R_t = 3/4, t = 1, \ldots, T$ (giving $R = 1/2$), encoding computations can be saved in the following way. First, we pick $3N/2T$ systematic bits for trellis 1 and generate the corresponding $N/2T$ parity bits, using a number of computations that is linear in N. Then, we work around the ring and for each trellis pick $N/2T$ systematic bits and generate the corresponding $N/2T$ parity bits. When all but two trellises have been encoded, the last two trellises are used to form a binary vector that when multiplied by a previously computed $N/T \times N/T$ binary matrix yields the final set of N/T parity bits. The computations for the last step dominate and require approximately N^2/T^2 binary operations. For $R_{\text{avg}} = 3/4, R = 1/2$, $T = 3$, the first method described above takes $N^2/4$ operations, whereas the second method takes $N^2/9$ operations.

As with homogeneous TCCs, when $T > 2$ ring-connected TCCs can be iteratively decoded using a variety of schedules. In my simulations, the trellises are processed sequentially while passing probabilities around the ring in one direction. Iterative decoding continues until a valid codeword is found or until 100 iterations are completed.

The performance was estimated for an $N = 131,070, T = 3$ ring-connected TCC with $n_1 = n_2 = n_3 = 2/3$ and $R_1 = R_2 = R_3 = 3/4$, giving $R = 1/2$. Each rate 3/4 trellis used the generator polynomials $(12, 4, 17, 11)_{\text{octal}}$, which were found by trial and error. The constituent codeword bits were shared alternately with the two neighboring trellises. Figure 6.14 shows the performance of this ring-connected TCC. It performs significantly better than the homogeneous TCC and the low-density parity-check code and only 0.2 dB worse than the turbocode.

6.5   Decoding complexity of iterative decoders

The decoding complexities per iteration for low-density parity-check codes, turbocodes, and homogeneous TCCs vary as significantly as do their proximities to Shannon's limit. The decoding complexity for a low-density parity-check code is roughly $\Omega_{\text{GL}} = 6It$ multiplies per codeword bit, where I is the average number of iterations required to find the correct codeword, and t is the average number of checks with which each codeword bit participates [MacKay and Neal 1996].

For turbocodes and homogeneous TCCs, most of the computations are spent processing the constituent trellises. Each section of a bi-proper trellis requires roughly $6 \times 2^\nu$ multiplies to process, where 2^ν is the number of states in the regular trellis. For a turbocode with rate R and n_t constituent convolutional codes, there are NRn_t trellis sections in all, so that the decoding complexity for a turbocode is roughly $\Omega_{\text{TC}} = 6RIn_t2^\nu$ multiplies per codeword bit. For a homogeneous TCC, there are Nn_t trellis sections in all, so that the decoding complexity is roughly $\Omega_{\text{HTCC}} = 6In_t2^\nu$ multiplies per codeword bit.

For example, at $E_b/N_0 = 1.3$ dB, the $t \approx 3$ low-density parity-check code discussed in the previous section has $I = 11.2$ (David MacKay, personal communication), so $\Omega_{\text{GL}} = 202$ multiplies per codeword bit. The $R = 1/2$, $n_t = 2$, $\nu = 4$ turbocode has $I = 5.3$, so $\Omega_{\text{TC}} = 509$ multiplies per codeword bit. The $R = 1/2$, $n_t = 2$, $\nu = 4$ homogeneous TCC has $I = 10.5$, so $\Omega_{\text{HTCC}} = 2016$ multiplies per codeword bit.

6.6   Parallel iterative decoding

The decoding algorithm for low-density parity-check codes proposed by Gallager [1963] and later by MacKay and Neal [1996] is inherently a parallel algorithm. As described in Section 6.2.5, probability propagation in the Bayesian network for a low-density parity-check code consists of passing *sets* of messages back and forth between the codeword bits and the clamped parity-check variables. It turns out that the standard decoders for turbocodes and serially-concatenated convolutional codes are inherently *serial*. In this section, I consider a parallel message-passing schedule. Not only do these results shed light on the insensitivity of turbodecoding to the message-passing schedule, but they also introduce the possibility of highly parallel turbodecoding hardware.

6.6.1 Concurrent turbodecoding

If each chain in a turbocode is viewed as a single vertex, then turbodecoding can also be viewed as a "parallel" algorithm.[2] However, if each chain in a turbocode is viewed at a refined level (*e.g.*, Figure 6.8), then the standard turbodecoding algorithm is inherently serial. That is, when messages are passed as shown in Figure 6.9, most of the computations are used to compute messages that cannot be propagated in parallel.

Here, I consider *concurrent turbodecoding* in which messages are passed in a parallel fashion. One time step of concurrent turbodecoding consists of simultaneously passing messages in both directions on all graph edges in the Bayesian network for the code. (Although "concurrent" is not quite the right term for such a parallel algorithm, the term "parallel" is used in the other name for turbocodes, "parallel concatenated convolutional codes".) Notice that concurrent turbodecoding is not just a parallel implementation of standard turbodecoding. It is a different algorithm which may have different properties.

A naive approach to a hardware implementation of concurrent turbodecoding would be to build one simple processor for each vertex in the Bayesian network for a code. Of course, for reasonably long block lengths, a prohibitively large number of these processors would be needed for a fully parallel VLSI implementation of concurrent turbodecoding. In the following section, I empirically compare the time complexity of standard decoding with concurrent decoding, while ignoring practical implementation issues such as wiring complexity. In practice, a more space-efficient implementation (*e.g.*, time-shared processors) would be used at some detriment to the computational efficiency.

6.6.2 Results

The code used for the simulations was a rate 1/2 $K = 5,000$, $N = 10,000$ turbocode with two constituent convolutional codes, each with generator polynomials $(21/37)_{\text{octal}}$. The constituent chains were connected by a randomly selected permuter. Every second output of each constituent chain was punctured to get a rate of 1/2. For each of three values of E_b/N_0, the transmission of

---

[2]When there is more than one chain in a turbocode, messages may be passed between chains in either a serial or parallel manner.

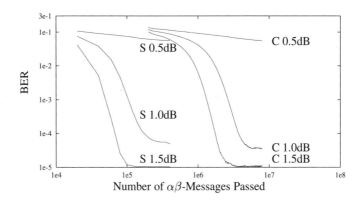

Figure 6.15
Performance of standard (S) and concurrent (C) turbodecoding when implemented on a serial computer, for 3 values of E_b/N_0.

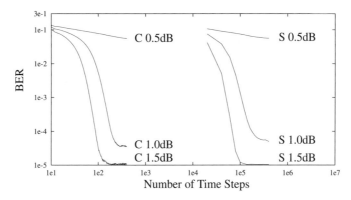

Figure 6.16
Performance of standard (S) and concurrent (C) turbodecoding when implemented on a parallel computer, for 3 values of E_b/N_0.

10^7 information bits was simulated, and the results are shown in Figures 6.15 and 6.16. Interestingly, for a given E_b/N_0 it appears that both algorithms converge to the same BER.

Figure 6.15 shows the BER versus the number of messages passed in the constituent chains, for standard and concurrent turbodecoding. (The computation of the messages passed in the constituent chain dominates the decoding time). The number of messages passed gives a good indication of decoding complexity on a serial computer. Not surprisingly, it is apparent that the standard algorithm is better suited to serial implementation. It is interesting that for a given BER, the concurrent decoding algorithm is roughly 30 times *slower* than the standard algorithm when implemented on a serial computer.

Figure 6.16 shows the BER versus the number of time steps for the case where 10,000 processors are available for concurrent turbodecoding. We assume that pipelining is *not* used for standard turbodecoding. For a given BER, the concurrent decoding algorithm is roughly 850 times *faster* than the standard algorithm when implemented on a parallel computer. If one processor is used for each half iteration of 5 iterations of standard turbodecoding in a pipeline fashion, standard decoding can be sped up by a factor of only 10 (extra pipeline stages do not improve the BER). Concurrent turbodecoding is still 85 times faster.

6.7 Speeding up iterative decoding by detecting variables early

The excellent bit error rate performance of iterative probability propagation decoders is achieved at the expense of a computationally burdensome decoding procedure. In this section, I present a method called *early detection* [Frey and Kschischang 1998] that can be used to reduce the computational complexity of a variety of iterative decoders. Using a confidence criterion, some information symbols, state variables and codeword symbols are detected early on in the iterative decoding procedure. In this way, the complexity of further processing is reduced with a controllable increase in BER. I present an easily implemented instance of this algorithm, called *trellis splicing*, that can be used with turbodecoding. For a simulated system of this type, I obtain a reduction in computational complexity of up to a factor of four, relative to a turbodecoder that performs the fewest iterations needed to achieve the same BER.

6.7.1 Early detection

It seems plausible that in some cases when iteratively decoding, some parts of the codeword may be more easily decoded than other parts. Although different parts of a codeword are usually inter-dependent, for particular noise patterns the coupling between certain parts may be weak. In these cases, it makes sense that the decoder should spend more computations on "tough" parts, and fewer computations on "easy" parts. During decoding, those parts that are deemed to be successfully decoded are clamped. Decoding computations are then focused on the remaining parts.

In general, the computation time of an iteration decreases with the number of variables detected early. So, in order to obtain the greatest speed-up, the decoder should early-detect as many variables as possible. However, an overly aggressive early-detection criterion will lead to a high rate of *erroneous* decisions, spoiling the BER performance. In addition to this constraint, the early-detection criterion should be relatively simple, so that the overhead of ascertaining which variables ought to be detected early does not overshadow the reduction in the computational complexity of subsequent iterative decoding. Here, I consider applying a threshold to the soft decisions for information bits, codeword bits, and state variables during decoding.

The soft decisions used for iterative decoding can be represented as log-odds ratios that approximate the true *a posteriori* log-odds ratios. The log-odds ratio for an information symbol, state variable, or codeword symbol z at iteration i given the channel output $\mathbf{y}$ is

$$\hat{L}^i(z = z') = \log \frac{\hat{P}^i(z = z'|\mathbf{y})}{\hat{P}^i(z \neq z'|\mathbf{y})}, \tag{6.31}$$

where $\hat{P}^i(z|\mathbf{y})$ is the approximation to the *a posteriori* distribution $P(z|\mathbf{y})$ produced at iteration i. I will let i be fractional when the meaning is clear. For example, in a turbodecoder with two constituent codes, $i = 0.5$ refers to quantities produced by processing the first constituent code for the first time. By monitoring the log-odds ratios, we hope to accurately determine when to detect variables early.

6.7.2   Early detection for turbocodes: Trellis splicing

Here, I consider early detection of information symbols only. Consider the simple two-state trellis shown in Figure 6.17a. Let u_k be the random variable for the information bit in the kth section of the trellis, and let s_k be the random variable for the state at the beginning of the kth section of the trellis. The edge in the kth section of the trellis that leaves state $s_k \in \{0, 1\}$ in response to information bit $u_k \in \{0, 1\}$ has an associated branch metric, $\gamma_k^{u_k}(s_k)$. These metrics are determined from the received signals and the *a priori* probabilities regarding the transmitted information bit values. (In a systematic code, the likelihoods for the noisy received information bits can be included in the *a priori* probabilities.) If $p(y_k|u_k, s_k)$ is the likelihood function for the kth received signal and $P(u_k)$ is the *a priori* probability for information bit u_k, then $\gamma_k^{u_k}(s_k) = P(u_k)p(y_k|u_k, s_k)$. The forward pass consists of computing the flows from these metrics in the forward direction. This results in a flow value $\alpha_k(s_k)$ for each state s_k at each section $k, k = 0 \ldots K - 1$, computed as $\alpha_{k+1}(0) = \gamma_k^0(0)\alpha_k(0) + \gamma_k^1(1)\alpha_k(1)$, and $\alpha_{k+1}(1) = \gamma_k^1(0)\alpha_k(0) + \gamma_k^0(1)\alpha_k(1)$. The backward pass simply consists of a flow computation in the reverse direction in order to obtain a flow value

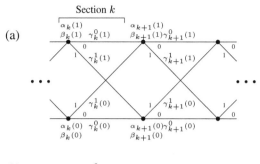

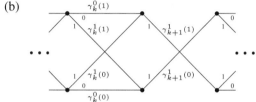

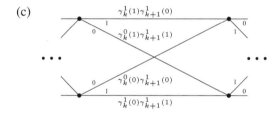

Figure 6.17
Trellis splicing. (a) shows a two-state trellis with edges accompanied by information bit labels and metrics and with nodes accompanied by flows. (b) and (c): If we know that information bit $k + 1$ has a value of 1, we can cut the corresponding section out of the trellis and splice the trellis back together, introducing new information bit labels and new metrics for the connecting edges.

$\beta_k(s_k)$ for each state at each section: $\beta_k(0) = \gamma_k^0(0)\beta_{k+1}(0) + \gamma_k^1(0)\beta_{k+1}(1)$, and $\beta_k(1) = \gamma_k^1(1)\beta_{k+1}(0) + \gamma_k^0(1)\beta_{k+1}(1)$. These two types of flow are combined to obtain the *a posteriori* log-odds ratio that each information bit is 1 versus 0, given the received signal sequence $\mathbf{y}$:

$$\log \frac{P(u_k = 1|\mathbf{y})}{P(u_k = 0|\mathbf{y})} = \log \frac{\alpha_k(0)\gamma_k^1(0)\beta_{k+1}(1) + \alpha_k(1)\gamma_k^1(1)\beta_{k+1}(0)}{\alpha_k(0)\gamma_k^0(0)\beta_{k+1}(0) + \alpha_k(1)\gamma_k^0(1)\beta_{k+1}(1)}. \quad (6.32)$$

The computational cost of each section in the forward-backward algorithm thus consists of the time spent computing the α's and β's for each state, as well as the time spent computing the *a posteriori* log-odds ratios. Although there are various useful techniques and approximations for decreasing this cost [Hagenauer, Offer and Papke 1996; Benedetto *et al.* 1996], such as the SOVA [Hagenauer, Offer and Papke 1996], I will define it as a basic computational unit, and refer to it as a trellis *section operation*.

Suppose that according to some early detection criterion, we decide that the value of information bit u_{k+1} is 1. (Here, I will consider early detection for information bits only.) As a consequence, the trellis simplifies to the one shown in Figure 6.17b. The trellis can be simplified further by multiplying out the path metrics, giving the trellis shown in Figure 6.17c. Note that not only have the path metrics changed, but also the transitions now correspond to different information bit values. In general, portions of the trellis corresponding to early-detected information bits can be cut away, and the remaining segments spliced together with new path metrics and new information bit edge labels. If the values of b information bits are known, the spliced trellis will be b sections shorter, leading to a computational savings of b section operations for each future forward-backward sweep.

In order to implement trellis splicing, an integer array must be used to determine the state transitions, $(s_k, u_k) \longrightarrow s_{k+1}$. Whereas in the original trellis this mapping is very regular, after trellis splicing it is usually not. (*E.g.*, the information bits associated with the outgoing edges of the kth state in Figure 6.17c have *opposite* values compared to those in Figure 6.17a.) The use of this array slightly increases the computational complexity of each section operation. Also, the array must be modified each time a section is cut away. However, both of these computational costs are insignificant compared to the cost of the basic section operation. In the implementation of trellis splicing used for the experiments presented in Section 6.7.3, I found that the percentage of cpu time spent on trellis splicing was less than 6%. The integer array also requires extra memory. However, the total memory used actually *decreases* during decoding while using trellis splicing. When a single section is cut away, the memory liberated by the elimination of γs, αs and βs more than makes up for the extra integer array memory introduced. Moreover, if sections adjacent to the first are cut away, the transition array is simply modified, so that the memory associated with the γs, αs and βs of the adjacent sections is completely recovered.

6.7.3 Experimental results

I simulated trellis splicing at $E_b/N_0 = 0.1, 0.2$ and 0.3 dB, for a rate 1/3 unpunctured turbocode that had 10,000 information bits, identical constituent en-

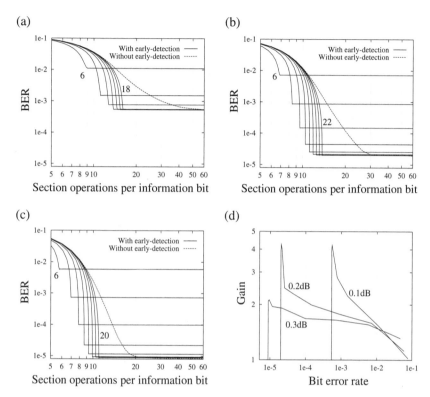

Figure 6.18
BER performance of turbodecoding with and without early detection for thresholds increasing by 2, for (a) $E_b/N_0 = 0.1$ dB, (b) $E_b/N_0 = 0.2$ dB, and (c) $E_b/N_0 = 0.3$ dB. (c) shows the computational gain for turbodecoding with early detection compared to turbodecoding without early detection as a function of BER, for $E_b/N_0 = 0.1, 0.2$, and 0.3 dB.

coders $(21, 37)_{\text{octal}}$, and a randomly drawn permuter. After each half-iteration of turbodecoding, the log-odds ratio of each information bit was compared with a threshold in order to decide whether or not the bit should be detected early. For each value of the threshold, the number of bit errors and the number of section operations were averaged over the transmission of 20,000 information vectors. Figs. 6.18a, b, and c show plots of BER versus average number of section operations per information bit decoded, for a variety of thresholds. The curves for turbodecoding *without* early detection are also shown. In these simulations, a fixed number of decoding iterations were performed for each block.

For a given BER, the computational complexity of decoding can be reduced the most compared to standard turbodecoding by using the threshold that corresponds to the curve in each figure that bottoms out at the prespecified BER. Thus, the locus of points corresponding to the heels of the curves gives the optimal achievable BER-complexity performance. Using these curves, we can answer the question, "At a specified E_b/N_0 and BER, what is the computational gain obtained by using early detection compared to using fewer decoding iterations without early detection?" The locus of points described above is interpolated in Figure 6.18d which shows the computational gain as a function of BER for the different values of E_b/N_0. For all three values of E_b/N_0, the greatest computational gain is obtained near the minimal BER.

7 Future Research Directions

My goal in this book was to present to the reader a unified graphical model framework for describing problems and developing algorithms in the areas of pattern classification, unsupervised learning, data compression, and channel coding. The previous four chapters have shown how graphical models and various inference and learning algorithms can be applied to problems in these areas. In this chapter, I hope to give the reader a sense for some of what is to come in the near future of graphical models research in machine learning and digital communication.

7.1 Modularity and abstraction

> I basically know of two principles for treating complicated systems in simple ways; the first is the principle of modularity and the second is the principle of abstraction. I am an apologist for computational probability in machine learning, and particularly for graphical models and variational methods, because I believe that probability theory implements these two principles in deep and intriguing ways — namely through factorization and through averaging. Exploiting these two mechanisms as fully as possible seems to me to be the way forward in machine learning.
>
> Michael I. Jordan
> Massachusetts Institute of Technology, 1997

Both in machine learning and digital communication, the goal is to perform inference in learned or designed models. Graphical models describe how a probabilistic description of a system can be factored into local functions. Exact inference consists of abstracting variables correctly according to probability theory, by marginalization. In intractable models, the approximate inference algorithms reviewed in Chapter 2 make abstraction tractable by approximately averaging over variables, whether by ignoring cycles in the graph, by using samples, by using approximating distributions, or by using inverse models.

Surely the next (current?) leap forward in machine learning will take advantage of the modular structure that we know is present in natural data. Data-driven algorithms (*e.g.*, nearest neighbor methods) ignore this structure.

In digital communication, the presence of modularity is clear in such areas as data networks. The need for modularity in channel coding is less obvious, since the codes that Shannon used to prove that capacity is achievable were in fact completely random, albeit impractical to decode. However, the excellent performance of trellis-constrained codes (*e.g.*, turbocodes) indicates that near-Shannon limit performance can be obtained using highly-structured codes. In fact, this modularity is *necessary* for the approximate inference algorithms to work so well.

I think one important direction for further research is to develop inference algorithms that can figure out what should *not* be abstracted. For example, in variational inference, a parametric distribution is fit to the hidden variables. The form of this distribution influences the degree to which abstraction takes place. How do we choose this form? We certainly choose it so that it can be optimized easily. What other considerations are important? In fact, the most appropriate form of the variational distribution will even depend on the current input. As another example, loopy probability propagation ignores the cycles in the model graph. However, a small number of cycles can be processed quite easily, so why not take into account only those cycles that are most important for the current inference?

7.2   Faster inference and learning

> The two fundamental problems are first to choose a probabilistic model capable of learning interesting things, and second to find ways of implementing inference in that model — approximately, of course. I'd like to comment on the latter problem. I think all our favourite implementation methods — Gibbs sampling, overrelax-ation, hybrid Monte Carlo, variational methods, EM, gradient de-scent — are all too creepy-crawly slow. Of course, they're really snappy compared with the algorithms they replaced, but I think inference and learning should be even quicker. The world isn't an adversary. It should be possible to solve many learning prob-lems in a couple of iterations through a reasonable data set, rather than thousands. It may be too much to ask for a one-shot learning method, but maybe we should be looking for one-and-a-half-shot learning algorithms.
>
> David J.C. MacKay
> Cambridge University, 1997

By using *any* fast inference algorithm while learning, the generalized expec-tation maximization algorithm will favor models for which the approximate inference algorithm works well. However, taken to the extreme, this approach will produce useless models in which we can make fast (and meaningless) inferences. It seems that there is a need for new cost functions that favor fast, but *good* probabilistic inferences.

Currently, the speed of inference is indirectly controlled by the number of iterations of loopy probability propagation, the Monte Carlo sample size, the simplicity of the variational distribution, and the simplicity of the recognition network. Is there a way to formulate a Lyapunov function that directly measures closeness to the correct answer *and* the number of iterations needed to get there?

With regards to learning, how does a machine recognize when it is finished learning? If the relative improvement in the cost function is measured, learning may go on indefinitely. Simply stopping learning after a specified time has elapsed does not guarantee the time was used efficiently. In Monte Carlo Bayesian learning, how does the sampler know when to stop? If the sampler is given 10 minutes, how should it proceed to obtain the "best" possible sample?

7.3 Scaling up to the brain

> The brain is amazingly good at converting images into internal representations of their real causes. This could be the result of a huge collection of co-adapted clever tricks, but I think it is far more likely to be the result of a clever, general-purpose learning algorithm that can efficiently suck structure out of the rich sensory input. The search for this learning algorithm is one of the most exciting areas of science and is also of great technological importance. Graphical models are currently the most promising direction, but we do not yet know how to fit very large, hierarchical models to data in a computationally tractable way. It feels as if we are quite close to a really powerful learning algorithm, but something is still missing: None of the current algorithms scale well and as a result we can only tackle toy problems.

> Geoffrey E. Hinton
> University of Toronto, 1997

Why do current approximate inference and learning algorithms not scale well? It is certainly true that for richly-connected neural networks, the time needed for exact inference scales exponentially with the number of units. We would like our approximate algorithms to scale roughly linearly with the number of units. Is this too much to ask for? I don't believe so, for scale is a double-edged sword. The greater the number of sensory inputs, the less ambiguity there tends to be in the inference. There is usually one explanation for a visual scene — multimodal inferences such as the orientation of the Necker cube are rare in everyday life. It seems to me that we need to find approximate algorithms that can allocate resources more efficiently in large networks.

Another important research topic is the interaction between the model and the approximate inference algorithm during learning, and how this interaction can help the scaling problem. Different types of model will be best-suited to different types of approximate inference algorithm. In unsupervised learning, the generalized expectation maximization algorithm favors models for which the approximate inference algorithm works well. Which properties of this interaction influence performance under scaling, and how can these properties be used to improve inference?

7.4   Improving model structures

> For me, estimating joint distributions is a bit like playing God. You can't do everything!
>
> Vladimir Vapnik
> AT & T – Research, 1997

The premise of using estimates of the joint distribution to classify patterns is that by learning the natural generative process that produces each class of pattern, our machine can do a good job of classifying a test pattern by identifying the most appropriate generative process. In fact, if our joint distribution estimates are correct, this method is optimal. However, modelling the full joint distribution over the input patterns in this way is much more difficult than modelling the conditional probability of the class identity given the input pattern (as is done, *e.g.*, in Le Cun *et al.* [1989] and Vapnik [1998]). In the former case, the machine tries to learn all aspects of the data, whereas in the latter case the machine tries to focus on only those aspects that influence the classification probability. While modelling conditional probabilities is more direct, it also ignores possible generalizations that can be made from apparently irrelevant input features to features that are relevant to the classification task.

A valid concern about attempts to model the full joint distribution is that the suboptimal solutions based on limited data sets may perform worse than simpler conditional probability estimates. As with much of neural network research, we find inspiration from cognitive science: Real neural networks *do* try to model everything in a mostly unsupervised fashion, and they succeed quite remarkably. Additional inspiration comes from the field of Bayesian learning, where proponents argue that given enough computer power, we ought to use models that are as complex as we believe the data to be, and then average over model predictions:

> For problems where we do not expect a simple solution, the proper
> Bayesian approach is therefore to use a model of a suitable type
> that is as complex as we can afford computationally, regardless of
> the size of the training set.
>
> Radford M. Neal [1996]

Of course, "Bayesian Bayesian networks" will require significant computational resources and so we will need to find appropriate models. What are the right models?

To date, research on learning in intractable graphical models with hidden variables has focused mainly on "vanilla" layered architectures of units with identical activation functions (*e.g.*, sigmoid units, noisy-or combination functions). Clearly, these models are not most appropriate for a wide variety of real-world learning problems. It appears the time is right for a "killer application" of a latent-variable graphical model that will undoubtably use a well-thought out model structure. For example, it is probably a good idea to build in whatever physics are known, and leave some underlying physical parameters to be estimated or averaged over.

7.5 Iterative decoding

> To me, it is clear that turbocodes are the most significant develop-
> ment in channel coding since Shannon's original 1948 paper. Of
> course, they weren't invented in a vacuum and build on ideas that
> came before, but nevertheless they are a truly remarkable discov-
> ery. Berrou *et al.* are primarily superb experimentalists, and they
> left plenty of work for the theorists to do. Some of the theorists
> have tackled the job of explaining why the classical turbocode
> construction should yield near-Shannon limit performance with
> optimal decoding. Some have found ways of modifying the clas-
> sical construction to obtain near-Shannon limit performance with
> manageable complexity in a variety of situations (*e.g.*, serial con-
> catenation, product codes, "self"-concatenation, *etc.*).
>
> However, right from the beginning, a few of us were vexed by
> the experimentally verified but theoretically unexplained iterative
> turbodecoding algorithm, which is, in my opinion, the key inno-
> vation of the French group. Turbodecoding is a low-complexity

close approximation to the exponentially hard problem of exact decoding of turbocodes. While no one yet fully understands just why turbodecoding works as well as it does, we now know that there is a close connection between turbodecoding and many other algorithms known in the cryptography (Baum-Welch), information theory (Gallager-Tanner-MacKay-Wiberg), signal processing (backward-forward, FFT), statistics (expectation maximization), and artificial intelligence (probability propagation, Shafer-Shenoy theory) communities. All of these algorithms share the common feature of being distributed message passing schemes on graphs of various sorts. (I am at work on a tutorial paper with S. Aji as co-author on the "generalized distributive law," which explains these connections.) However, unless the graph is a tree, these algorithms will not be exact, but (at best) are good approximations. Thus, turbodecoding and the Gallager-Tanner-MacKay-Wiberg algorithm are not fully understood, since the underlying graphs have cycles.

My own work is focused mainly on trying to provide a theoretically sound explanation for why these algorithms "work" when there are cycles. There have been small successes. The work of my group (Aji, Horn, and me) and that done independently by Weiss has pretty much cleared up the "one cycle" case. This is interesting but not directly relevant to turbodecoding since for classical turbocodes, the underlying graph is a bipartite graph with many cycles. (On the other hand it is directly relevant to the decoding of tail-biting codes.)

However, I believe that the success of turbodecoding will ultimately be found to be a special case of a theorem that says that the generalized distributive law, when applied iteratively to bipartite graphs with many cycles (and probably a broader class of graphs with cycles) using the sum-product semiring, gives, with high probability, decisions (though not conditional probabilities) on the hidden variables that are the same as those given by the brute force approach. I predict these theorems will be discovered in the next few years. (Of course, I hope we at Caltech will be the discoverers, but I am less confident of that!)

Robert J. McEliece
California Institute of Technology, 1997

7.6   Iterative decoding in the real world

Real-world channels are not Gaussian. They have nonlinearities, bursty noise, multiple users, multiple reflections, delay constraints, and so on. An important direction for future research in digital communication is to extend the success of trellis-constrained codes such as turbocodes and low-density parity-check codes to real-world channels. One appealing approach is to build a graphical model that takes into account some of the effects mentioned above. Nonlinear channels can be modelled using (possibly parameterized) nonlinear conditional probabilities in the graphical model; bursty noise can be taken into account by a two-state ("bursty" versus "nonbursty") Markov model for the channel; each user in a multiple user system can attach extra graphical models that account for the other users; and so on. Optimal decoding is then a matter of inference in the total graphical model, and suboptimal decoding is accomplished using an approximate inference technique.

7.7   Unification

I think a great deal of perspective can be obtained by describing known algorithms in terms of inference and learning in graphical models. For example, we already know of many algorithms that are essentially probability propagation in appropriate graphical models: the forward-backward algorithm, Kalman filtering, extended Kalman filtering, the fast-Fourier transform, Gallager's iterative decoder and turbodecoding. What other connections can be made between known algorithms and the other inference techniques for graphical models? As these connections become clear, we can explore the use of different inference algorithms. How well does variational inference work for decoding turbocodes? Can we use Helmholtz machine recognition networks to assist decoding? How well does iterative probability propagation work for learning intractable graphical models? What new inference algorithms can be applied to new problems that can be described in terms of graphical models? I believe that in answering these questions and similar ones, we are sure to discover new fundamental connections and new powerful algorithms for inference and learning.

References

Aji, S. M. and McEliece, R. J. (1997). A general algorithm for distributing information in a graph. In *Proceedings of IEEE International Symposium on Information Theory*.

Amari, S.-I. (1985). *Differential-Geometrical Methods in Statistics, Lecture Notes in Statistics vol. 28*. Springer, New York NY.

Amari, S.-I., Cichocki, A., and Yang, H. (1996). A new learning algorithm for blind signal separation. In Touretzky, D. S., Mozer, M. C., and Hasselmo, M. E., editors, *Advances in Neural Information Processing Systems 8*. MIT Press, Cambridge MA.

Bahl, L. R., Cocke, J., Jelinek, F., and Raviv, J. (1974). Optimal decoding of linear codes for minimizing symbol error rate. *IEEE Transactions on Information Theory*, 20:284–287.

Baum, L. E. and Petrie, T. (1966). Statistical inference for probabilistic functions of finite state markov chains. *Annals of Mathematical Statistics*, 37:1559–1563.

Becker, S. and Hinton, G. E. (1992). A self-organizing neural network that discovers surfaces in random-dot stereograms. *Nature*, 355:161–163.

Bell, A. J. and Sejnowski, T. J. (1995). An information maximization approach to blind separation and blind deconvolution. *Neural Computation*, 7:1129–1159.

Benedetto, S., Divsalar, D., Montorsi, G., and Pollara, F. (1996). Soft-ouput decoding algorithms in iterative decoding of parallel concatenated convolutional codes. Submitted to *IEEE International Conference on Communications*.

Benedetto, S. and Montorsi, G. (1996a). Iterative decoding of serially concatenated convolutional codes. *Electronics Letters*, 32:1186–1188.

Benedetto, S. and Montorsi, G. (1996b). Serial concatenation of block and convolutional codes. *Electronics Letters*, 32:887–888.

Benedetto, S., Montorsi, G., Divsalar, D., and Pollara, F. (1997). Serial concatenation of interleaved codes: Performance analysis, design, and iterative decoding. To appear in *IEEE Transactions on Information Theory*.

Berrou, C. and Glavieux, A. (1996). Near optimum error correcting coding and decoding: Turbo-codes. *IEEE Transactions on Communications*, 44:1261–1271.

Berrou, C., Glavieux, A., and Thitimajshima, P. (1993). Near Shannon limit error-correcting coding and decoding: Turbo codes. In *Proceedings of the IEEE International Conference on Communications*.

Bishop, C. M., Svensén, M., and Williams, C. K. I. (1997). Gtm: the generative topographic mapping. To appear in *Neural Computation*.

Blahut, R. E. (1990). *Digital Transmission of Information*. Addison-Wesley Pub. Co., Reading MA.

Breiman, L., Friedman, J. H., Olshen, R. A., and Stone, C. J. (1984). *Classification and regression trees*. Wadsworth, Blemont CA.

Calderbank, A. R. and Sloane, N. J. A. (1987). New trellis codes based on lattices and cosets. *IEEE Transactions on Information Theory*, 33:177.

Chandler, D. (1987). *Introduction to Modern Statistical Mechanics*. Oxford University Press, New York NY.

Chow, C. K. (1957). An optimum character recognition system using decision functions. *IRE Transactions on Electronic Computing*, 6:247–254.

Comon, P., Jutten, C., and Herault, J. (1991). Blind separation of sources. *Signal Processing*, 24:11–20.

Cooper, G. F. (1990). The computational complexity of probabilistic inference using Bayesian belief networks. *Artificial Intelligence*, 42:393–405.

Cover, T. M. and Thomas, J. A. (1991). *Elements of Information Theory*. John Wiley & Sons, New York NY.

Dagum, P. (1993). Approximating probabilistic inference in Bayesian belief networks is NP-hard. *Artificial Intelligence*, 60:141–153.

Dagum, P. and Chavez, R. M. (1993). Approximating probabilistic inference in Bayesian belief networks. *IEEE Transactions on Pattern Analysis and Machine Intelligence*, 15(3):246–255.

Daut, D. G., Modestino, J. W., and Wismer, L. D. (1982). New short constraint length convolutional code constructions for selected rational rates. *IEEE Transactions on Information Theory*, 28(5):794–800.

Dayan, P. and Hinton, G. E. (1996). Varieties of Helmholtz machine. *Neural Networks*, 9:1385–1403.

Dayan, P., Hinton, G. E., Neal, R. M., and Zemel, R. S. (1995). The Helmholtz machine. *Neural Computation*, 7:889–904.

Dayan, P. and Zemel, R. S. (1995). Competition and multiple cause models. *Neural Computation*, 7:565–579.

Dempster, A. P., Laird, N. M., and Rubin, D. B. (1977). Maximum likelihood from incomplete data via the EM algorithm. *Proceedings of the Royal Statistical Society*, B-39:1–38.

Devroye, L. (1986). *Nonuniform Random Variate Generation*. Springer-Verlag, New York NY.

Divsalar, D. and Pollara, F. (1995). Turbo-codes for PCS applications. In *Proceedings of the International Conference on Communications*, pages 54–59.

Duane, S., Kennedy, A. D., Pendleton, B. J., and Roweth, D. (1987). Hybrid Monte Carlo. *Physical Letters B*, 195:216–222.

Duda, R. O. and Hart, P. E. (1973). *Pattern Classification and Scene Analysis*. John Wiley, New York NY.

Fletcher, R. (1987). *Practical methods of optimization*. John Wiley & Sons, New York NY.

Foldiak, P. (1990). Forming sparse representations by local anti-hebbian learning. *Biological Cybernetics*, 64:165–170.

Forney, Jr., G. D. (1973). The Viterbi algorithm. *Proceedings of the IEEE*, 61(3):268–277.

Forney, Jr., G. D. (1988). Coset codes - Part I: Introduction and geometrical classification. *IEEE Transactions on Information Theory*, 34:1123.

Forney, Jr., G. D. (1997). Approaching AWGN channel capacity with coset codes and multilevel coset codes. Submitted to *IEEE Transactions on Information Theory*.

Frey, B. J. (1997a). Continuous sigmoidal belief networks trained using slice sampling. In Mozer, M. C., Jordan, M. I., and Petsche, T., editors, *Advances in Neural Information Processing Systems 9*. MIT Press, Cambridge MA. Available at http://www.cs.utoronto.ca/~frey.

Frey, B. J. (1997b). Variational inference for continuous sigmoidal Bayesian networks. In *Sixth International Workshop on Artificial Intelligence and Statistics*.

Frey, B. J. and Hinton, G. E. (1996). Free energy coding. In Storer, J. A. and Cohn, M., editors, *Proceedings of the Data Compression Conference 1996*. IEEE Computer Society Press. Available at http://www.cs.utoronto.ca/~frey.

Frey, B. J. and Hinton, G. E. (1997). Efficient stochastic source coding and an application to a Bayesian network source model. *The Computer Journal*, 40(2/3).

Frey, B. J. and Hinton, G. E. (1998). Variational learning in non-linear Gaussian belief networks. To appear in *Neural Computation*; available at http://www.cs.utoronto.ca/~frey.

Frey, B. J. and Kschischang, F. R. (1997). Probability propagation and iterative decoding. In *Proceedings of the 34th Allerton Conference on Communication, Control and Computing 1996*. Available at http://www.cs.utoronto.ca/~frey.

Frey, B. J. and Kschischang, F. R. (1998). Early detection and trellis splicing: Reduced-complexity iterative decoding. *IEEE Journal on Selected Areas in Communications*, 16:153–159.

Frey, B. J., Kschischang, F. R., Loeliger, H. A., and Wiberg, N. (1998). Factor graphs and algorithms. In *Proceedings of the 35th Allerton Conference on Communication, Control and Computing 1997*.

Frey, B. J. and MacKay, D. J. C. (1998a). A revolution: Belief propagation in graphs with cycles. In Jordan, M. I., Kearns, M. I., and Solla, S. A., editors, *Advances in Neural Information Processing Systems 10*. MIT Press. Available at http://www.cs.utoronto.ca/~frey.

Frey, B. J. and MacKay, D. J. C. (1998b). Trellis-constrained codes. In *Proceedings of the 35th Allerton Conference on Communication, Control and Computing 1997*.

Gallager, R. G. (1963). *Low-Density Parity-Check Codes.* MIT Press, Cambridge MA.

Geman, S. and Geman, D. (1984). Stochastic relaxation, Gibbs distribution and the Bayesian restoration of images. *IEEE Transactions on Pattern Analysis and Machine Intelligence,* 6:721–741.

Ghahramani, Z. and Jordan, M. I. (1998). Factorial hidden Markov models. *Machine Learning,* 29:245–273.

Gilks, W. R. and Wild, P. (1992). Adaptive rejection sampling for Gibbs sampling. *Applied Statistics,* 41:337–348.

Goodman, L. A. (1970). The multivariate analysis of qualitative data: Interaction among multiple classifications. *Journal of the American Statistical Association,* 65:226–256.

Hagenauer, J., Offer, E., and Papke, L. (1996). Iterative decoding of binary block and convolutional codes. *IEEE Transactions on Information Theory,* 42(2):429–445.

Hammersley, J. M. and Handscomb, D. C. (1964). *Monte Carlo Methods.* Chapman and Hall, London England.

Heckerman, D. and Geiger, D. (1995). Learning Bayesian networks: a unification for discrete and Gaussian domains. In Besnard, P. and Hanks, S., editors, *Proceedings of the Eleventh Conference on Uncertainty in Artificial Intelligence.* Morgan Kaufmann.

Hinton, G. E., Dayan, P., Frey, B. J., and Neal, R. M. (1995). The wake-sleep algorithm for unsupervised neural networks. *Science,* 268:1158–1161.

Hinton, G. E. and Ghahramani, Z. (1997). Generative models for discovering sparse distributed representations. *Philosophical Transactions of the Royal Society of London B,* 352:1177–1190.

Hinton, G. E. and Sejnowski, T. J. (1986). Learning and relearning in Boltzmann machines. In Rumelhart, D. E. and McClelland, J. L., editors, *Parallel Distributed Processing: Explorations in the Microstructure of Cognition,* volume I, pages 282–317. MIT Press, Cambridge MA.

Hinton, G. E. and Zemel, R. S. (1994). Autoencoders, minimum description length and Helmholtz free energy. In Cowan, J. D., Tesauro, G., and Alspector, J., editors, *Advances in Neural Information Processing Systems 6.* Morgan Kaufmann.

Hofmann, R. and Tresp, V. (1996). Discovering structure in continuous variables using Bayesian networks. In Touretzky, D., Mozer, M., and Hasselmo, M., editors, *Advances in Neural Information Processing Systems 8*. MIT Press.

Huffman, D. A. (1952). A method for the construction of minimum redundancy codes. *Proceedings of the Institute of Radio Engineers*, 40:1098–1101.

Imai, H. and Hirakawa, S. (1977). A new multilevel coding method using error-correcting codes. *IEEE Transactions on Information Theory*, 23:371–377. Correction, Nov. 1977, p. 784.

Jaakkola, T. and Jordan, M. I. (1997). A variational approach to Bayesian logistic regression models and their extensions. In *Sixth International Workshop on Artificial Intelligence and Statistics*.

Jaakkola, T., Saul, L. K., and Jordan, M. I. (1996). Fast learning by bounding likelihoods in sigmoid type belief networks. In Touretzky, D. S., Mozer, M. C., and Hasselmo, M. E., editors, *Advances in Neural Information Processing Systems 8*. MIT Press.

Jordan, M. I. (1995). Why the logistic function? A tutorial discussion on probabilities and neural networks. Technical Report Computational Cognitive Science 9503, MIT, Cambridge MA.

Kalos, M. H. and Whitlock, P. A. (1986). *Monte Carlo Methods, Volume I: Basics*. John Wiley, New York NY.

Kinderman, R. and Snell, J. L. (1980). *Markov Random Fields and Their Applications*. American Mathematical Society, Providence USA.

Kschischang, F. R. and Frey, B. J. (1998). Iterative decoding of compound codes by probability propagation in graphical models. *IEEE Journal on Selected Areas in Communications*, 16:219–230. Available at http://www.cs.utoronto.ca/~frey.

Lauritzen, S. L. (1996). *Graphical Models*. Oxford University Press, New York NY.

Lauritzen, S. L., Dawid, A. P., Larsen, B. N., and Leimer, H. G. (1990). Independence properties of directed Markov fields. *Networks*, 20:491–505.

Lauritzen, S. L. and Spiegelhalter, D. J. (1988). Local computations with probabilities on graphical structures and their application to expert systems. *Journal of the Royal Statistical Society B*, 50:157–224.

Lauritzen, S. L. and Wermuth, N. (1989). Graphical models for associations between variables, some of which are qualitative and some quantitative. *Annals of Statistics*, 17:31–57.

Le Cun, Y., Boser, B., Denker, J. S., Henderson, D., Howard, R. E., Hubbard, W., and Jackel, L. D. (1989). Back-propagation applied to handwritten zip code recognition. *Neural Computation*, 1:541–551.

Lee, E. A. and Messerschmitt, D. G. (1994). *Digital Communication*. Kluwer Academic Publishers, Norwell MA.

Lin, S. and Costello, Jr., D. J. (1983). *Error Control Coding: Fundamentals and Applications*. Prentice-Hall Inc., Englewood Cliffs NJ.

Lodge, J., Young, R., Hoeher, P., and Hagenauer, J. (1993). Separable MAP 'filters' for the decoding of product and concatenated codes. In *Proceedings of IEEE International Conference on Communications*, pages 1740–1745.

MacKay, D. J. C. (1995). Bayesian neural networks and density networks. *Nuclear Instruments and Methods in Physics Research*, 354:73–80.

MacKay, D. J. C. (1997a). Good codes based on very sparse matrices. Submitted to *IEEE Transactions on Information Theory*.

MacKay, D. J. C. (1997b). Maximum likelihood and covariant algorithms for independent component analysis. Unpublished manuscript available at `http://wol.ra.phy.cam.ac.uk/mackay`.

MacKay, D. J. C. (1998). Information Theory, Inference and Learning Algorithms. Book in preparation, currently available at `http://wol.ra.phy.cam.ac.uk/mackay`.

MacKay, D. J. C. and Neal, R. M. (1995). Good codes based on very sparse matrices. In Boyd, C., editor, *Cryptography and Coding. 5th IMA Conference*, number 1025 in Lecture Notes in Computer Science, pages 100–111. Springer, Berlin Germany.

MacKay, D. J. C. and Neal, R. M. (1996). Near Shannon limit performance of low density parity check codes. *Electronics Letters*, 32(18):1645–1646. Reprinted in *Electronics Letters*, vol. 33, March 1997, 457–458.

McCullagh, P. and Nelder, J. A. (1983). *Generalized Linear Models*. Chapman and Hall, London England.

McEliece, R. J., MacKay, D. J. C., and Cheng, J. F. (1998). Turbo-decoding as an instance of Pearl's 'belief propagation' algorithm. *IEEE Journal on Selected Areas in Communications*, 16.

Meng, X. L. and Rubin, D. B. (1992). Recent extensions of the EM algorithm (with discussion). In Bernardo, J. M., Berger, J. O., Dawid, A. P., and Smith, A. F. M., editors, *Bayesian Statistics 4*. Clarendon Press, Oxford England.

Metropolis, N., Rosenbluth, A. W., Rosenbluth, M. N., Teller, A. H., and Teller, E. (1953). Equation of state calculation by fast computing machines. *Journal of Chemical Physics*, 21:1087–1092.

Movellan, J. R. and McClelland, J. L. (1992). Learning continuous probability distributions with symmetric diffusion networks. *Cognitive Science*, 17:463–496.

Neal, R. M. (1992). Connectionist learning of belief networks. *Artificial Intelligence*, 56:71–113.

Neal, R. M. (1993). Probabilistic inference using Markov chain Monte Carlo methods. Unpublished manuscript available over the internet by ftp at `ftp://ftp.cs.utoronto.ca/pub/radford/review.ps.Z`.

Neal, R. M. (1996). *Bayesian Learning for Neural Networks*. Springer-Verlag, New York NY.

Neal, R. M. (1997). Markov chain Monte Carlo methods based on "slicing" the density function. University of Toronto, Dept. of Statistics Technical Report No. 9722.

Neal, R. M. and Hinton, G. E. (1993). A new view of the EM algorithm that justifies incremental and other variants. Unpublished manuscript available over the internet by ftp at `ftp://ftp.cs.utoronto.ca/pub/radford/em.ps.Z`.

Pearl, J. (1986). Fusion, propagation, and structuring in belief networks. *Artificial Intelligence*, 29:241–288.

Pearl, J. (1987). Evidential reasoning using stochastic simulation of causal models. *Artificial Intelligence*, 32:245–257.

Pearl, J. (1988). *Probabilistic Reasoning in Intelligent Systems*. Morgan Kaufmann, San Mateo CA.

Peterson, C. and Anderson, J. R. (1987). A mean field theory learning algorithm for neural networks. *Complex Systems*, 1:995–1019.

Potamianos, G. G. and Goutsias, J. K. (1993). Partition function estimation of Gibbs random field images using Monte Carlo simulations. *IEEE Transactions on Information Theory*, 39:1322–1332.

Rabiner, L. (1989). A tutorial on hidden Markov models and selected applications in speech recognition. *Proceedings of the IEEE*, 77:257–286.

Rasmussen, C. E. (1996). *Evaluation of Gaussian Processes and Other Methods for Non-Linear Regression.* Department of Computer Science, University of Toronto, Toronto Canada. Doctoral dissertation (ftp://ftp.cs.toronto.edu/pub/carl/thesis.ps.gz).

Rasmussen, C. E., Neal, R. M., Hinton, G. E., van Camp, D., Revow, M., Ghahramani, Z., Kustra, R., and Tibshirani, R. (1996). *The DELVE Manual.* University of Toronto, Toronto Canada. http://www.cs.utoronto.ca/~delve.

Ripley, B. D. (1987). *Stochastic Simulation.* John Wiley, New York NY.

Rissanen, J. (1989). *Stochastic Complexity in Statistical Inquiry.* World Scientific, Singapore.

Rissanen, J. and Langdon, G. G. (1976). Arithmetic coding. *IBM Journal of Research and Development*, 23:149–162.

Saul, L. K., Jaakkola, T., and Jordan, M. I. (1996). Mean field theory for sigmoid belief networks. *Journal of Artificial Intelligence Research*, 4:61–76.

Saund, E. (1995). A multiple cause mixture model for unsupervised learning. *Neural Computation*, 7:51–71.

Schubert, L. K. (1976). Extending the expressive power of semantic networks. *Artificial Intelligence*, 7:163–198.

Shannon, C. E. (1948). A mathematical theory of communication. *Bell System Technical Journal*, 27:379–423, 623–656.

Sheykhet, I. I. and Simkin, B. Y. (1990). Monte Carlo method in the theory of solutions. *Computer Physics Reports*, 12:67–133.

Smyth, P., Heckerman, D., and Jordan, M. I. (1997). Probabilistic independence networks for hidden markov probability models. *Neural Computation*, 9(2):227–270.

Spiegelhalter, D. J. (1986). Probabilistic reasoning in predictive expert systems. In Kanal, L. N. and Lemmer, J. F., editors, *Uncertainty in Artificial Intelligence*, pages 47–68. North Holland, Amsterdam.

Spiegelhalter, D. J. (1990). Fast algorithms for probabilistic reasoning in influence diagrams, with applications in genetics and expert systems. In Oliver, R. M. and Smith, J. Q., editors, *Influence Diagrams, Belief Nets, and Decision Analysis*, pages 361–384. John Wiley & Sons, New York NY.

Spiegelhalter, D. J. and Lauritzen, S. L. (1990). Sequential updating of conditional probabilities on directed graphical structures. *Networks*, 20:579–605.

Tanner, R. M. (1981). A recursive approach to low complexity codes. *IEEE Transactions on Information Theory*, 27:533–547.

Tibshirani, R. (1992). Principal curves revisited. *Statistics and Computing*, 2:183–190.

Ungerboeck, G. (1982). Channel coding with multilevel/phase signals. *IEEE Transactions on Information Theory*, 28(1).

Vapnik, V. (1998). *Statistical Learning Theory*. John Wiley, New York NY.

Viterbi, A. J. and Omura, J. K. (1979). *Principles of Digital Communication and Coding*. McGraw-Hill, New York NY.

Vorobev, N. N. (1962). Consistent families of measures and their extensions. *Theory of Probability and Applications*, 7:147–163.

Wachsmann, U. and Huber, J. (1995). Power and bandwidth efficient digital communication using turbo-codes in multilevel codes. *European Transactions on Telecommunications*, 6(5):557–567.

Wallace, C. S. (1990). Classification by minimum-message-length inference. In S. G. Akl, *et. al..*, editor, *Advances in Computing and Information — ICCI 1990*, number 468 in Lecture Notes in Computer Science. Springer, Berlin Germany.

Wiberg, N. (1996). *Codes and Decoding on General Graphs*. Department of Electrical Engineering, Linköping University, Linköping Sweden. Doctoral dissertation.

Wiberg, N., Loeliger, H.-A., and Kötter, R. (1995). Codes and iterative decoding on general graphs. *European Transactions on Telecommunications*, 6:513–525.

Wicker, S. (1995). *Error Control Systems for Digital Communications and Storage*. Prentice-Hall Inc., Englewood Cliffs NJ.

Witten, I. H., Neal, R. M., and Cleary, J. G. (1987). Arithmetic coding for data compression. *Communications of the ACM*, 30:520–540.

Woods, W. A. (1975). What's in a link? Foundations for semantic networks. In Bobrow, D. and Collins, A., editors, *Representation and understanding*, pages 35–72. Academic Press, New York NY.

Wright, S. (1921). Correlation and causation. *Journal of Agricultural Research*, 20:557–585.

Zemel, R. E. (1993). *A minimum description length framework for unsupervised learning*. Department of Computer Science, University of Toronto, Toronto Canada. Doctoral dissertation.

Zhang, J. (1993). The mean field theory in EM procedures for blind Markov random field image restoration. *IEEE Transactions on Image Processing*, 2:27–40.

Index